A Beginner's Guide to

Written by Beth Taylor and Jennifer Zeiger

Cross-stitch designs by Shiho Akaike

Illustrations by Shiho Akaike

Photography by Christopher Hiltz

Additional images from Shutterstock.com

Louis Weber, CEO
Publications International, Ltd.
8140 Lehigh Avenue
Morton Grove, IL 60053

ISBN: 978-1-64558-991-4

Manufactured in China.

8 7 6 5 4 3 2 1

Let's get social!

@Publications_International

@PublicationsInternational

www.pilbooks.com

Table of Contents

SNARKY

309

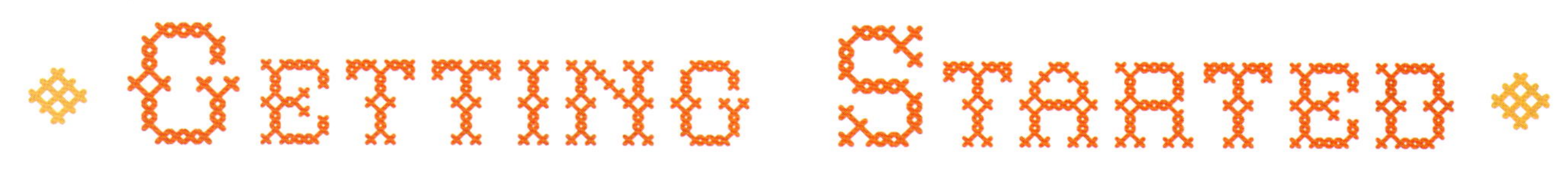

SUPPLIES

If you can count or read a chart, you can do counted cross-stitch. Aside from a design chart to follow, here are some supplies you need.

Fabrics

Most counted cross-stitch is done on Aida fabric or evenweave fabric. Aida fabric is woven in square blocks and evenweave is woven with single threads. On Aida fabric, a cross-stitch is worked over one square block. On evenweave fabric, a cross-stitch is worked "over two threads."

Aida

Aida fabric is perfect for beginners. Its precise, square-patterned weave creates visible holes that make Aida simple to use. Aida fabric is available in a variety of different counts, including 6, 8, 11, 14, 16, and 18. The most common is 14-count Aida, and it is this fabric on which the pattern dimensions in this book are based. The count indicates how many squares there are per inch of fabric. For example, 14-count Aida has 14 squares per inch.

Evenweave

The term *evenweave* refers to fabric having the same number of threads per inch vertically and horizontally. The thread count for evenweave fabric indicates the number of threads per inch. For example, 22-count evenweave fabric has 22 horizontal threads and 22 vertical threads per inch. The greater the thread count per inch, the finer the fabric.

Other Materials

A number of other materials can be used for cross-stitching. Plastic canvas, vinyl, perforated paper, perforated metal, and even baskets with a fairly even weave can be cross-stitched. You can also purchase ready-made items with panels of Aida cloth for cross-stitching.

Floss

Embroidery floss, or thread, is available in many forms and colors. You can buy it in your local craft store in skeins, hanks, spools, or balls. Most embroidery floss consists of six strands twisted together. The six-strand cotton embroidery floss is generally cut into 18-inch lengths for stitching. Use two of the six strands for cross-stitching on 14-count Aida. You will usually use one or two strands for back-stitching. Refer to individual patterns for how many strands to use.

Needles

Most cross-stitching is done with a tapestry needle. Tapestry needles have blunt, rounded tips and long oval eyes. Needles come in various sizes. As a general rule, the smaller the needle size, the greater the length of the needle and eye. A size 24 needle is recommended for cross-stitching on 14-count Aida.

For French knots and backstitches, some people prefer a sharper, finer embroidery needle.

When incorporating beads into a design, a beading needles works best. Beading needles are long and thin enough to pass easily through the holes in the beads.

Needle Threaders

As the name suggests, needle threaders help you thread the embroidery floss through the eye of the needle.

To use a needle threader, slide the folded wire of the threader through the eye of the needle. Insert the floss through the folded wire loop of the threader. Draw the wire loop and floss back through the eye of the needle.

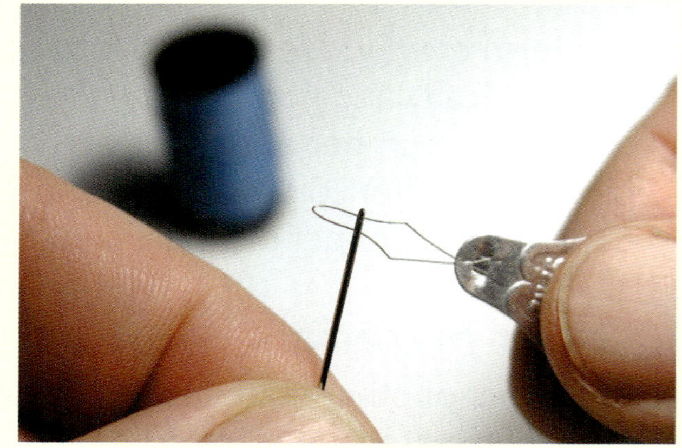

Embroidery Hoops

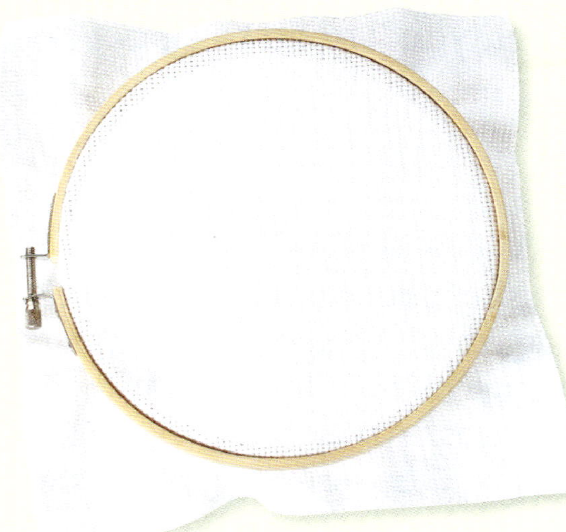

Embroidery hoops consist of two rings made of wood or plastic. They hold your fabric between the two rings so that your fabric is stretched out evenly while you stitch. You can use an embroidery hoop if you like, but it is not necessary for cross-stitching on Aida cloth. If you do use an embroidery hoop, be sure to remove it when not working on your piece so the creases will be easier to remove later.

To use an embroidery hoop, first place the fabric over the smaller inner ring. Then place the larger outer ring over the fabric. Press until the bottom ring fits snugly inside the top ring. Gently tug the edges of the fabric until the fabric is taut. Tighten the hoop's screw.

Scissors

You will want a pair of small, sharp embroidery scissors for cutting embroidery floss. Use a pair of dressmaking shears to cut Aida fabric.

Thread Organizers

For projects with numerous floss colors, it helps to organize your threads. Before starting your project, you can organize your floss by color with a thread organizer. You can purchase a thread organizer at your local craft store, or you can make your own. To make one, punch holes for each floss color in a piece of cardboard or a stiff piece of paper. Label each hole with the floss shade number or pattern symbol for reference. Cut the floss into manageable lengths of about 18 inches. Fold in half and loop through separate holes in the thread organizer.

GATHERING MATERIALS

Before embarking on any cross-stitch project, you'll need to select and prepare your materials.

Selecting Needles

Different needles are designed for different jobs. When selecting a needle, consider the fabric and the job at hand. You will do most of your counted cross-stitch with a tapestry needle. Tapestry needles have a large eye to accommodate multiple strands of floss and a blunt tip that passes through holes in the fabric without tearing fibers. The size of your tapestry needle depends on your fabric. While tapestry needle sizes may vary slightly between manufacturers, use the table below as a general guide.

Needle size	Fabric
18	6-count Aida / 10-count evenweave
22	11-count Aida / 22-25-27 count evenweave
24	14-count Aida / 28-count evenweave
26	16-count Aida / 32-count evenweave
28	18-count Aida / 36-55 count evenweave

Some other useful needles you can purchase:

Embroidery or crewel needles are thinner than tapestry needles and have a long eye and sharp tip.

Chenille needles are thicker than embroidery needles and have a long eye and sharp tip.

Beading Needles are long and very thin, used for stitching beads to fabric in cross-stitch designs. Tapestry needles are too big for this work.

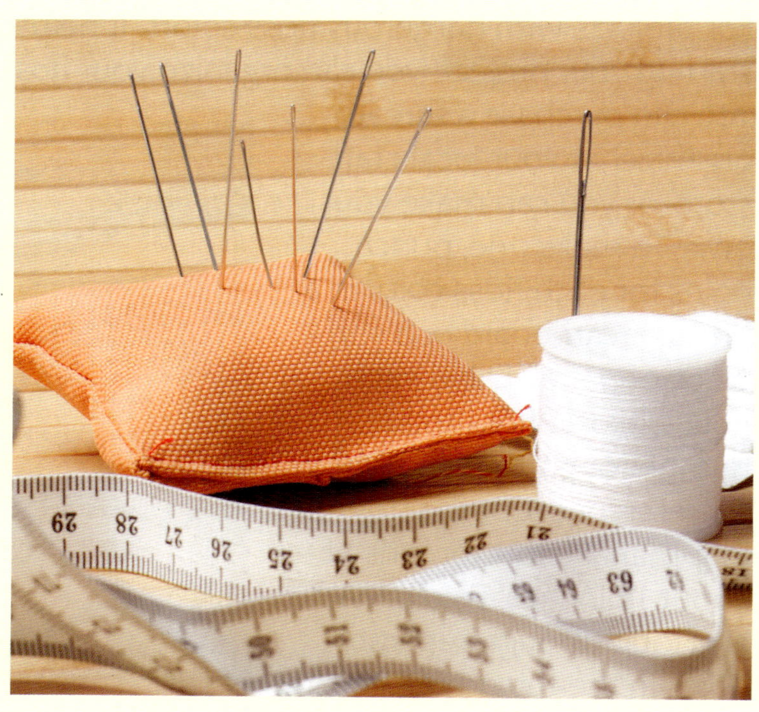

Selecting Fabrics

Here are some things to keep in mind when selecting fabrics for your projects:

- Aida is best for beginners. It's woven in blocks, giving the fabric obvious holes for the needle to go through.
- Quarter stitches and three-quarter stitches are harder to make on Aida because the needle goes through the middle of a square, which doesn't have a hole.
- Cross-stitches are worked over one square block with Aida fabric; on linen and other evenweaves, cross-stitches are generally worked "over two threads," so the needle enters alternating holes.
- Most evenweave fabrics are softer and less stiff than Aida.
- The dimensions and stitch counts provided for the patterns in this book assume the use of 14-count Aida.
- Each square on the charts in this book represents one block of Aida cloth or two threads of evenweave fabric.

Fabric Size

Many patterns will tell you how large a piece of fabric you will need for the design. When cutting fabric to size, allow some extra space for a border to protect yourself should you not get the design centered exactly. If the design will be framed or made into a pillow, add at least 3 inches on each of the sides. Cut fabric evenly along the vertical and horizontal threads.

Locating the Center

Locating the center of your fabric is important so you can center the design. Fold fabric lightly in half horizontally and then in half vertically to find the center. The center is where the folds intersect.

You can locate the center of the design chart by following the arrows on the sides. You can also count up or over to another point on the chart and then count the corresponding number of squares on your cloth to find the same place.

Reading the Chart

A cross-stitch design chart, or pattern, is made up of small squares on a grid. The squares on the chart correspond to the squares on the fabric. Each stitch is represented by a symbol or line on the chart. Once you locate an item on the chart, find it in the key. The key tells you the color, stitch, and number of strands to use. Many charts have darker grid lines surrounding 10 x 10 sections to make it easier to count your stitches and keep your place. Blank squares on the chart indicate fabric squares to be left unstitched.

When cross-stitching on Aida, each square on the chart represents a square block on the fabric. When cross-stitching on evenweave fabric, each square on the chart represents two fabric threads.

USING THE FINISHED PRODUCT

There are countless ways to use or display a finished cross-stitch piece. Here are just a few common ways to get you started.

Framing

There are specially-made frames that are designed to stabilize and display your cross-stitch. You can also use a regular frame; you just need to give your project a little added stability first:

Step 1: Cut a foam board, cardboard, or other sturdy backing material to size. One way to do this is trace around the frame's glass, then cut the backing along the traced lines.

Step 2: Center your project on the backing and wrap the excess fabric tightly around to the back. Make sure the design is taut across the front. Pin it in place.

Step 3: Staple, use a hot glue gun, or sew opposite edges of the piece together to secure the excess fabric to the backing. Remove the pins once the fabric is secure.

Bookmark or Banner

There are a number of products you can use to give your cross-stitching added strength and stability so you can use it as a bookmark or display it as a banner. Here are a few:

- Interfacing or stabilizer (add this before you start stitching, and stitch through your Aida or other fabric and the interface at the same time)
- Fabric adhesive (add this after you are done stitching)
- Fusible bonding web (add this heat-activated adhesive to the back of your completed project to permanently glue it to sturdy backing fabric)

Adding to an Object

Add a cross-stitch design to a pillowcase, towel, t-shirt, tote bag, or other fabric item. You can plan ahead and stitch the pattern directly to the item. For this, you'll need your needles, floss, and pattern, plus:

- Waste canvas
- Interface or stabilizer (to keep stretchy fabric in place)
- Item to which you're adding the design

Step 1: Cut the waste canvas and the interface or stabilizer to the same dimensions you would any other fabric.

Step 2: Layer your materials with the waste canvas on top, then the item you're stitching onto, then the interface. Position everything at the spot you want the design to appear. Pin everything in place or secure it with some basic basting stitches.

Step 3: Stitch as you normally would, counting your stitches on the waste canvas.

Step 4: Follow the manufacturers' directions to remove excess waste canvas and interface.

Cross-stitch-ready Items

You can find many items that come with a section that's made for you to cross-stitch, including bibs, towels, greeting cards, and more. All you need to do is fit the pattern to the item and start stitching!

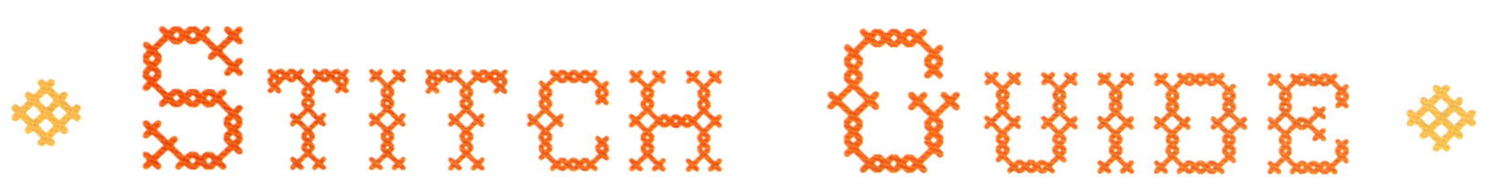

BASIC STITCHES

The seven stitches commonly used in cross-stitch are cross-stitch, backstitch, half stitch, quarter stitch, three-quarter stitch, Smyrna stitch, and French knot. Half stitches, quarter stitches, and three-quarter stitches are sometimes called fractional stitches. These and the Smyrna stitch are more difficult than the cross-stitch or backstitch.

Cross-stitch (X)

There are two common cross-stitching methods. One method completes each individual cross-stitch before moving on to the next. The other method makes a row of half stitches, then returns, making the half stitches in the other direction to complete the Xs.

Making a Single Cross-stitch

Step 1: Bring the needle from the back of the fabric through a hole to the front of the fabric. Make a diagonal stitch, bringing the needle up at 1 and down at 2.

Step 2: Bring the needle up at 3 and down at 4 to complete a single cross-stitch.

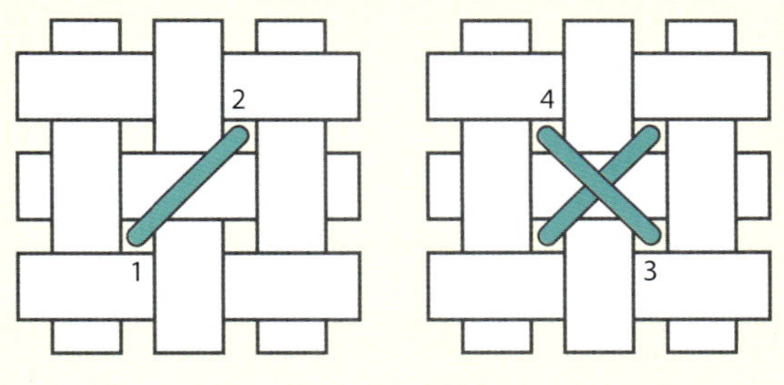

Making a Row of Cross-stitches

Step 1: Bring the needle up from the back of the fabric at 1 and down at 2. Continue making a row of half stitches, bringing the needle up at 3, down at 4, up at 5, down at 6, and so on.

Step 2: Now make a row of half stitches in the opposite direction to complete the stitches. Bring the needle up at 7, down at 8, up at 9, down at 10, and so on until the row of cross-stitches is complete.

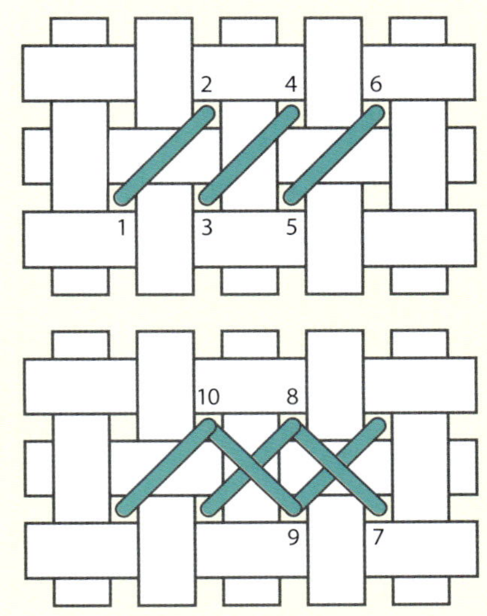

Vertical Cross-stitch

Step 1: Make a column of half stitches, bringing the needle up at 1, down at 2, up at 3, down at 4, up at 5, and down at 6.

Step 2: Cross the stitches in the opposite directions, bringing the needle up at 7, down at 8, up at 9, down at 10, and so on.

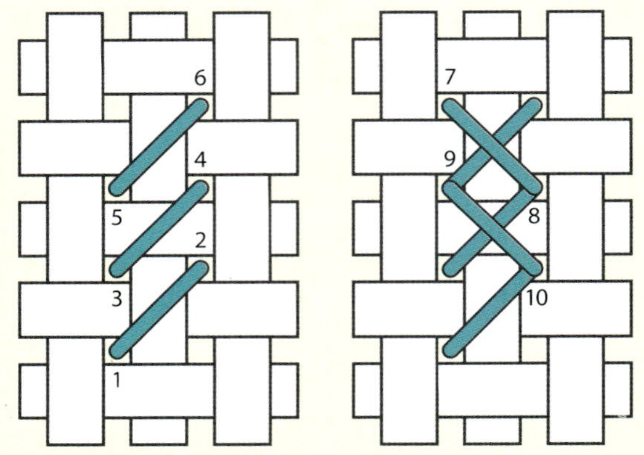

Backstitch (BS)

When backstitching, pass the needle back down through the fabric at the same space as the previous backstitch. Bring the needle up at 1, down at 2, up at 3, down at 4, up at 5, down at 6, and so on.

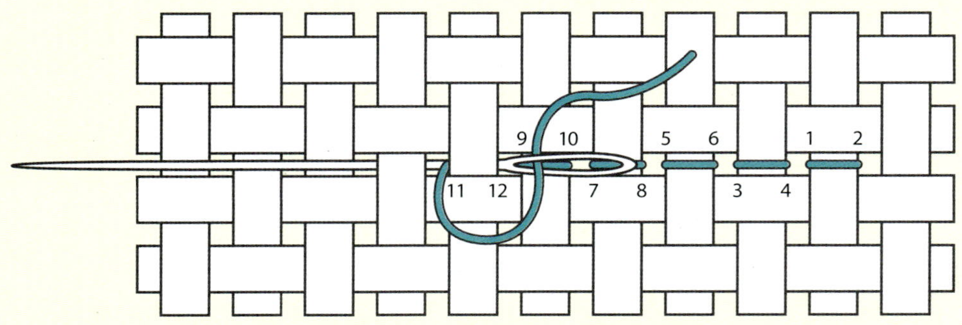

Half Stitch (1/2)

A half stitch is half of a full cross-stitch. Make a diagonal stitch, bringing the needle up at 1 and down at 2. To make a row of half stitches, bring the needle up at 3, down at 4, up at 5, down at 6, and so on.

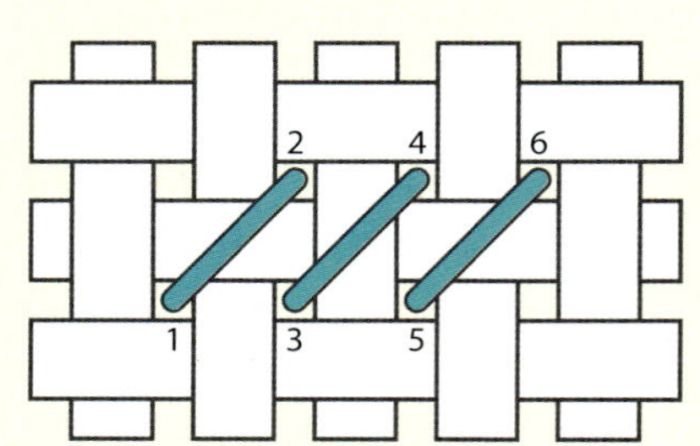

Quarter Stitch (1/4)

To make a quarter stitch, bring the needle up at 1. Then bring the needle down at 2, through the solid center of the square. Quarter stitches can be made in all directions.

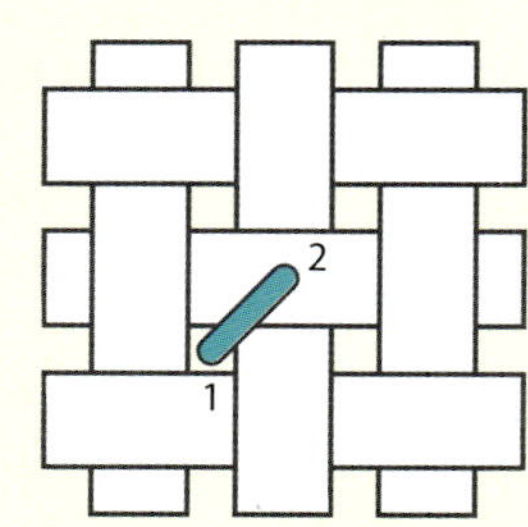

Three-quarter Stitch (3/4)

Bring the needle up at 1 and down at 2. Bring the needle up at 3 and down through the center of the square at 4 to complete the three-quarter stitch. Three-quarter stitches can be made in all directions.

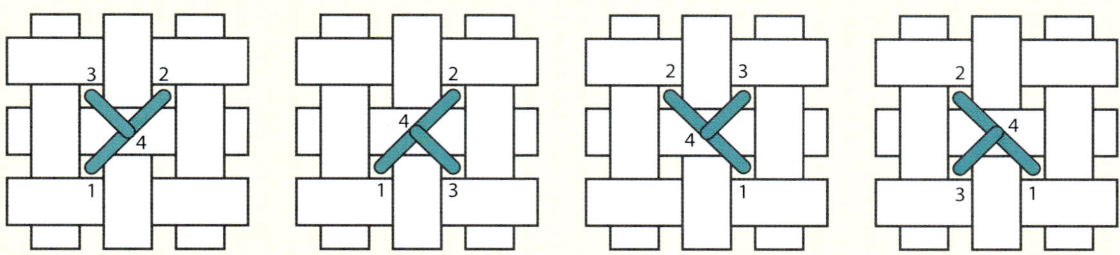

Smyrna Stitch (Spec)

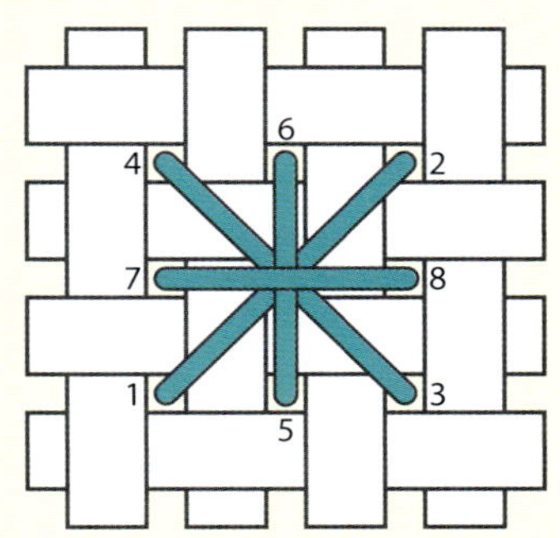

Smyrna stitch is also called double cross-stitch.

Bring the needle up at 1, down at 2, up at 3, down at 4, up at 5, down at 6, up at 7, and down at 8 to complete the Smyrna stitch.

French Knot (FK)

Bring the needle up to the front. Wrap the floss around the needle (once for a small knot, more for a larger knot). Pull the floss end gently until the wrapped floss tightens around the needle. Holding the floss taut with one hand, insert the needle next to where you brought it up. Draw the needle and floss until it must be released.

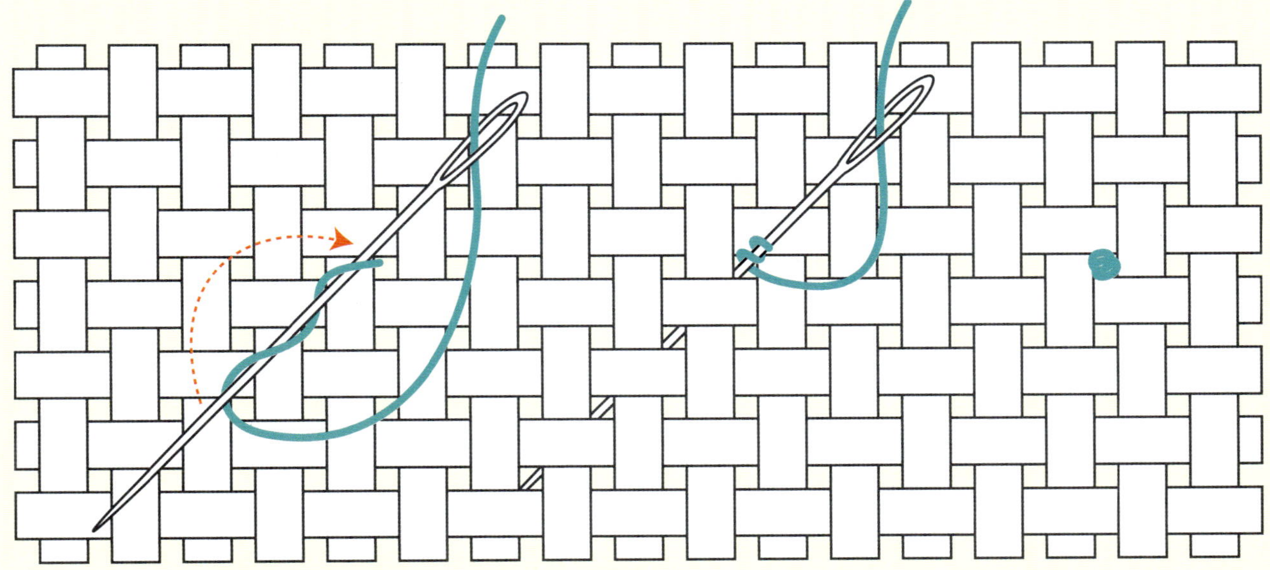

Stitching with Beads

The same charts can be used for counted beading. Small colored beads are sewn to the fabric to create the design. Use a beading needle (a very fine needle with a sharp point) and sewing thread the same color as the fabric.

Bring the needle up from the back of the fabric to the front. Pass the needle through the hole in the bead. Make a diagonal stitch (half of a full cross-stitch), passing the needle from the front of the fabric to the back. You can either work from left to right or from right to left, but be sure all stitches go in the same direction so the beads lie properly.

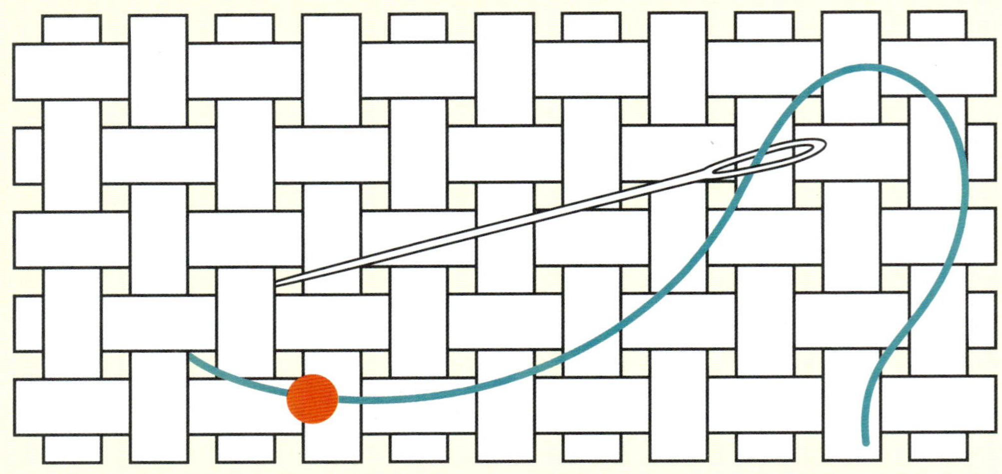

PREPARING TO STITCH

Separating Strands

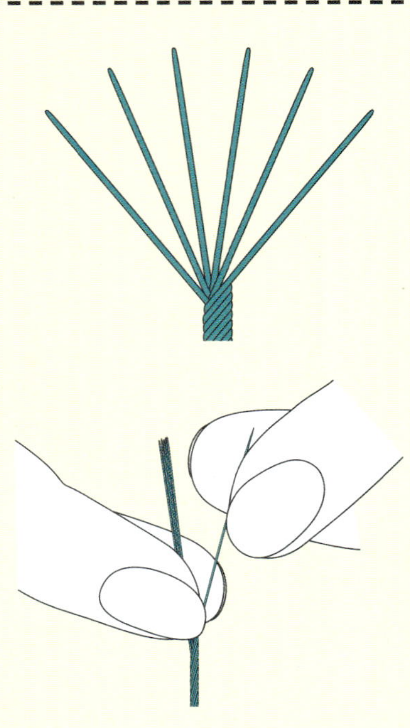

Most embroidery floss, or thread, consists of six strands twisted together. The number of strands you will use depends on the fabric count. For 14-count Aida fabric, you will typically use two strands of floss for cross-stitches and one or two strands for backstitches. Most patterns will specify the number of strands to use.

Tip: To rejoin strands of floss, hold them together at one end and gently stroke them until smooth. Then twirl them together to recombine.

Threading the Needle

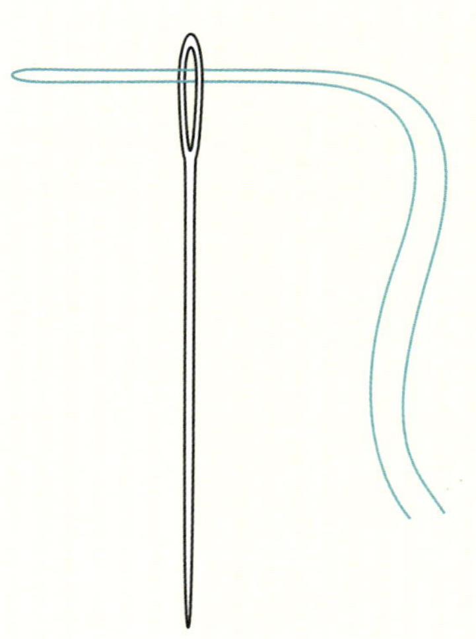

After you have separated the individual strands of floss, thread your tapestry needle with the required number of strands. Most cross-stitching on 14-count Aida is done with two strands.

Tip: If stitching with two strands of floss, you can cut a length of floss twice as long as you would normally use and separate one strand rather than two. You can then fold the strand of floss in half and thread the needle with both ends.

STARTING AND STOPPING

Select a floss color and stitch all of that color within an area. After you have separated the individual strands of floss, thread your tapestry needle with the required number of strands.

To start stitching, hold the end(s) of the floss behind the fabric until secured and covered over with a few stitches. This is sometimes called the "stitching over" method and is recommended for beginners. You may skip a few stitches to get from one area to another on the back of the fabric, but don't run floss behind an area that will not be stitched in the final piece because it will show through the fabric, particularly if the floss is a dark shade.

Loop Start

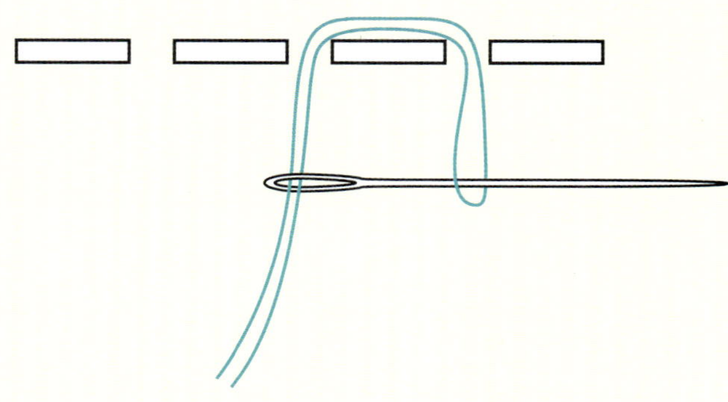

You can anchor the floss to your fabric with a loop. This method only works when stitching with an even number of strands. If stitching with an even number of strands, start with half of the total number of strands you need (e.g. for stitching with two strands, use one; for four strands, use two) and cut double the length you need. Fold in half and thread through the needle.

To start with a loop, bring the needle up from the back where you want your first stitch, leaving the looped end on the back side of the fabric. Make a half cross-stitch and bring the needle through the loop on the back side. Pull the floss until the loop is secure against the fabric.

Waste Knot Start

A waste knot is another way to anchor your floss. To start, knot one end of the floss and pass your needle through the fabric, from front to back, and about an inch from where your first cross-stitch will go. Bring your needle up from back to front at the starting point of your first cross-stitch. Stitch toward the knot, making sure your stitches cover the floss on the back. When you reach the knot, cut it from the front of the fabric and continue stitching.

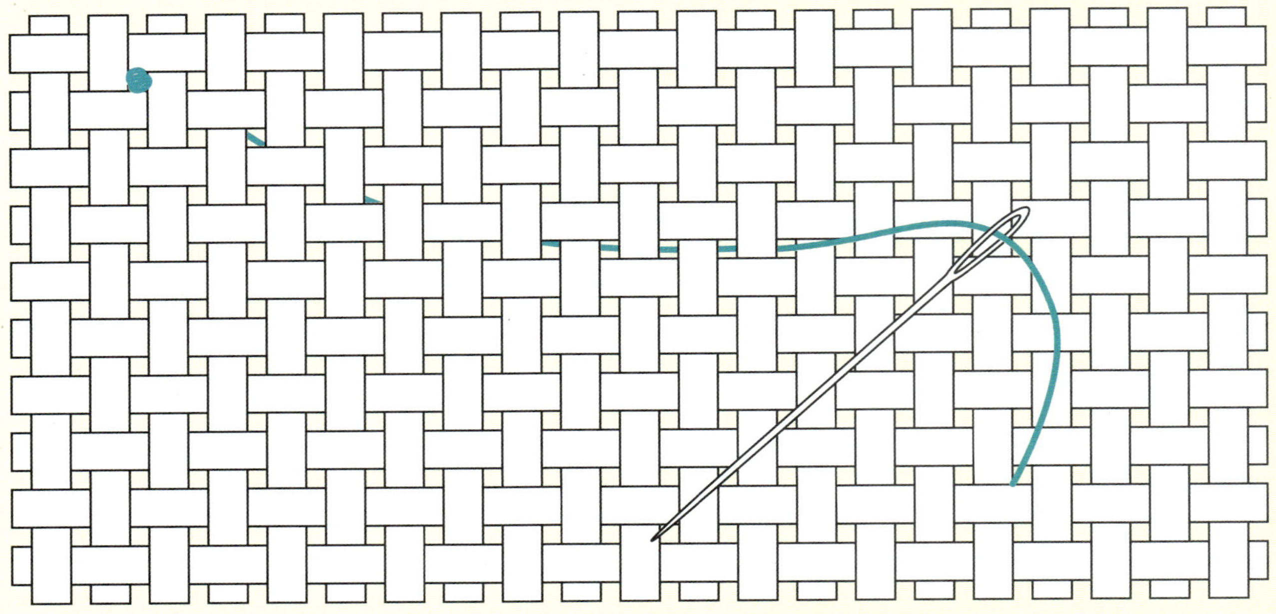

Stopping

To stop stitching, weave or run the floss under several stitches on the back side until secure. Clip the ends close to the work on the back. To resume stitching, re-thread the needle and secure the new floss by weaving or running it under several stitches on the back side.

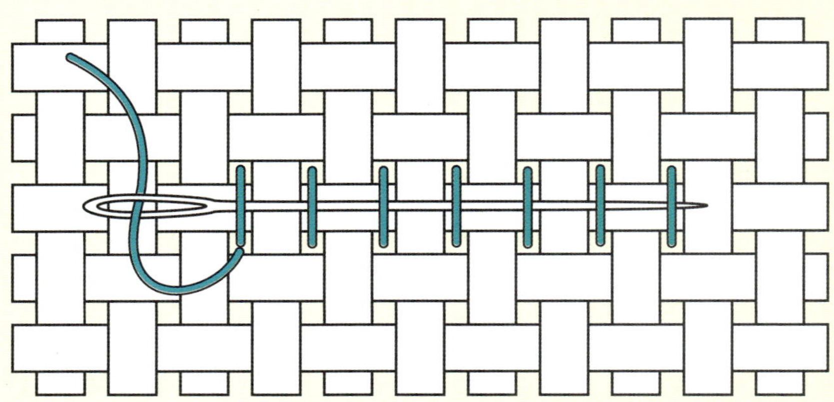

STITCHING TIPS

- Cross all stitches in the same direction. For horizontal rows, work the entire row of diagonal half stitches and then cross them coming back across the row.
- Start stitching in the center of the fabric and work out from there.
- Stitch with the darker colors first, then finish with the lighter colors.
- Avoid running floss across the back side of the fabric to jump to a new design area, especially with dark colors. It can show on the front. Only run floss across the back with the jump is short and the floss is a light color.
- For neat, uniform cross-stitches, keep your tension consistent throughout.
- Work all cross-stitches and fractional stitches first. Then work any back-stitches. If French knots are used, work these last.
- Keeping your hands clean is the best way to keep your cross-stitch project clean.

Inspirational
You are my
SUNSHINE

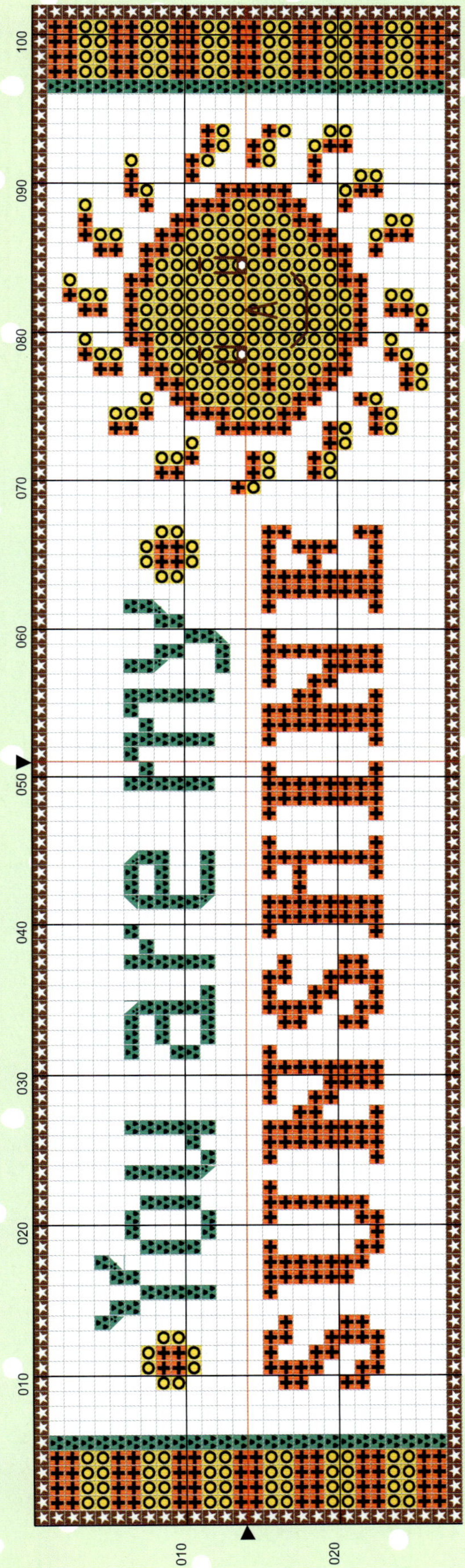

Design size:

102w x 28h stitches (7.3" x 2")

Instructions:

Following the general instructions on pages 13–19, stitch in 2 strands according to the chart. Backstitch the details on the sun's face in brown floss. For the bottom part of each eye, use brown floss to make a horizontal half stitch across the bottom half of the square. Horizontal half stitches are the same as full cross-stitches, but use half the space. Refer to page 11 for ways to increase the stability of your piece to use it as a bookmark.

Tip:

Even though "half stitch" is in its name, the horizontal half stitch is worked the same way as a full cross-stitch. The only difference is that the horizontal half stitch is made over the top or bottom half of an Aida square. The stitch should look like a shorter cross-stitch.

2 strands		
Cross-stitch	✚	Pumpkin
	O	Canary Yellow
	☢	Bright Green
	★	Medium Brown
Back-stitch	—	Medium Brown
Horiz half stitch	⬢	Medium Brown
Half stitch	☢	Bright Green

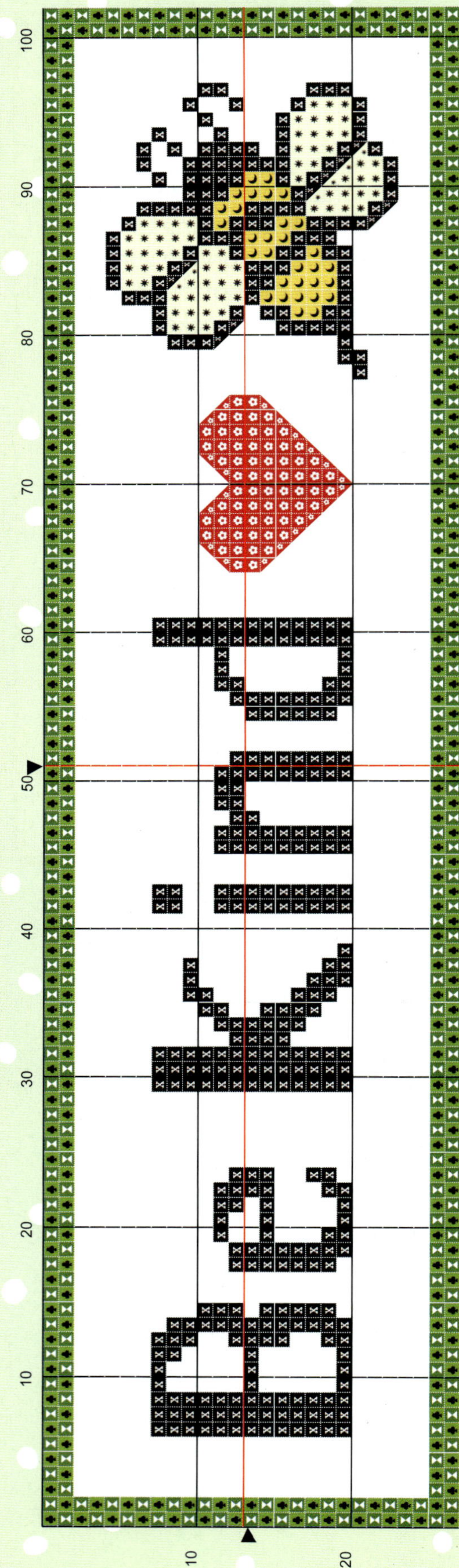

Design size:

102w x 28h stitches (7.2" x 2")

Instructions:

Following the general instructions on pages 13–19, stitch in 2 strands according to the chart. Refer to page 11 for ways to increase the stability of your piece to use it as a bookmark.

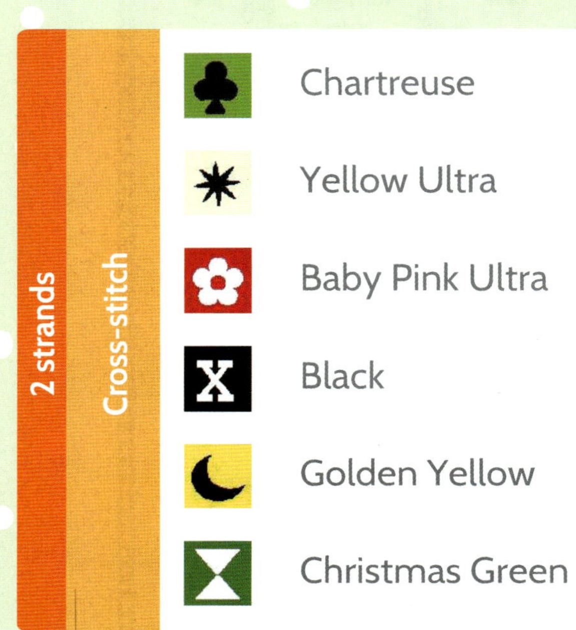

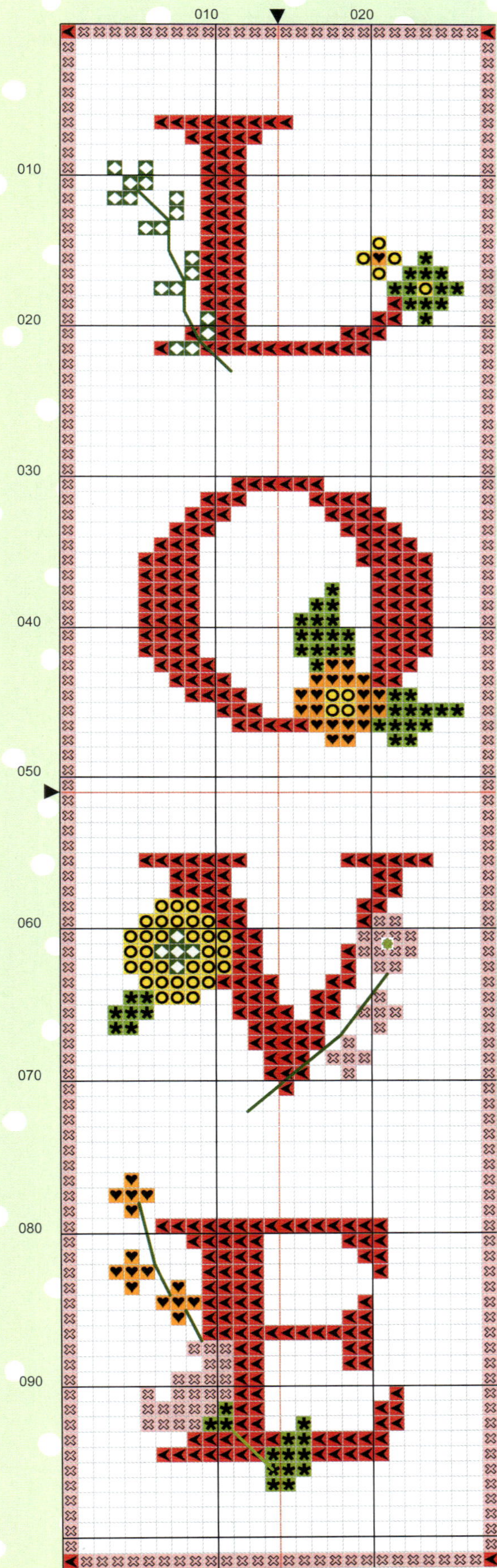

Design size:

28w x 102h stitches (2" x 7.3")

Instructions:

Following the general instructions on pages 13–19, stitch in 2 strands according to the chart. When all cross-stitching is done, backstitch the flower stems in green. Stitch the French knot in the center of the pink flower last, using light parrot green. Refer to page 11 for ways to increase the stability of your piece to use it as a bookmark.

Tip:

Fringed edges work best on bookmarks that have a complete stitched border. This prevents the fabric from unraveling within the bookmark's border.

2 strands	Cross-stitch	Dusty Rose
		Canary Yellow
		Dark Baby Pink
		Light Parrot Green
		Dark Parrot Green
		Tangerine
	Backstitch	Light Parrot Green
		Dark Parrot Green
	French knot	Light Parrot Green

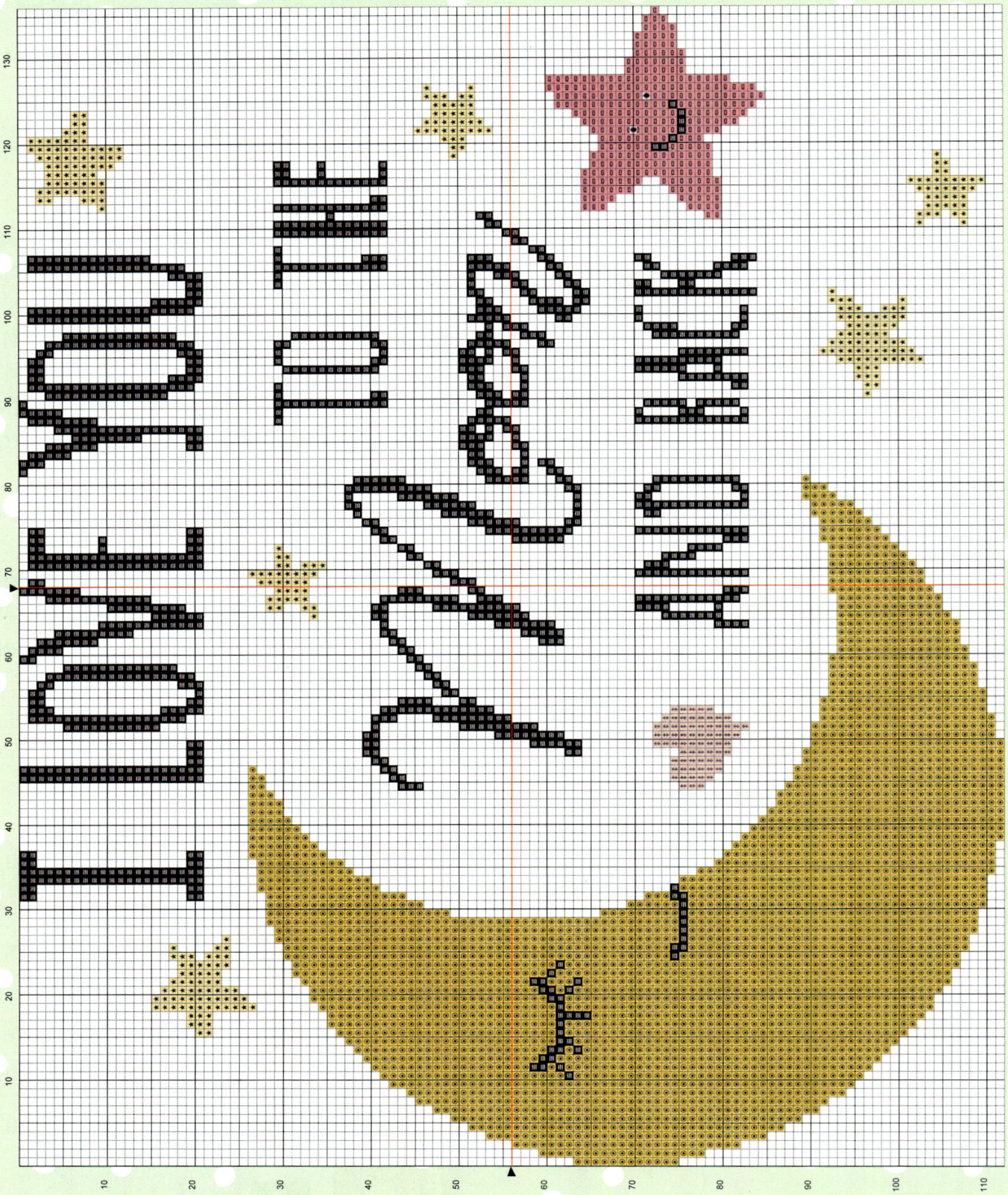

Design size:

136w x 112h stitches (9.7'' x 8'')

Instructions:

Following the general instructions on pages 13–19, stitch in 2 strands according to the chart. When all cross-stitching is done, use French knots to add the star's eyes. Allow yourself a little extra fabric around the edges if you intend to frame your design.

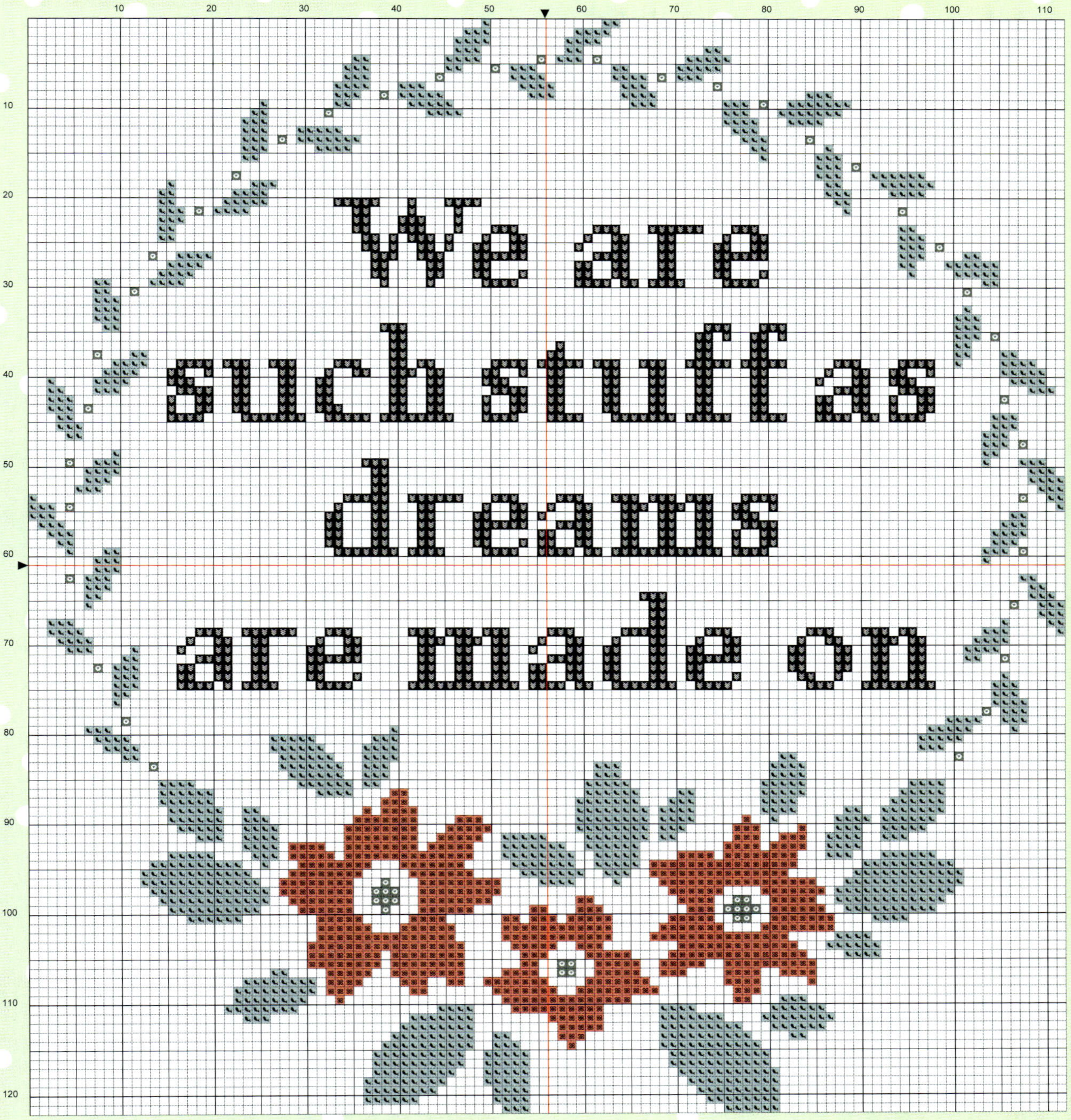

Design size:
112w x 122h stitches (8" x 8.7")

Instructions:
Following the general instructions on pages 13–19, stitch in 2 strands according to the chart. Allow yourself a little extra fabric around the edges if you intend to frame your design.

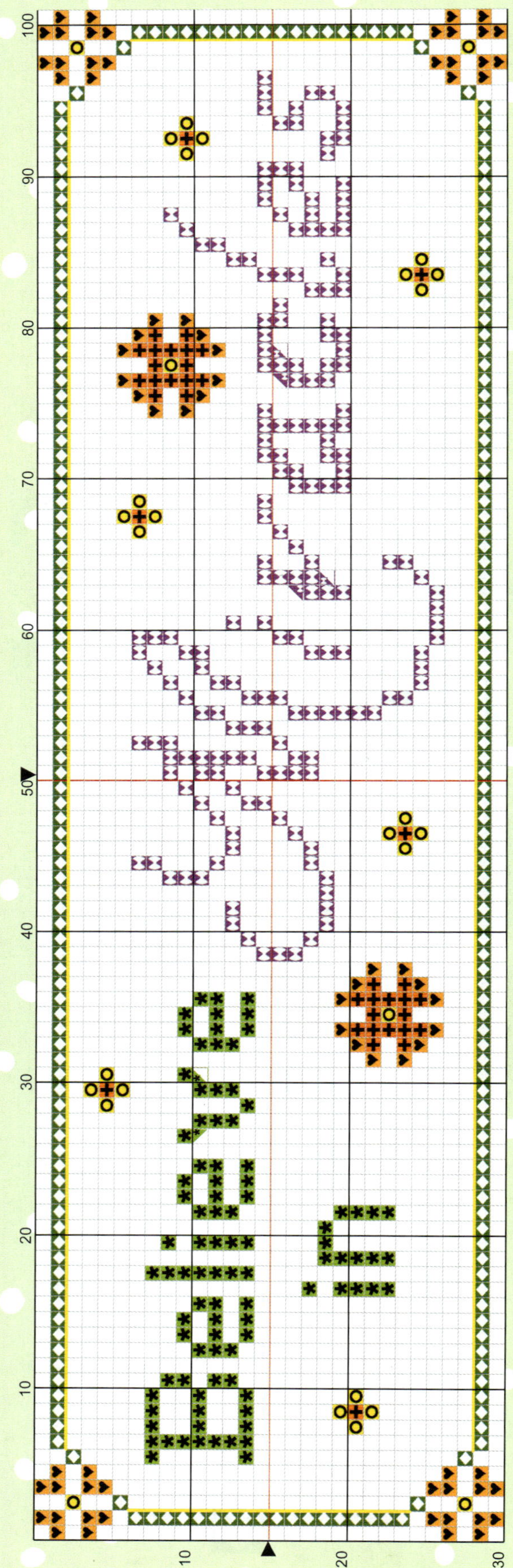

Design size:

101w x 30h stitches (7.2" x 2.1")

Instructions:

Following the general instructions on pages 13–19, stitch in 2 strands according to the chart. Squares in the chart that are only half filled use a half stitch. When all cross-stitching is done, backstitch the border in canary yellow. Refer to page 11 for ways to increase the stability of your piece to use it as a bookmark.

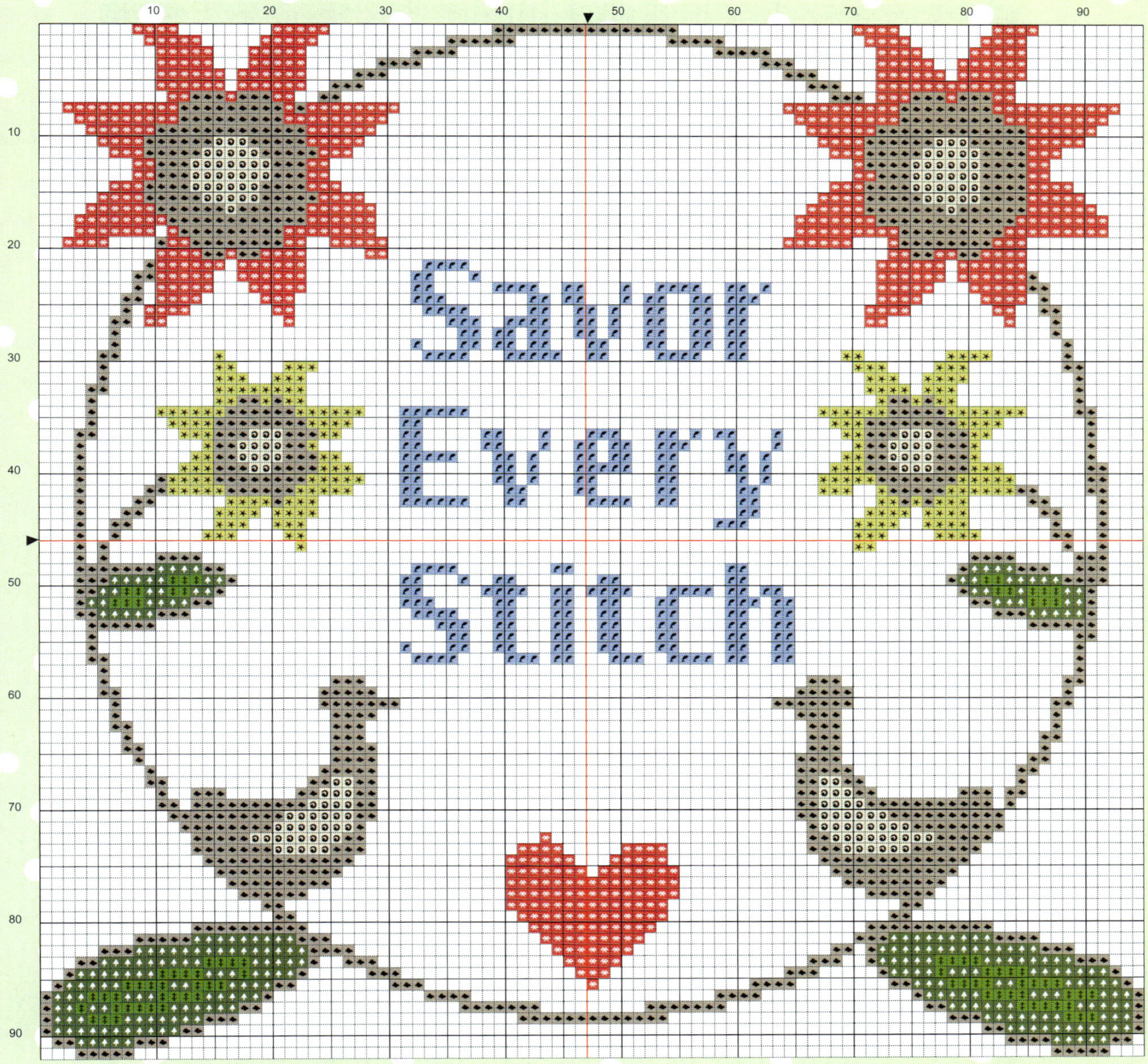

Design size:
95w x 92h stitches
(6.8" x 6.6")

Instructions:
Following the general instructions on pages 13–19, stitch in 2 strands according to the chart. Allow yourself a little extra fabric around the edges if you intend to frame your design.

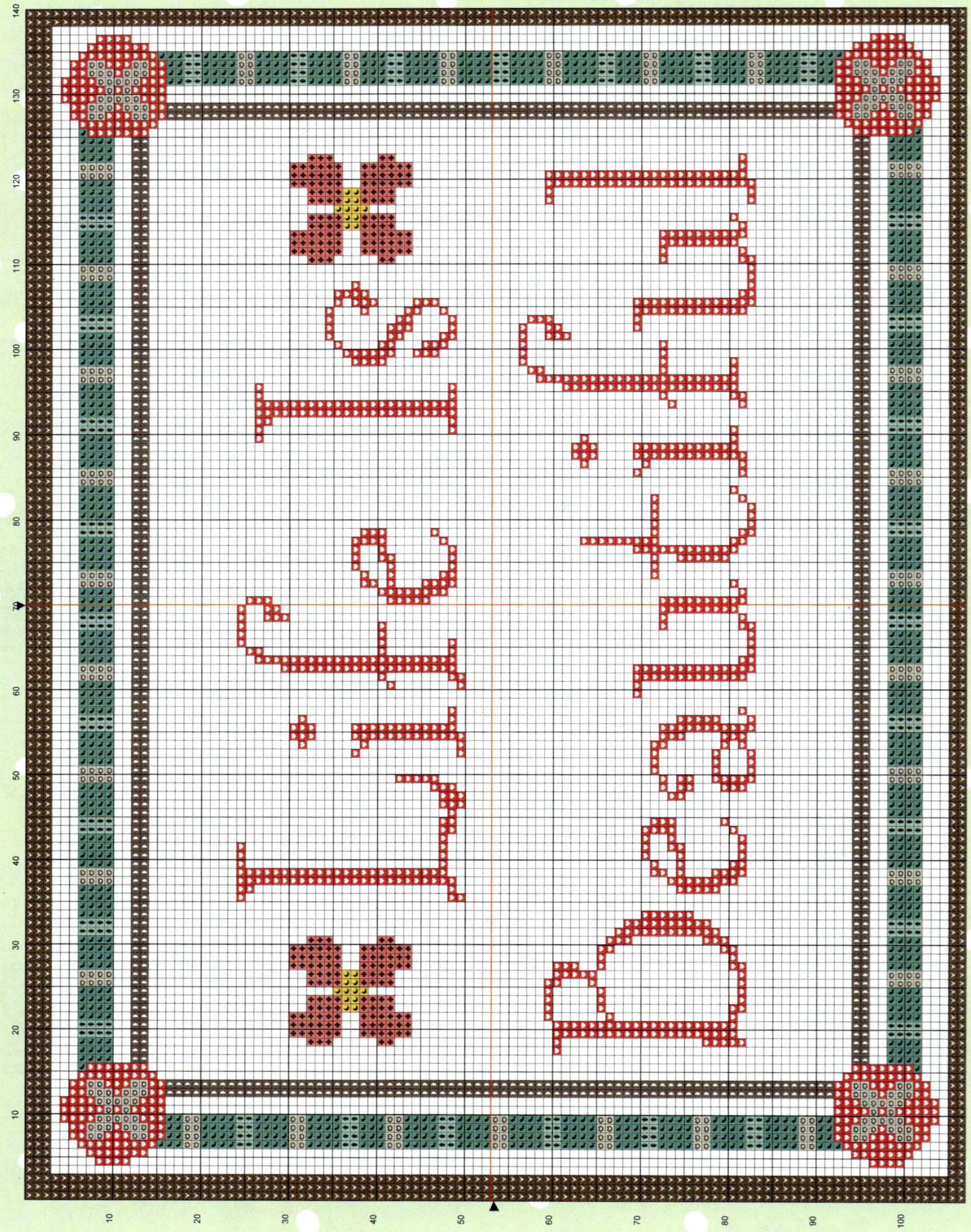

Design size:

140w x 107h stitches (10" x 7.6")

Instructions:

Following the general instructions on pages 13–19, stitch in 2 strands according to the chart. Allow yourself a little extra fabric around the edges if you intend to frame your design.

Design size:
126w x 98h stitches (9" x 7")

Instructions:
Following the general instructions on pages 13–19, stitch in 2 strands according to the chart. Allow yourself a little extra fabric around the edges if you intend to frame your design.

2 strands

Cross-stitch

▚	Coffee
▲	Jade
♣	Chartreuse

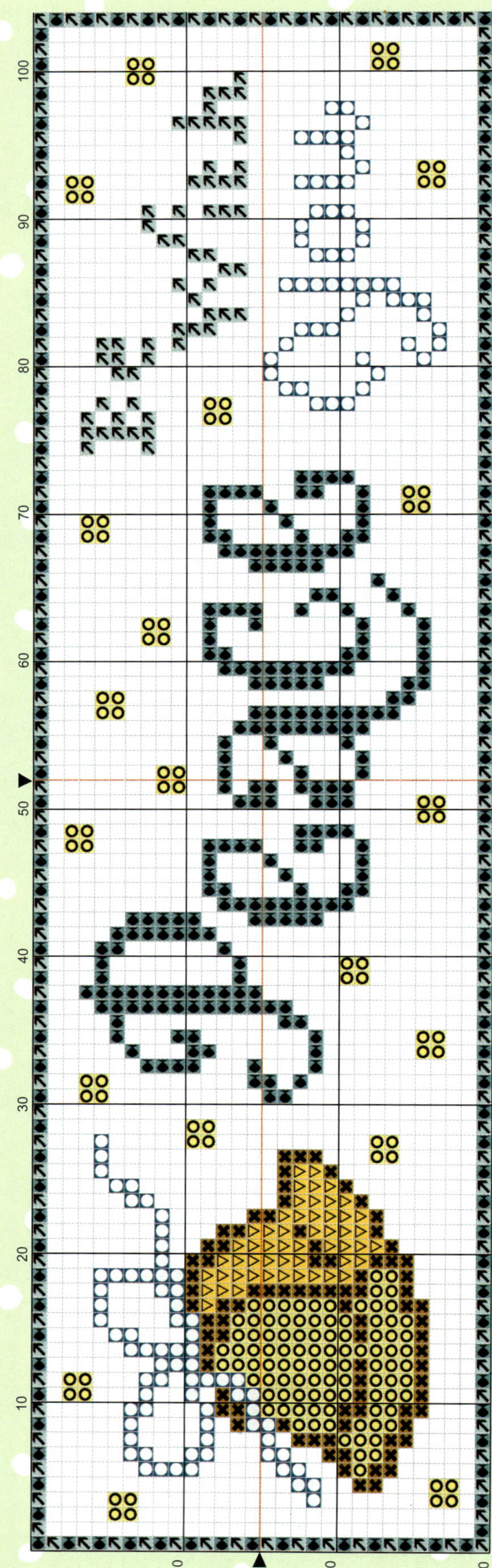

Design size:

104w x 30h stitches (7.4" x 2.1")

Instructions:

Following the general instructions on pages 13–19, stitch in 2 strands according to the chart. Refer to page 11 for ways to increase the stability of your piece to use it as a bookmark.

Tip:

Allow about an extra half-inch of fabric beyond the stitched border on each side if you wish to fringe the edges. After completing the stitching, gently pull loose strands of cloth around the edges up to the cross-stitched border.

Design size:
126w x 125h stitches (9" x 8.9")

Instructions:
Following the general instructions on pages 13–19, stitch in 2 strands according to the chart. Allow yourself a little extra fabric around the edges if you intend to frame your design.

2 strands	Cross-stitch	
		Teal
		Electric Blue
		Baby Pink
		Cornflower Blue

Design size:

30w x 104h stitches (2.1" x 7.4")

Instructions:

Following the general instructions on pages 13–19, stitch in 2 strands according to the chart. When all cross-stitching is done, backstitch the stems of the apples in the tree with green floss. Leave empty white squares around the text unstitched. Refer to page 11 for ways to increase the stability of your piece to use it as a bookmark.

2 strands	Cross-stitch	Bright Red
		Light Beige-Brown
		Bright Orange-Red
		Light Brown
		Dark Hunter Green
		Medium Cocoa Brown
		Green
		Chartreuse
		Light Shell Pink
		Light Avocado Green
		Avocado Green
		Light Sky Blue
	Backstitch	Green

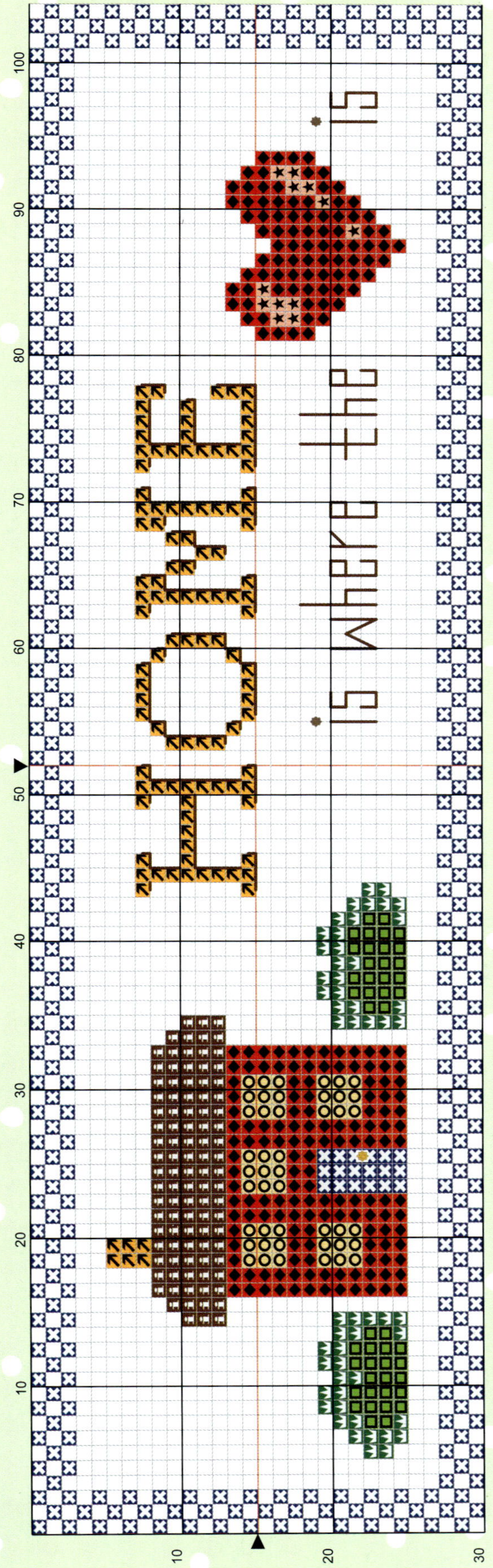

Design size:

104w x 30h stitches (7.4" x 2.1")

Instructions:

Following the general instructions on pages 13–19, stitch in 2 strands according to the chart. When all cross-stitching is done, backstitch the words in the second line of text and the solid lines around "Home"; dot the I's with French knots. Add a French knot of medium autumn gold for the doorknob. Refer to page 11 for ways to increase the stability of your piece to use it as a bookmark.

2 strands

Cross-stitch	O	Light Autumn Gold
	↗	Medium Autumn Gold
	◆	Light Christmas Red
	✖	Dark Bright Turquoise
	i	Medium Cocoa Brown
	♛	Green
	■	Bright Chartreuse
	★	Apricot
Backstitch	—	Medium Cocoa Brown
French knots	✸	Medium Autumn Gold
	✸	Medium Cocoa Brown

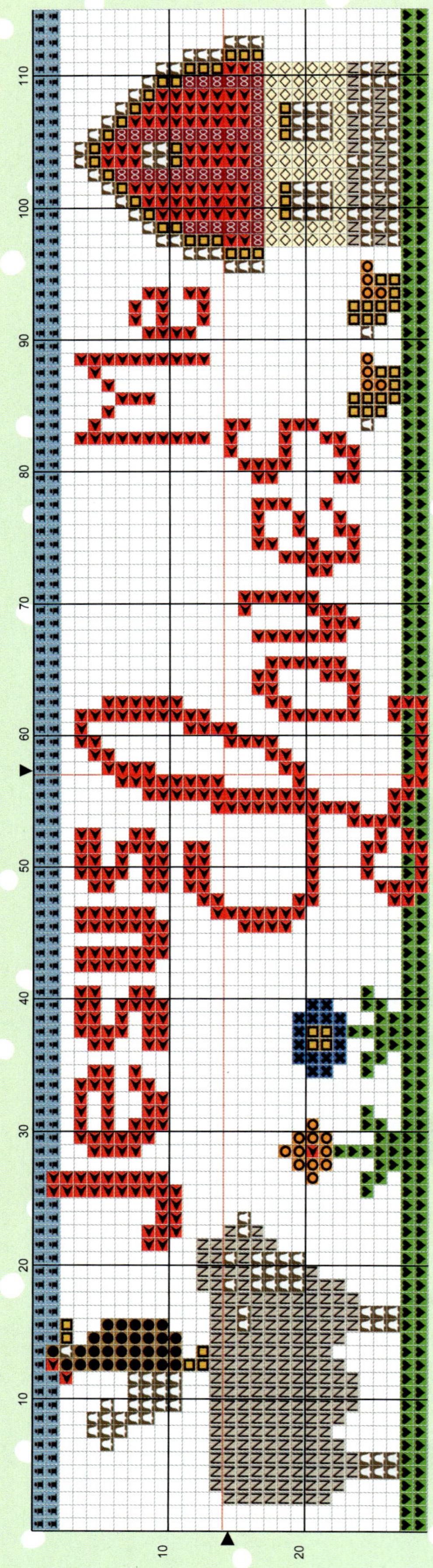

Design size:
115w x 29h stitches (8.2" x 2.1")

Instructions:
Following the general instructions on pages 13–19, stitch in 2 strands according to the chart. Refer to page 11 for ways to increase the stability of your piece to use it as a bookmark.

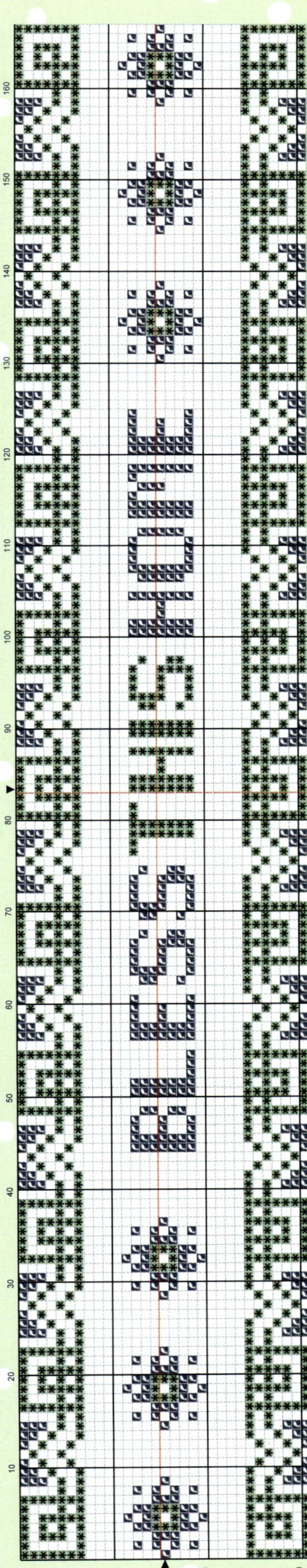

Design size:

167w x 31h stitches (11.9" x 2.2")

Instructions:

Following the general instructions on pages 13–19, stitch in 2 strands according to the chart. Start stitching from the center and work outward. Depending on how you are using this piece, you can lengthen or shorten the border; if space allows, you can add more space between the words.

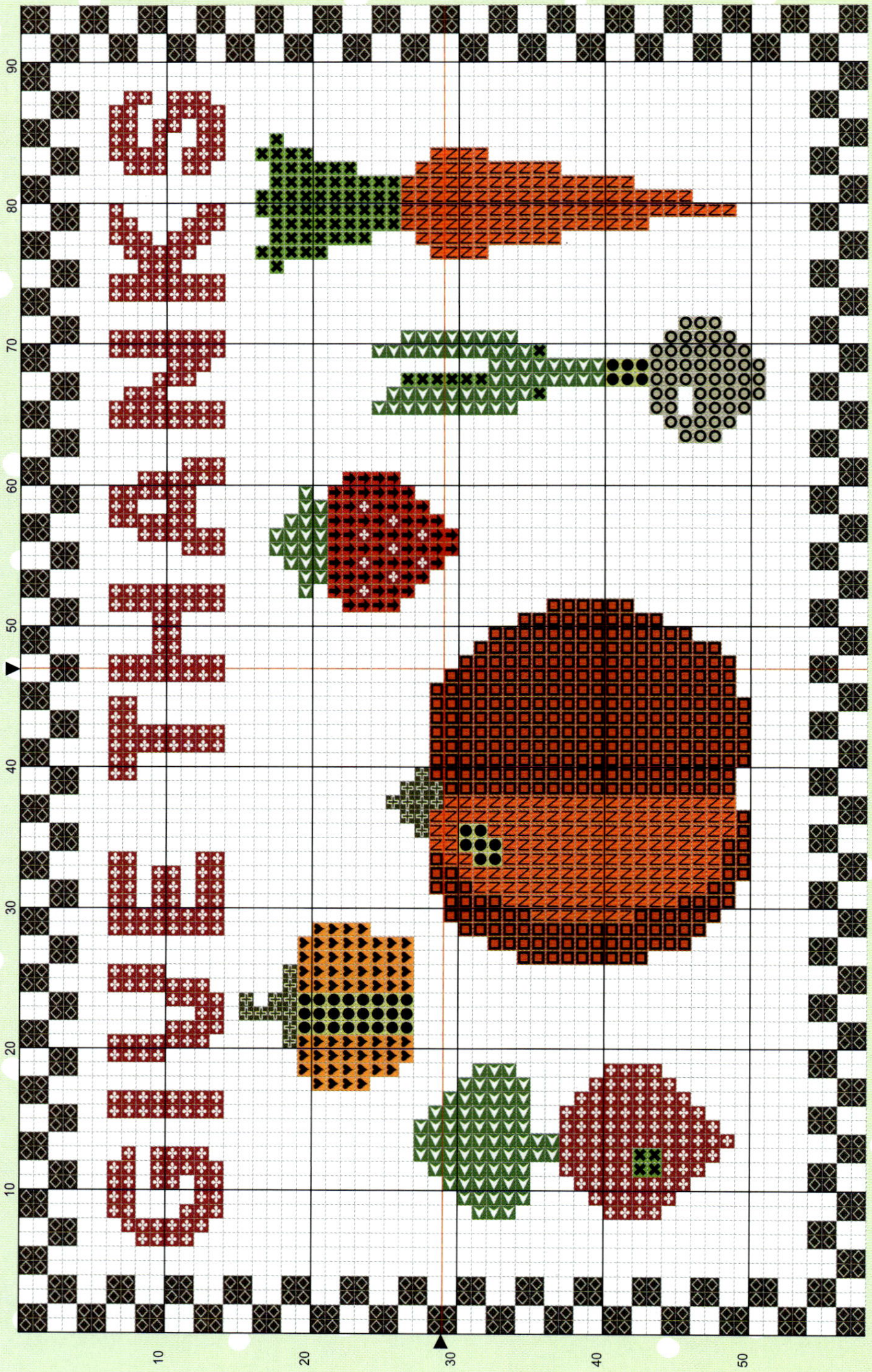

Design size:

94w x 58h stitches (6.7" x 4.1")

Instructions:

Following the general instructions on pages 13–19, stitch in 2 strands according to the chart. Allow yourself a little extra fabric around the edges if you intend to frame your design.

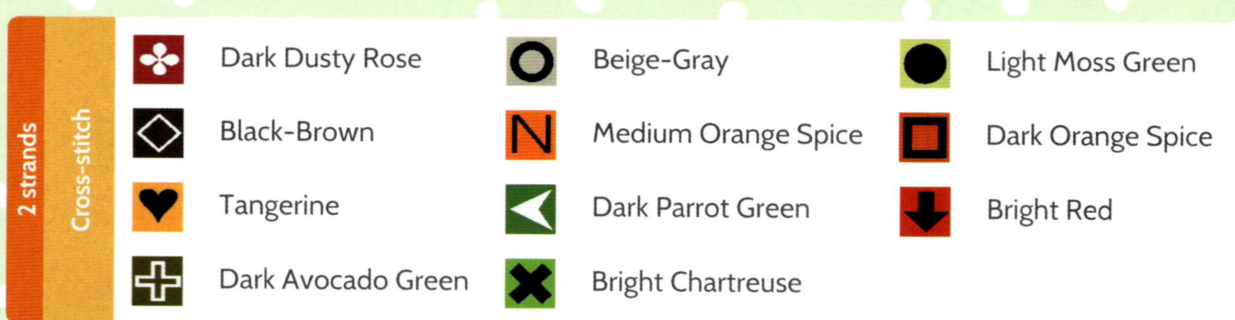

Design size:

41w x 28h stitches (2.9" x 2")

Instructions:

Following the general instructions on pages 13–19, stitch in 2 strands according to the chart.

Tip:

This design is a good size for a luggage tag. Trim the finished piece to fit inside a blank luggage tag case. If your case is visible from both sides, add your name and contact info on a card for the reverse side. This will also hide the threads on the back side of your design.

2 strands

Cross-stitch

	Black
	Light Christmas Red

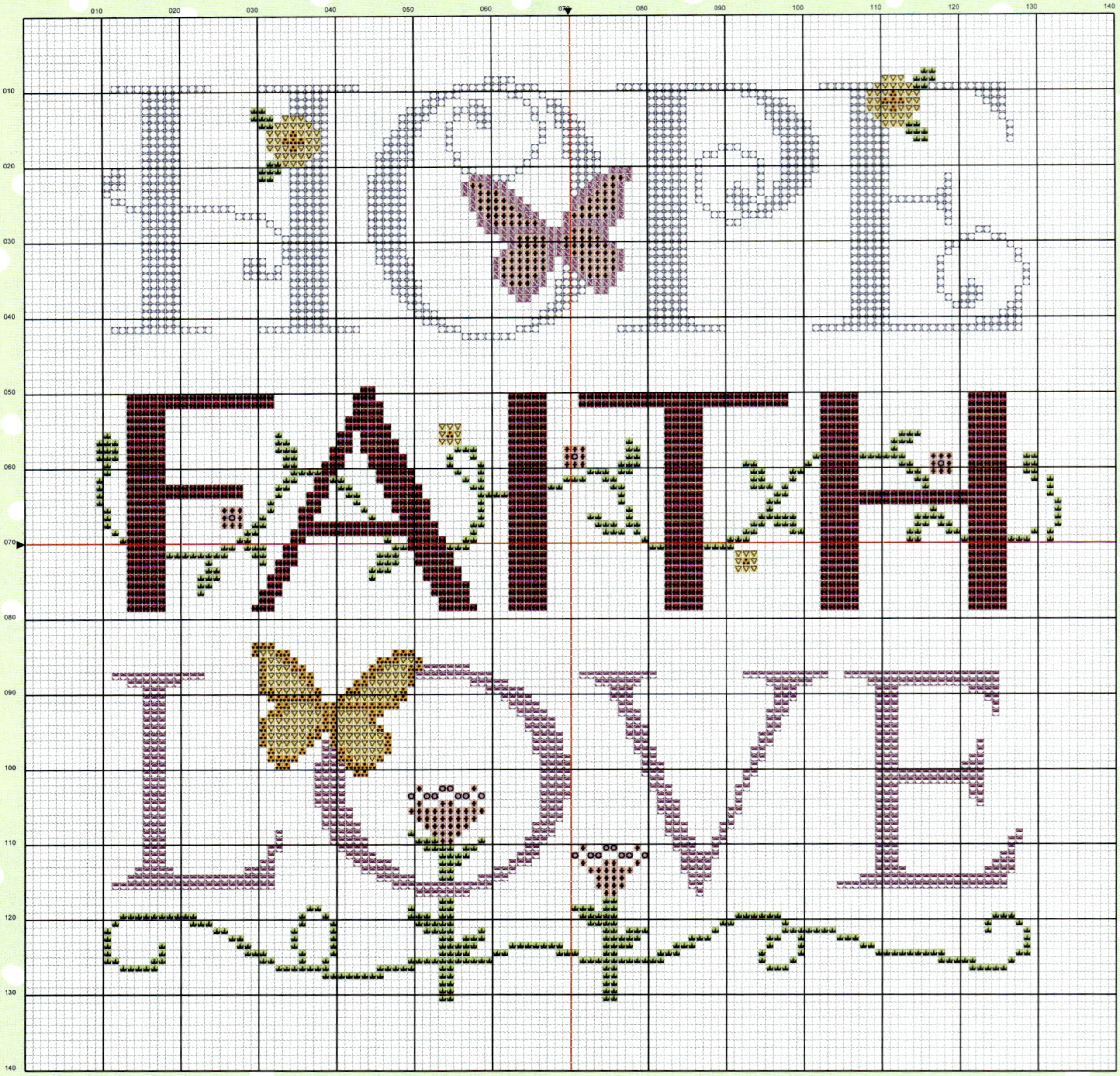

Design size:

140w x 140h stitches (10" x 10")

Instructions:

Following the general instructions on pages 13–19, stitch in 2 strands according to the chart. Allow a little extra fabric around the edges if you intend to frame your design.

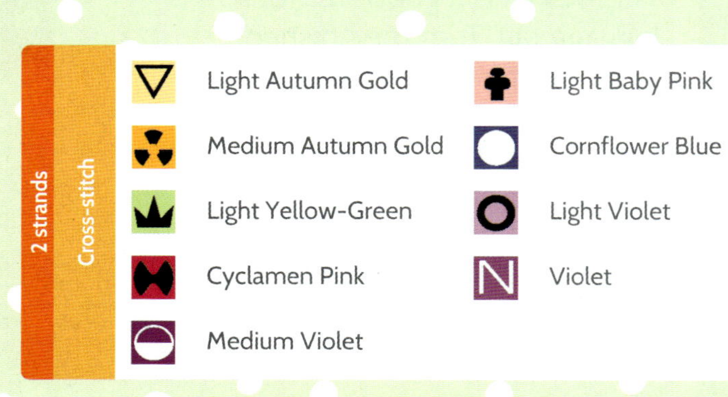

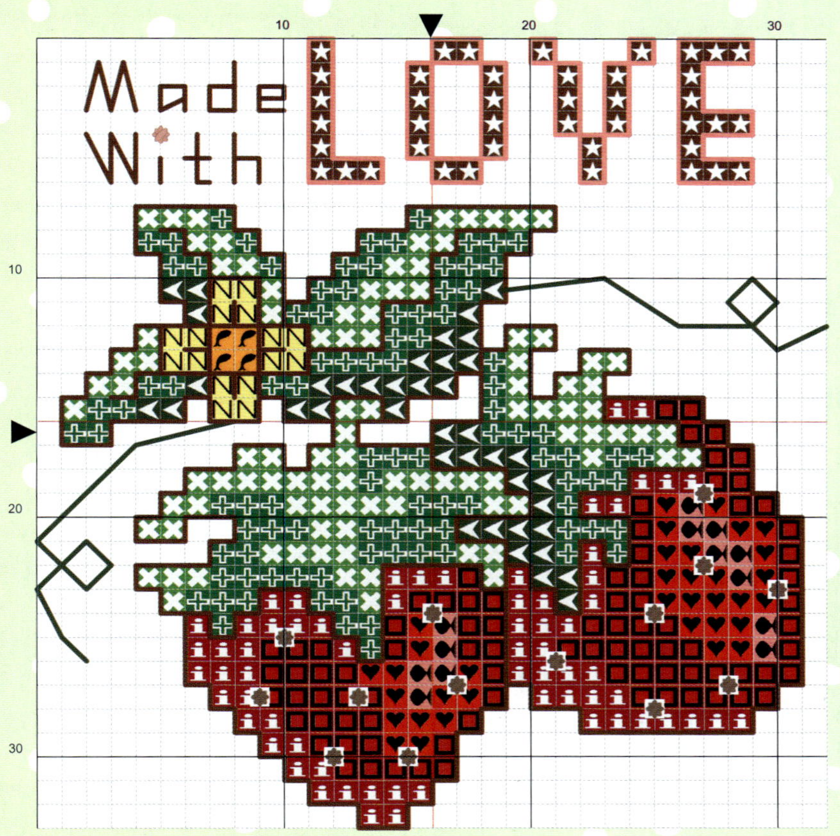

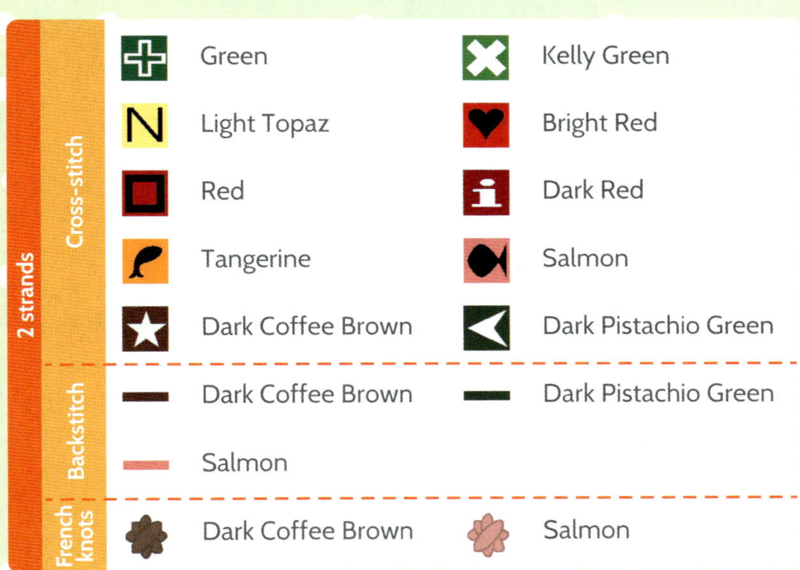

Design size:

32w x 33h stitches (2.3" x 2.4")

Instructions:

Following the general instructions on pages 13–19, stitch in 2 strands according to the chart. When all cross-stitching is done, backstitch the outline of the strawberries and "Made With" in brown floss. Stitch strawberry seeds with French knots in brown floss. Backstitch strawberry stems in dark pistachio green. With salmon floss, backstitch the outline around "Love" and dot the I with a French knot.

Tip:

This design is just the right size to use as a topper for a Mason jar. When your piece is complete, fill the jar with the desired contents. Cover the top of the jar lid with your cross-stitched fabric. Secure the lid and cross-stitched piece on the jar with the outer band.

Design size:

56w x 84h stitches (4" x 6")

Instructions:

Following the general instructions on pages 13–19, stitch in 2 strands according to the chart. Allow yourself a little extra fabric around the edges if you intend to frame your design.

2 strands · **Cross-stitch**

	Dark Mocha Beige		Medium Yellow-Green
	Dark Teal Green	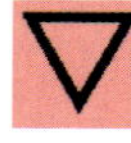	Baby Pink
	Brown-Gray		Light Leaf Green
	Dark Dusty Rose		

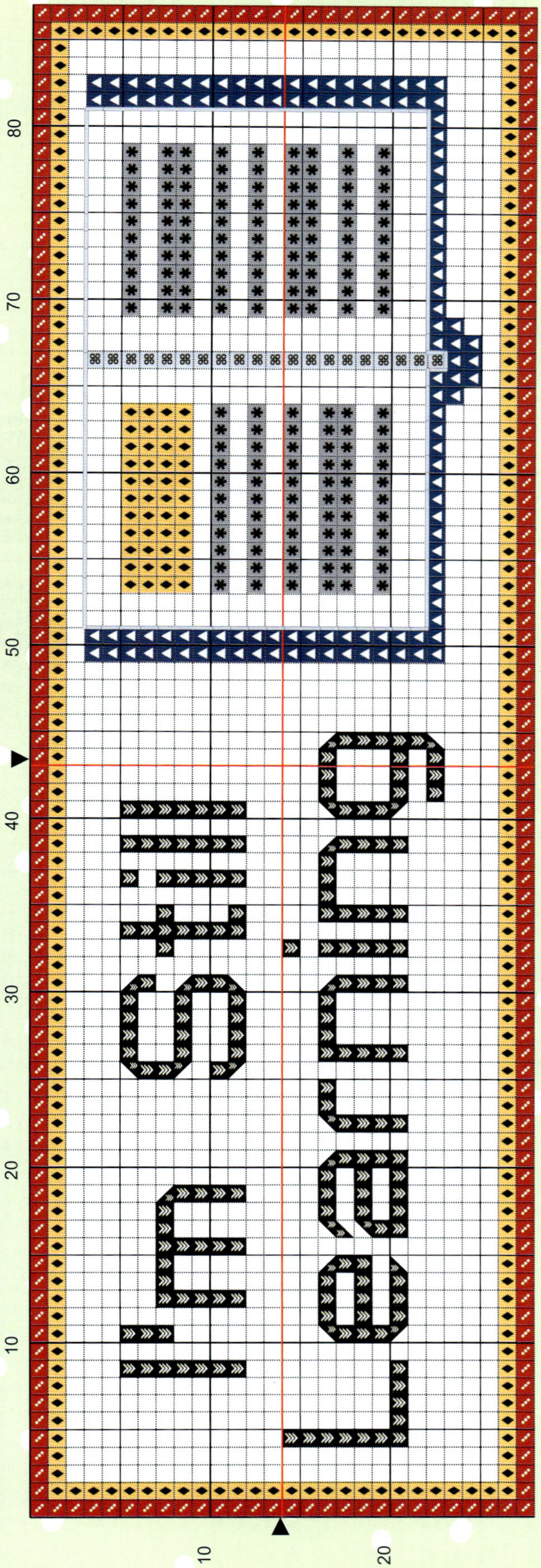

Design size:

87w x 28h stitches (6.2" x 2")

Instructions:

Following the general instructions on pages 13–19, stitch in 2 strands according to the chart. When all cross-stitching is done, backstitch the outline of the pages in blue purple floss. Refer to page 11 for ways to increase the stability of your piece to use it as a bookmark.

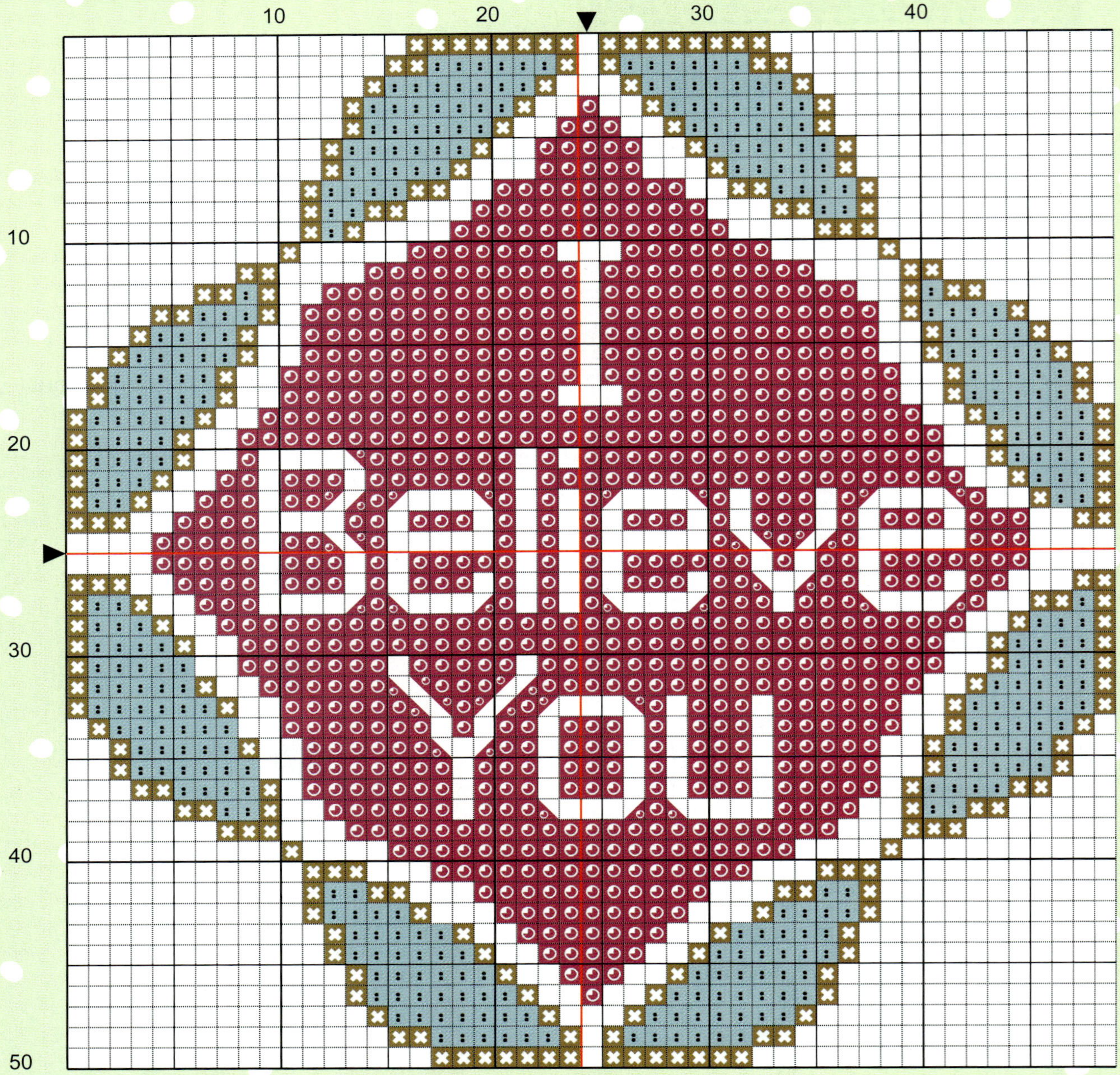

Design size:
49w x 50h stitches (3.5" x 3.6")

Instructions:
Following the general instructions on pages 13–19, stitch in 2 strands according to the chart. Allow yourself a little extra fabric around the edges if you intend to frame your design.

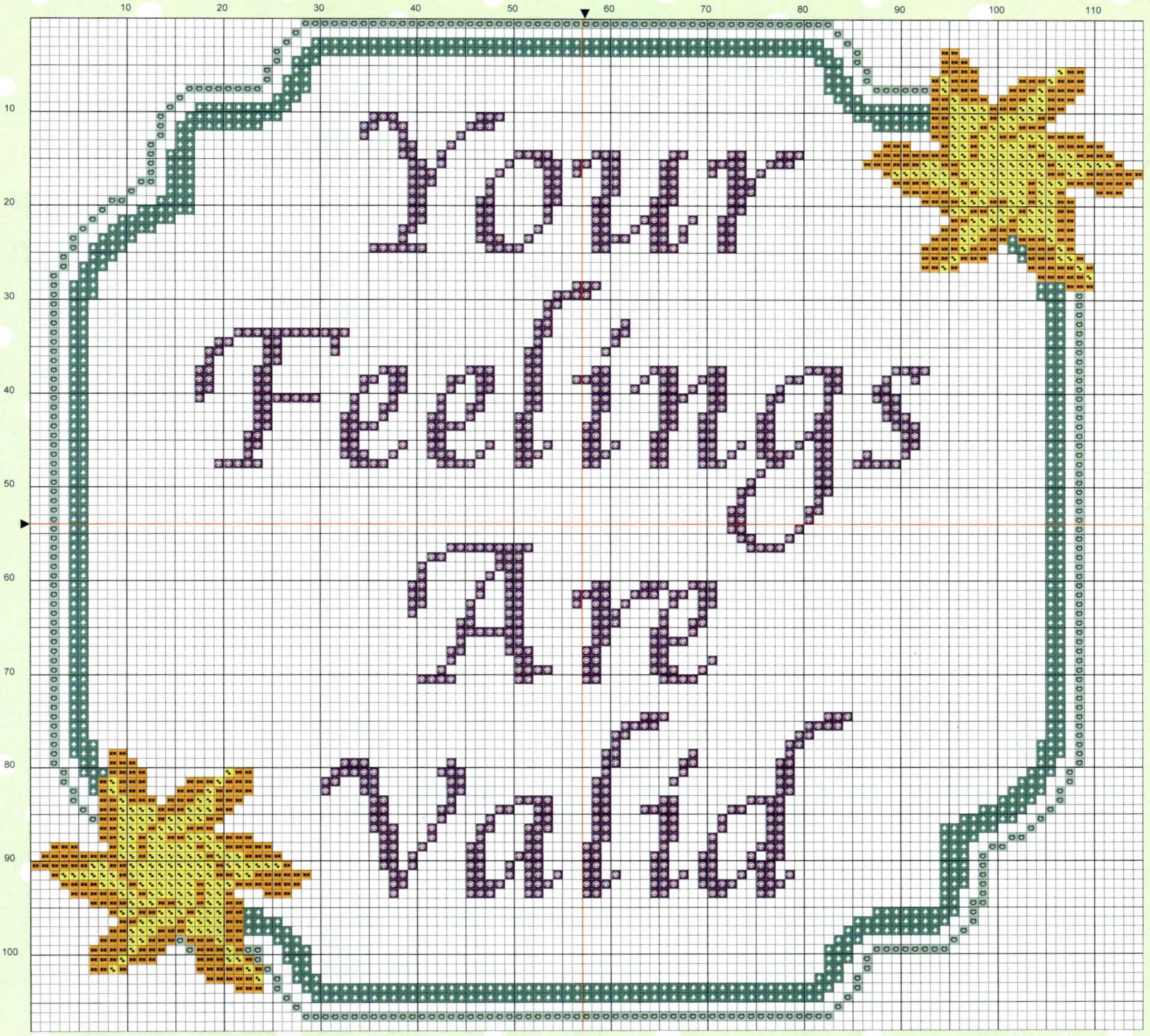

Design size:
115w x 108h stitches (8.2" x 7.7")

Instructions:
Following the general instructions on pages 13–19, stitch in 2 strands according to the chart. Allow yourself a little extra fabric around the edges if you intend to frame your design.

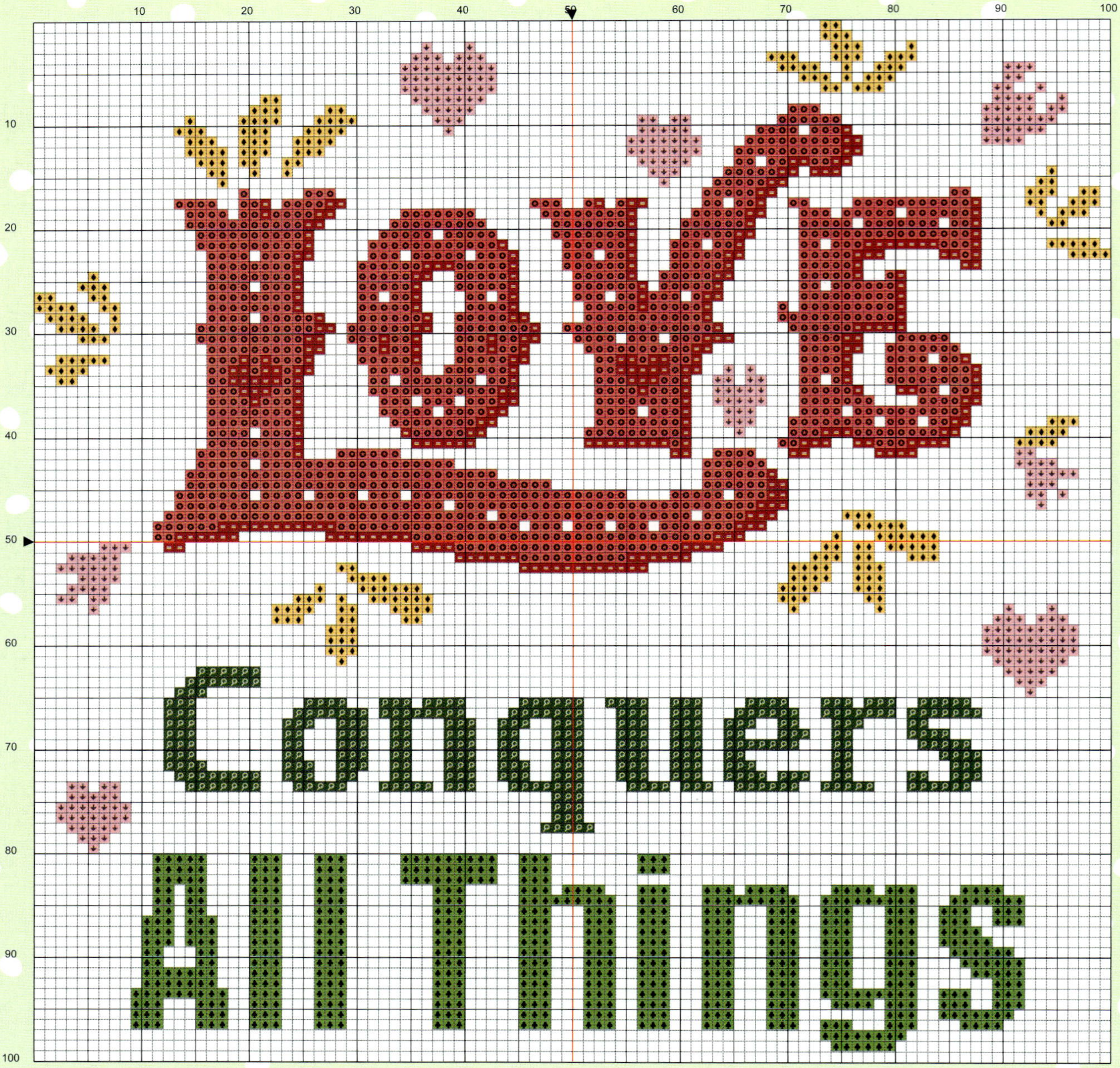

Design size:
100w x 100h stitches (7.1" x 7.1")

Instructions:
Following the general instructions on pages 13–19, stitch in 2 strands according to the chart. Allow yourself a little extra fabric around the edges if you intend to frame your design.

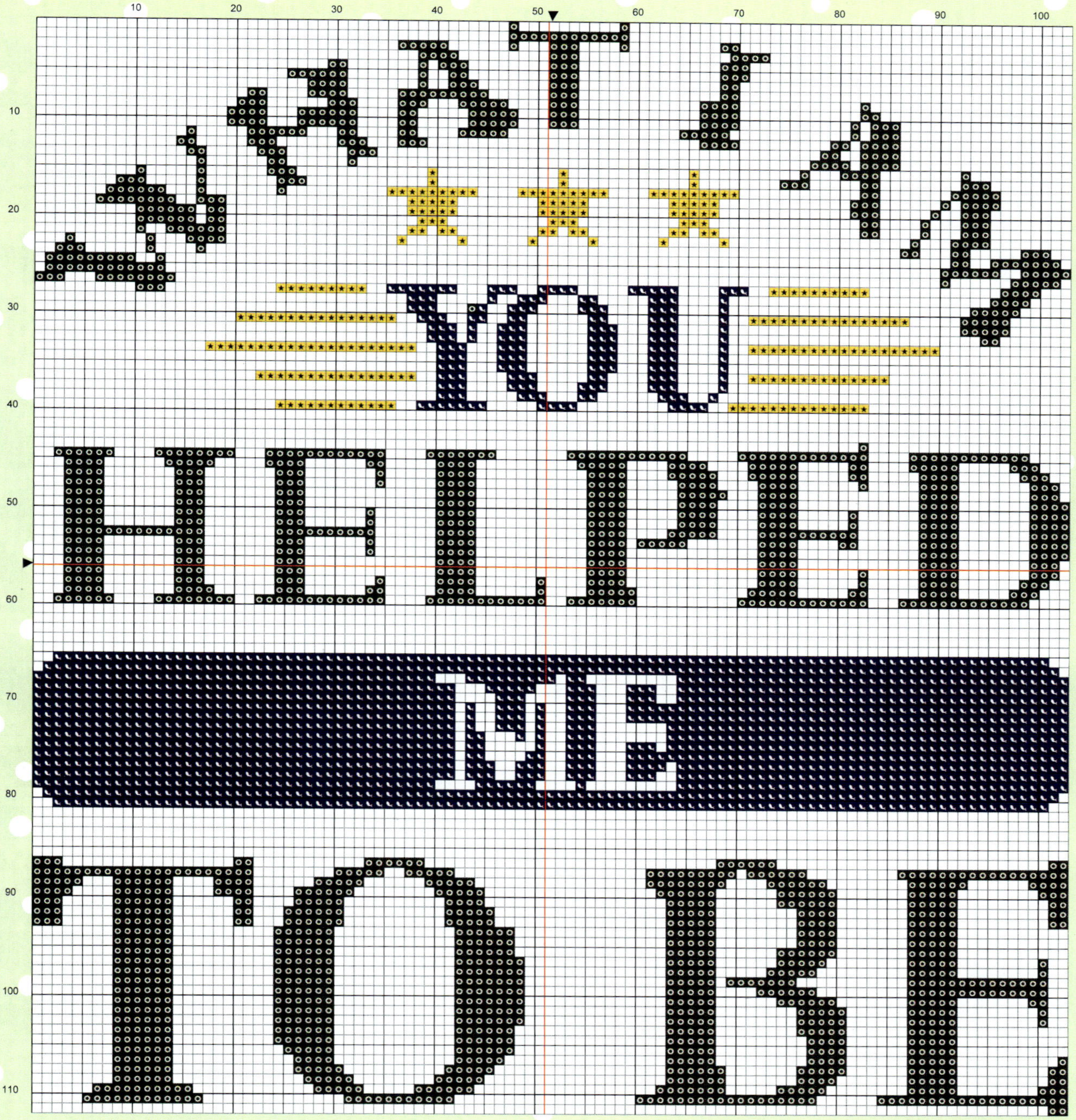

Design size:

103w x 112h stitches (7.4" x 8")

Instructions:

Following the general instructions on pages 13–19, stitch in 2 strands according to the chart. Allow yourself a little extra fabric around the edges if you intend to frame your design.

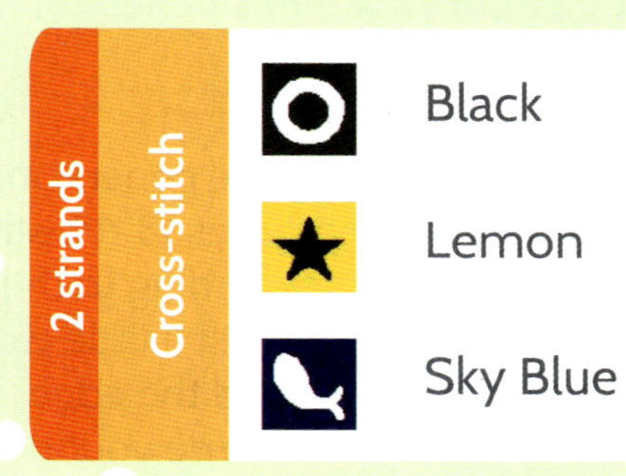

10 20 30 40 50 60 70 80 90

A Beautiful Thing Is Never Perfect

Design size:
99w x 99h stitches (7.1" x 7.1")

Instructions:
Following the general instructions on pages 13–19, stitch in 2 strands according to the chart. Allow yourself a little extra fabric around the edges if you intend to frame your design.

2 strands	Cross-stitch		
			Avocado Green
			Dusty Rose
			Blue Violet

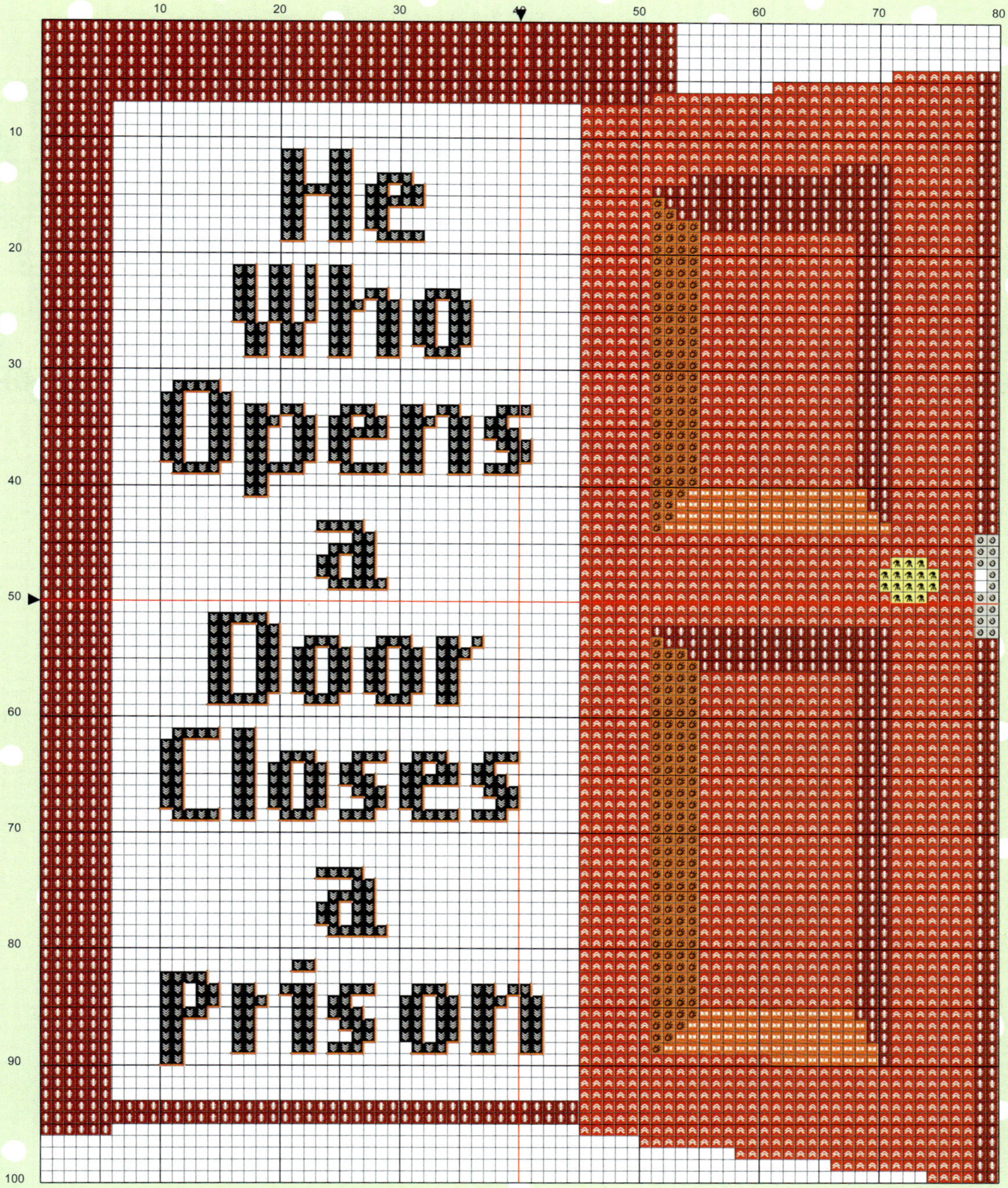

Design size:
80w x 100h stitches (5.7" x 7.1")

Instructions:
Following the general instructions on pages 13–19, stitch in 2 strands according to the chart. When all cross-stitching is done, backstitch the outline of the text in orange spice.

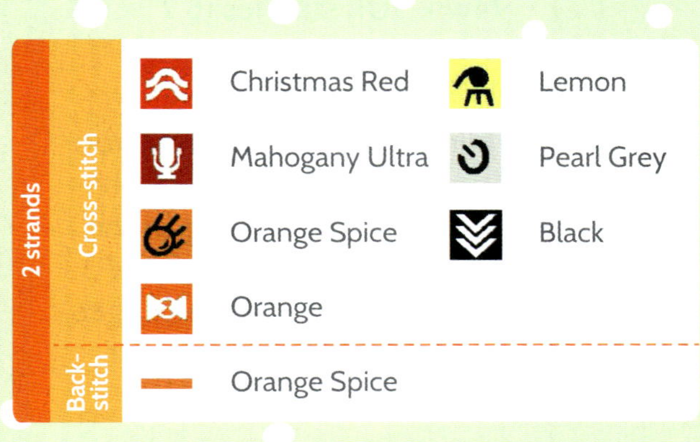

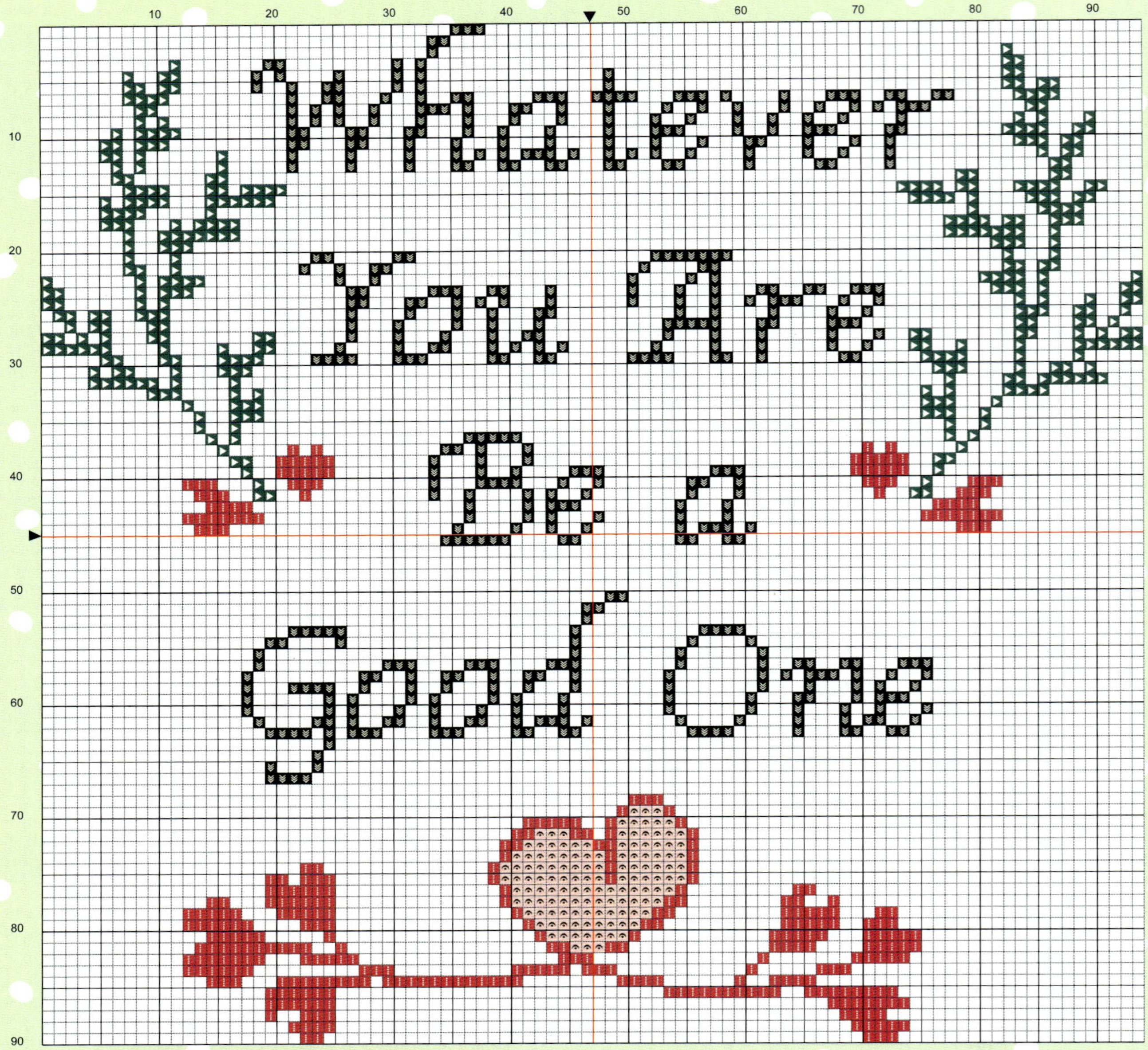

Design size:

94w x 90h stitches (6.7" x 6.4")

Instructions:

Following the general instructions on pages 13–19, stitch in 2 strands according to the chart. Allow yourself a little extra fabric around the edges if you intend to frame your design.

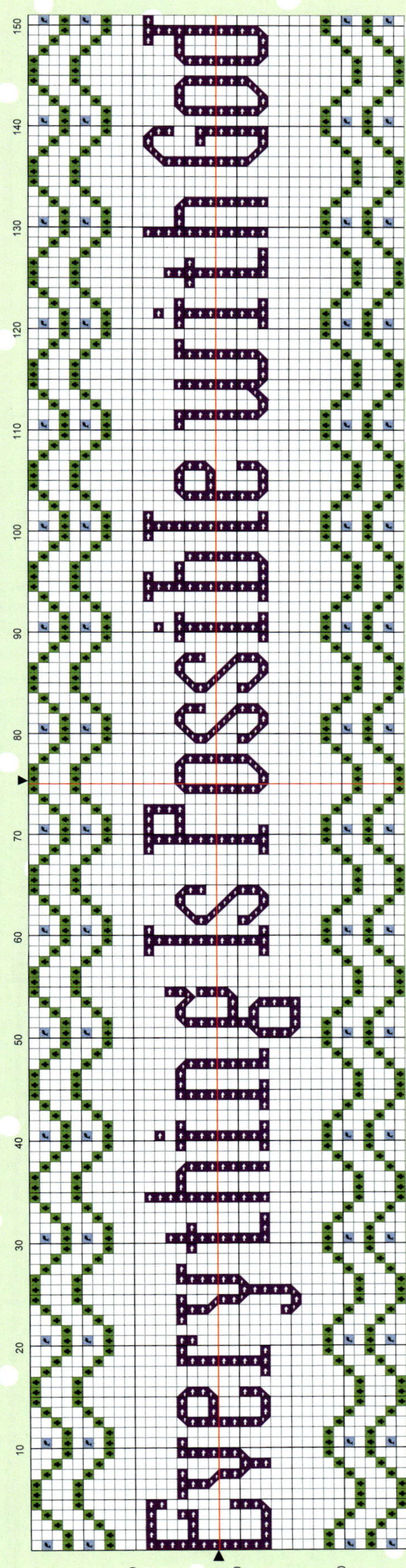

Design size:

151w x 36h stitches (10.8" x 2.6")

Instructions:

Following the general instructions on pages 13–19, stitch in 2 strands according to the chart. Squares in the chart that are only half filled use a half stitch. Refer to page 11 for ways to increase the stability of your piece to use it as a bookmark.

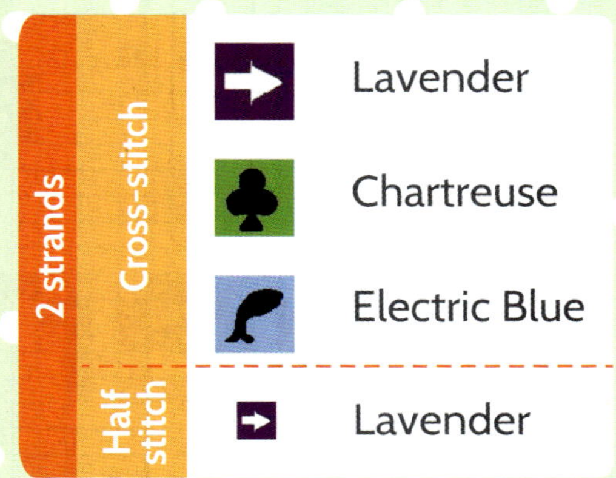

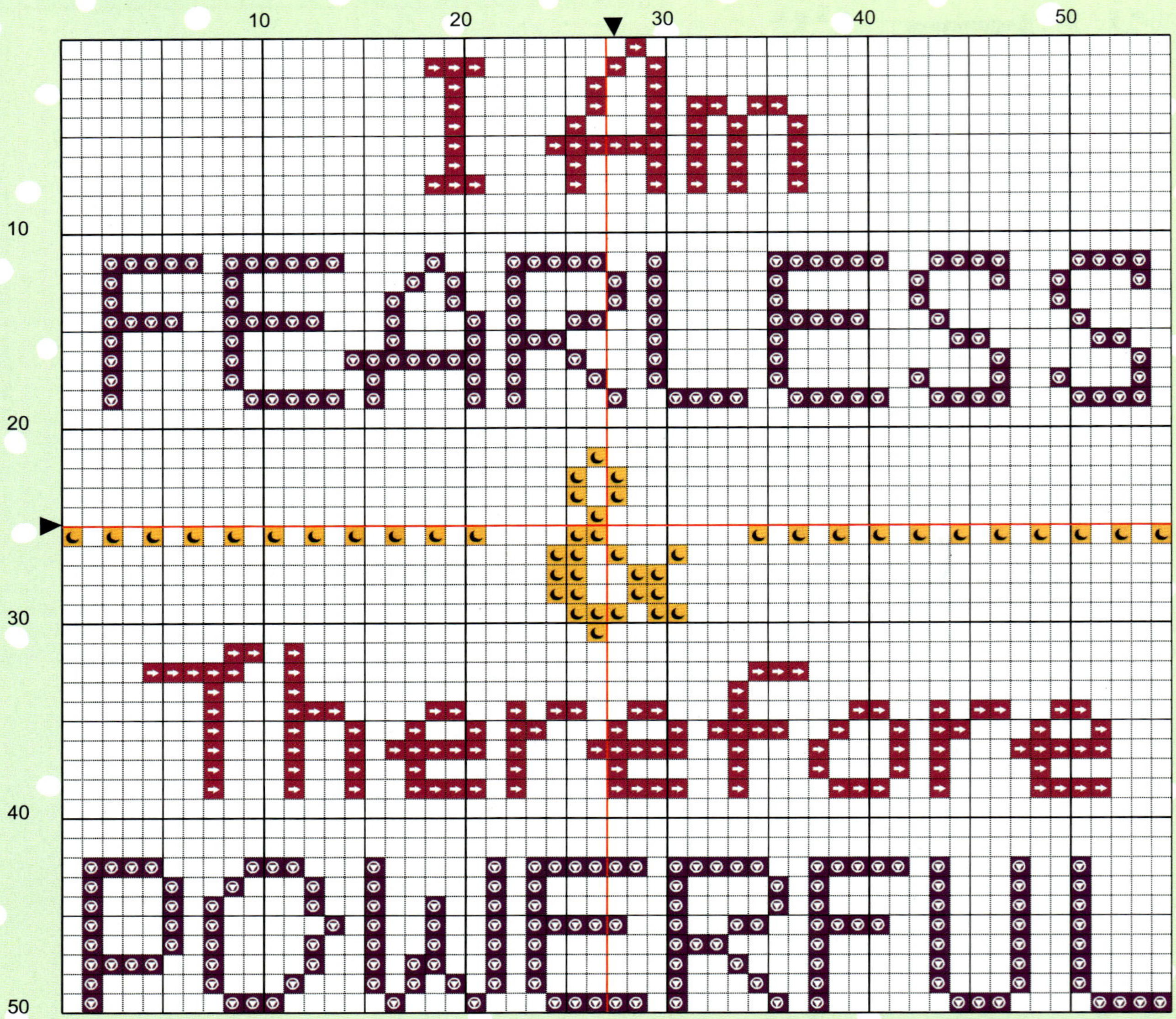

Design size:
55w x 50h stitches
(3.9" x 3.6")

Instructions:
Following the general instructions on pages 13–19, stitch in 2 strands according to the chart. Allow yourself a little extra fabric around the edges if you intend to frame your design.

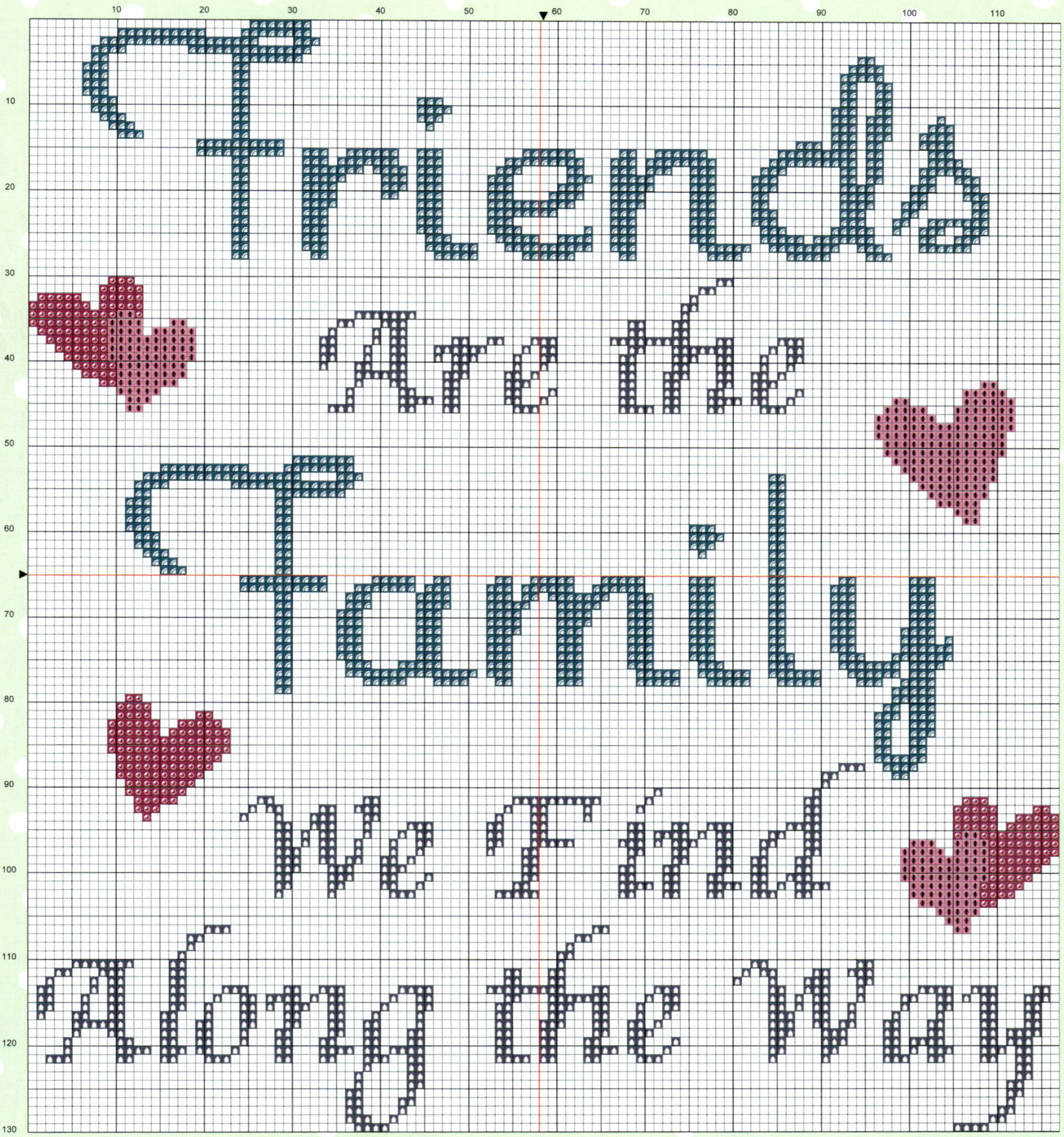

Design size:
117w x 130h stitches (8.4" x 9.3")

Instructions:
Following the general instructions on pages 13–19, stitch in 2 strands according to the chart. Allow yourself a little extra fabric around the edges if you intend to frame your design.

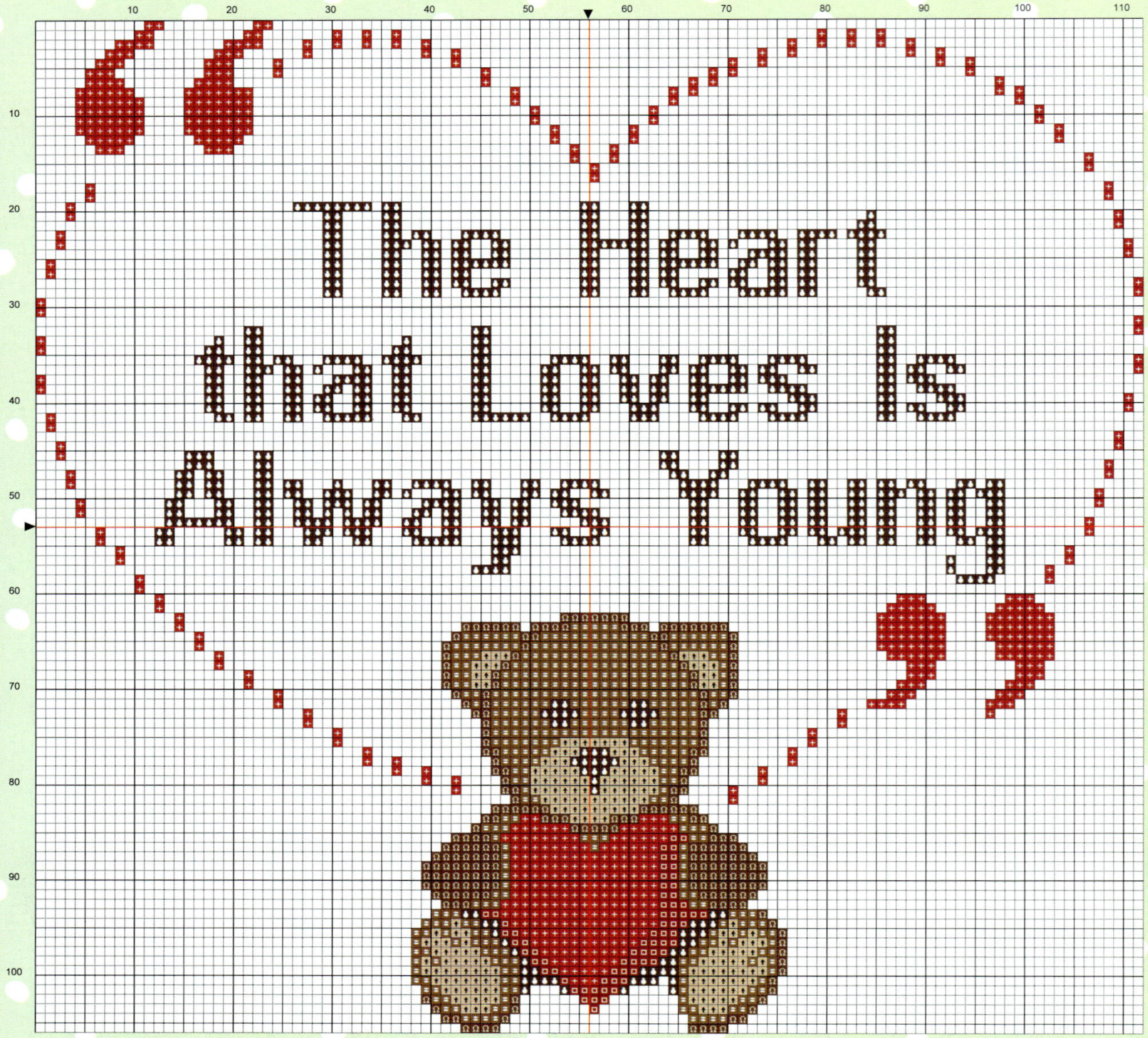

Design size:

112w x 112h stitches (8" x 7.6")

Instructions:

Following the general instructions on pages 13–19, stitch in 2 strands according to the chart. Allow yourself a little extra fabric around the edges if you intend to frame your design.

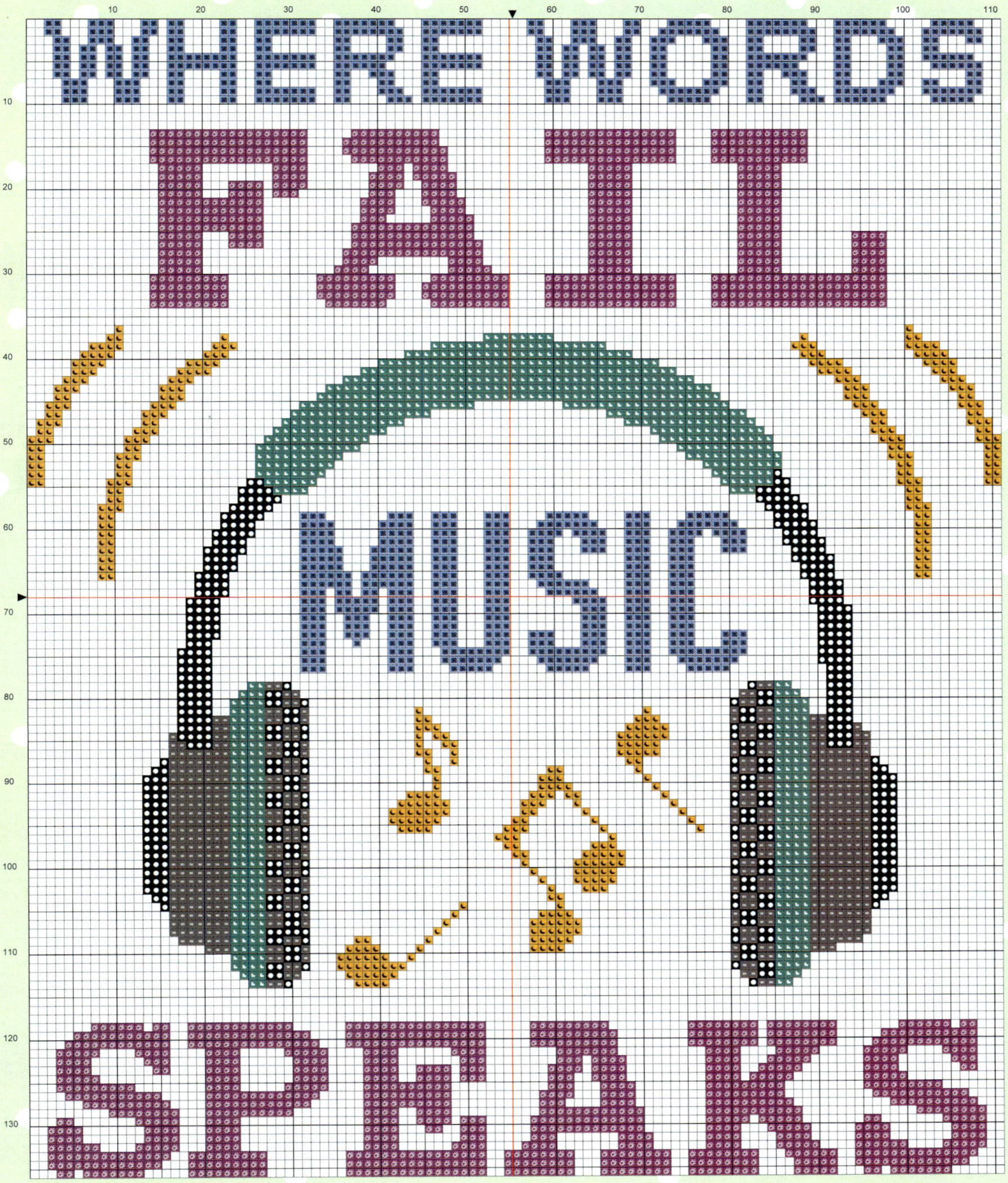

Design size:
111w x 136h stitches (7.9" x 9.7")

Instructions:
Following the general instructions on pages 13–19, stitch in 2 strands according to the chart. Allow yourself a little extra fabric around the edges if you intend to frame your design.

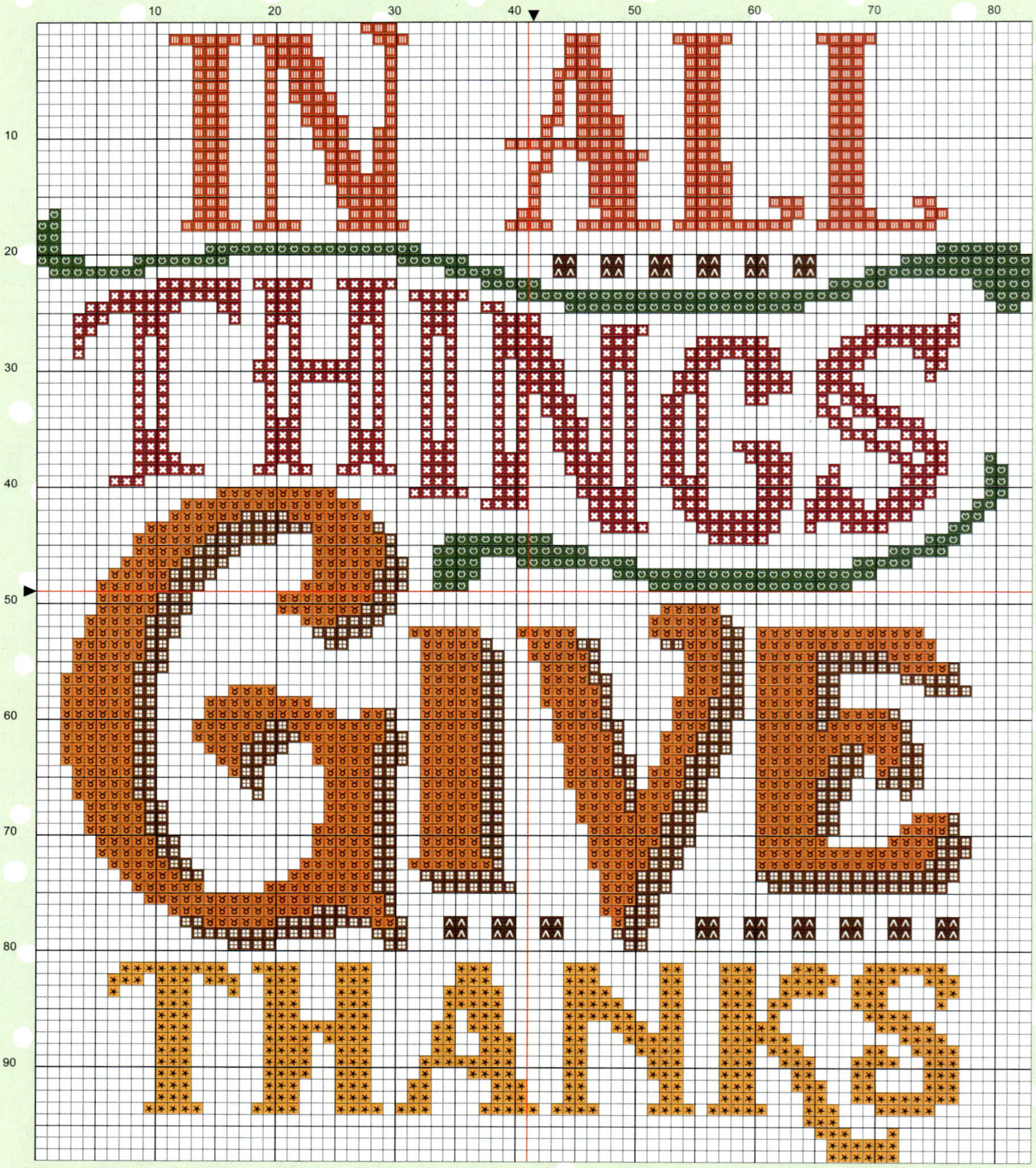

Design size:

83w x 98h stitches (5.9" x 7")

Instructions:

Following the general instructions on pages 13–19, stitch in 2 strands according to the chart. Allow yourself a little extra fabric around the edges if you intend to frame your design.

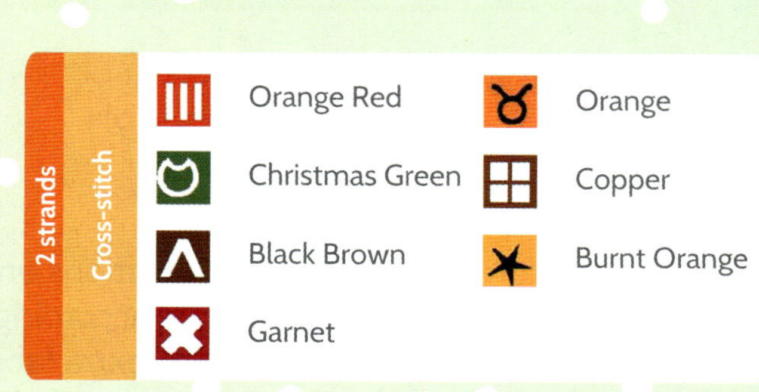

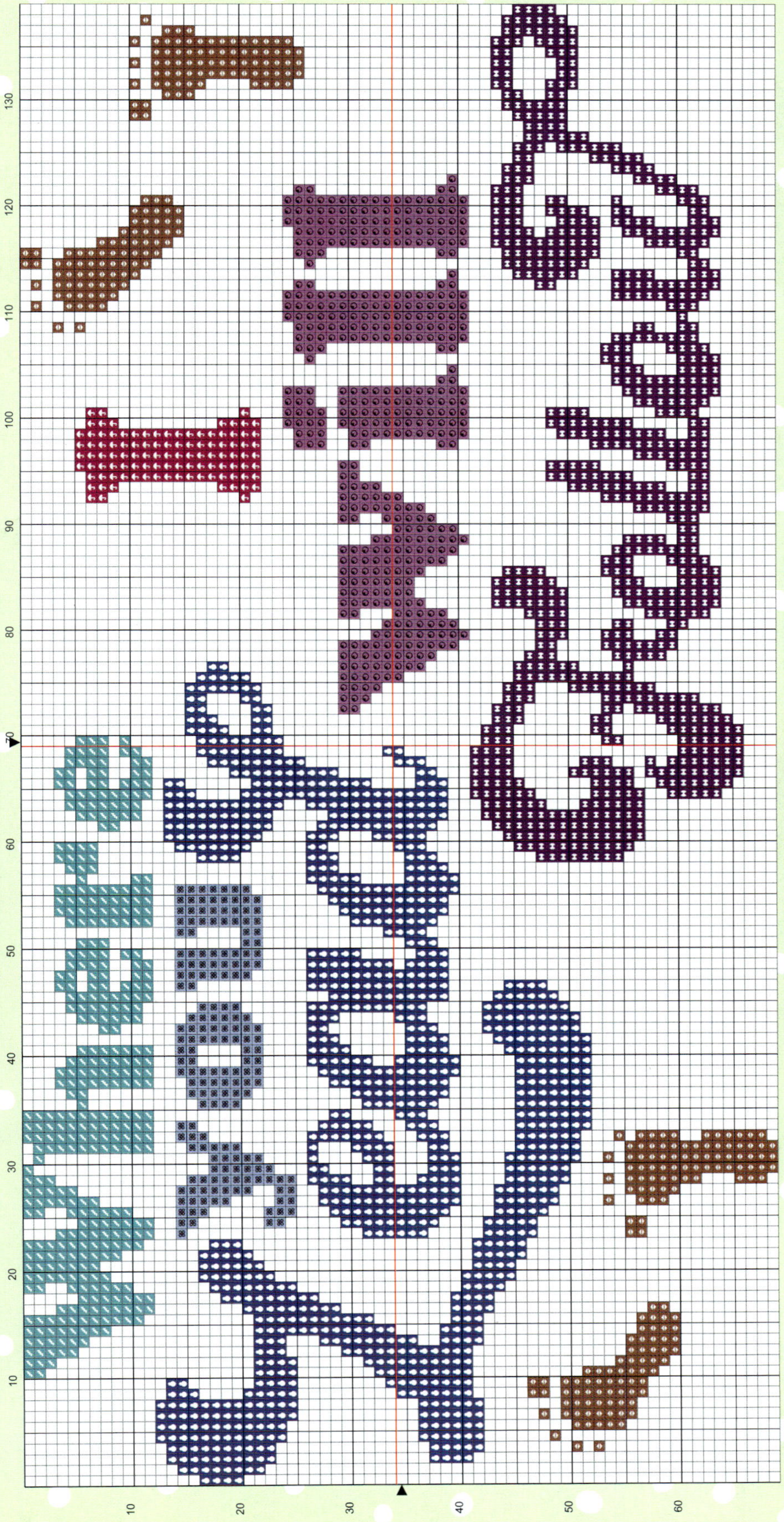

Design size:
139w x 69h stitches (9.9" x 4.9")

Instructions:
Following the general instructions on pages 13–19, stitch in 2 strands according to the chart. Allow yourself a little extra fabric around the edges if you intend to frame your design.

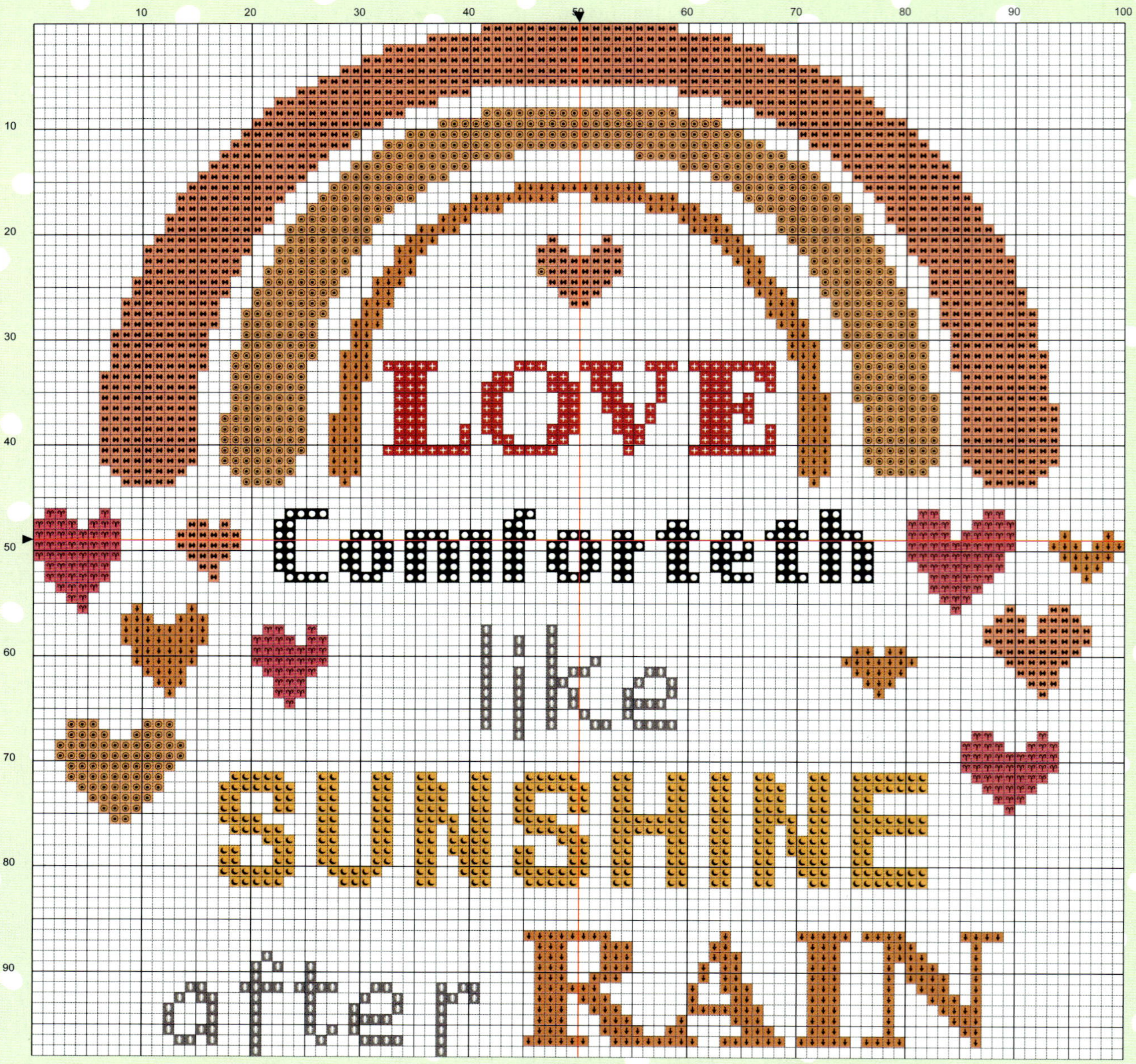

Design size:
100w x 98h stitches (7.1" x 7")

Instructions:
Following the general instructions on pages 13–19, stitch in 2 strands according to the chart. Allow yourself a little extra fabric around the edges if you intend to frame your design.

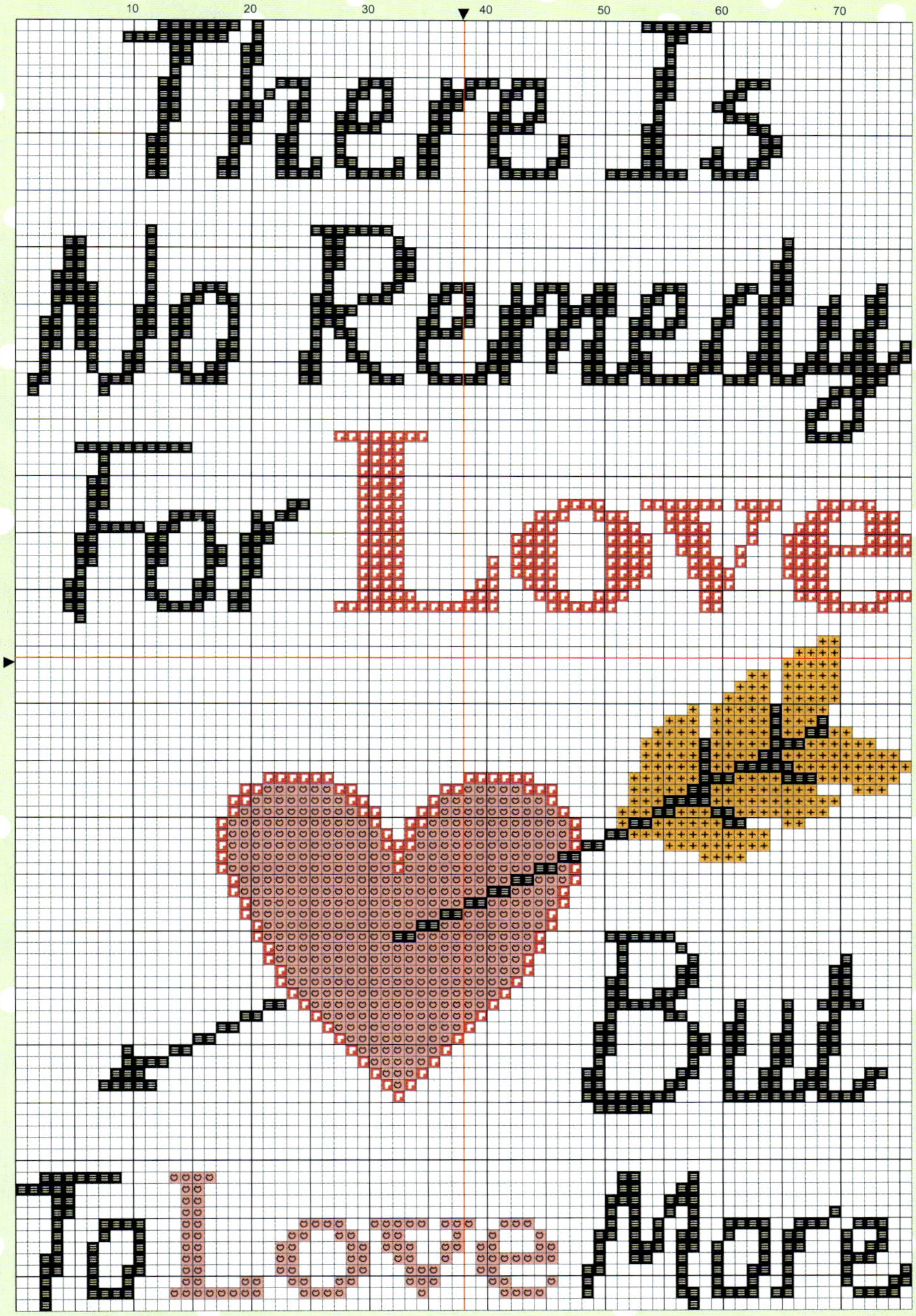

Design size:
76w x 113h stitches (5.4" x 8.1")

Instructions:
Following the general instructions on pages 13–19, stitch in 2 strands according to the chart. Allow yourself a little extra fabric around the edges if you intend to frame your design.

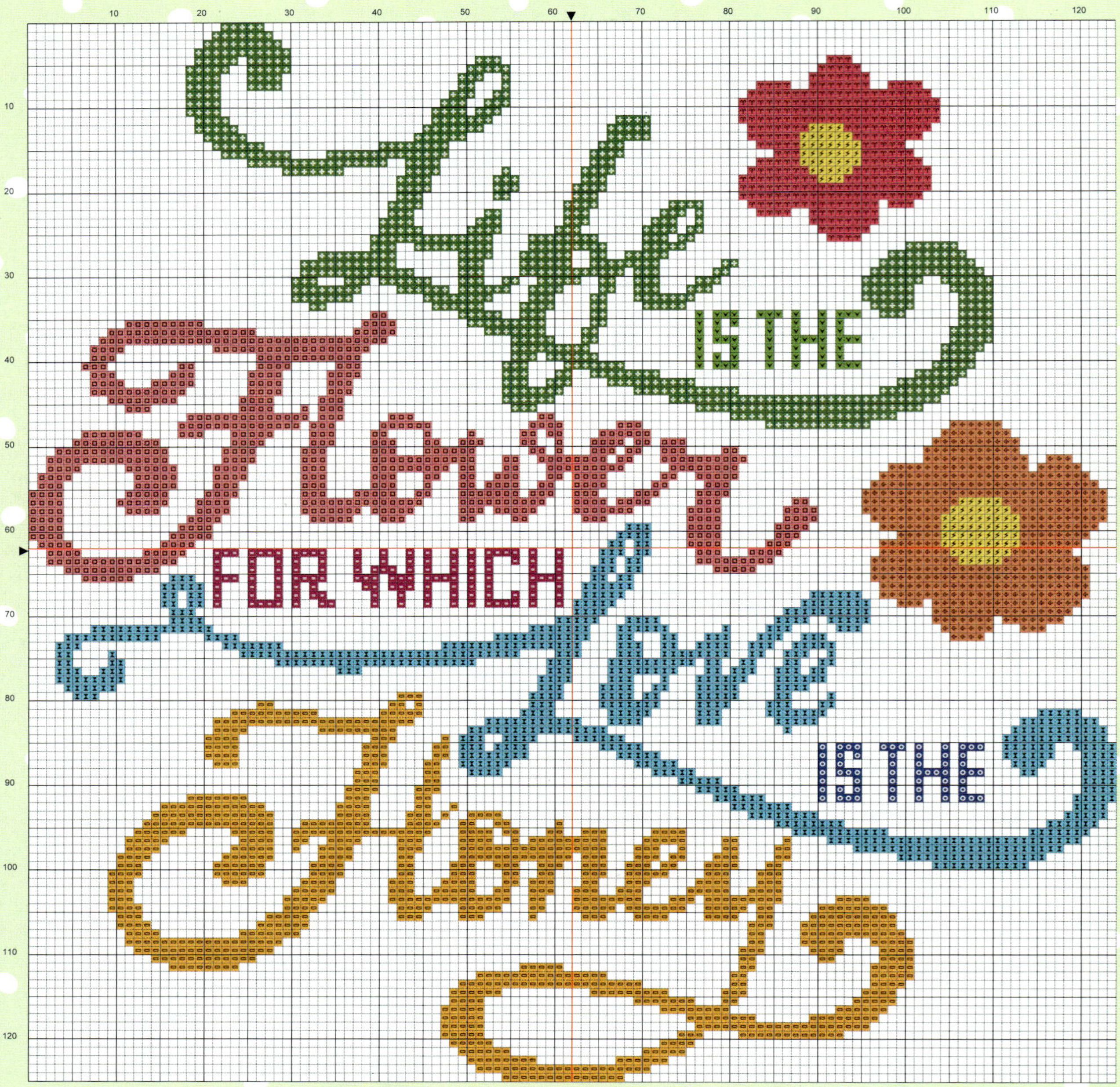

Design size:

124w x 125h stitches
(8.9" x 8.9")

Instructions:

Following the general instructions on pages 13–19, stitch in 2 strands according to the chart. Allow yourself a little extra fabric around the edges if you intend to frame your design.

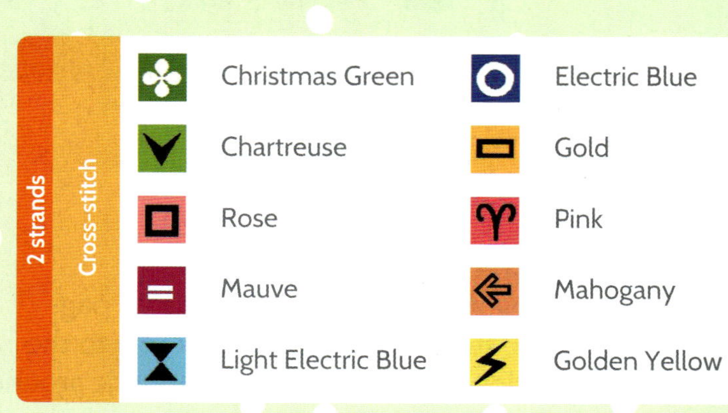

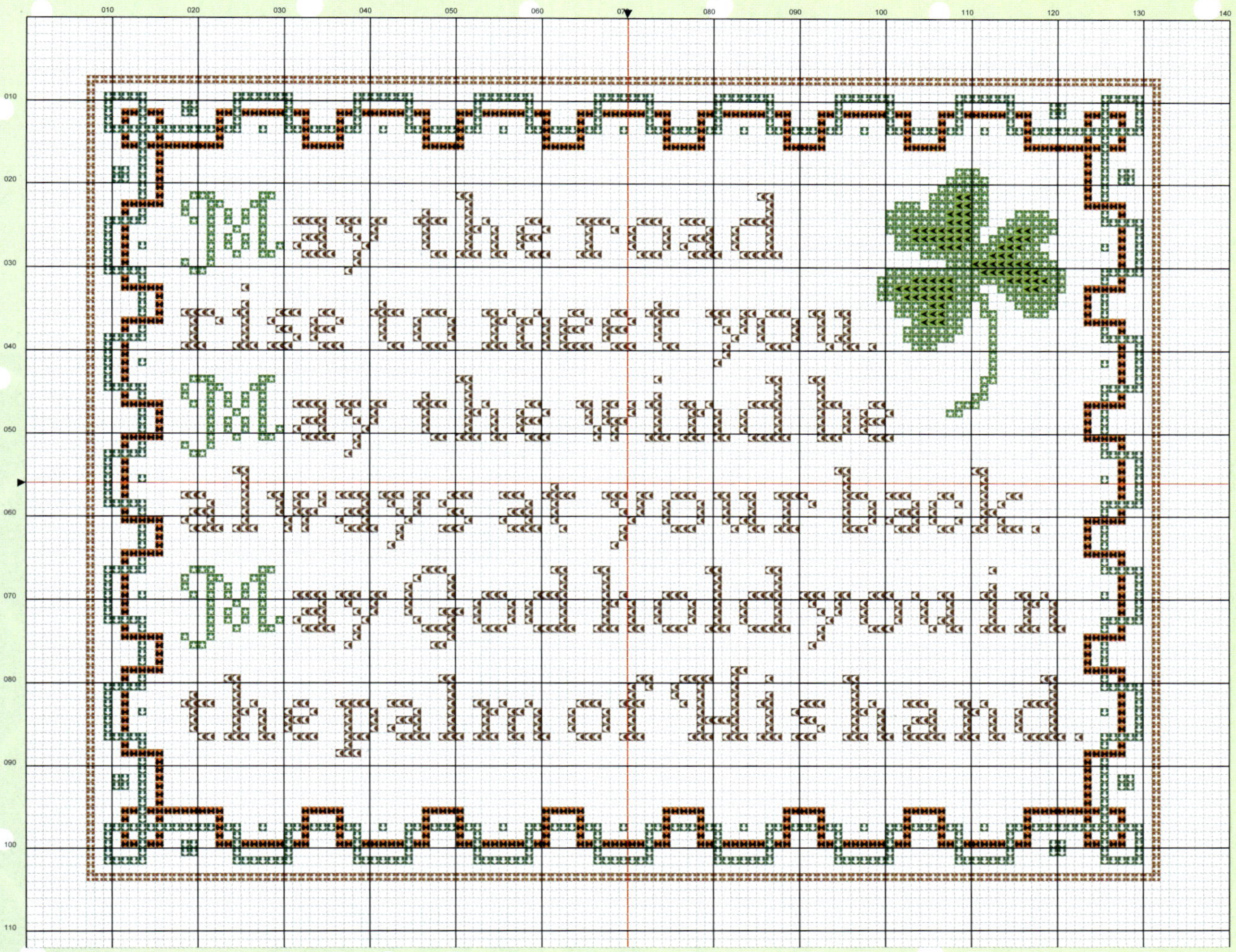

Design size:
112w x 140h stitches
(8" x 10")

Instructions:
Following the general instructions on pages 13–19, stitch in 2 strands according to the chart. Allow yourself a little extra fabric around the edges if you intend to frame your design.

NO PROB
llama
Silly

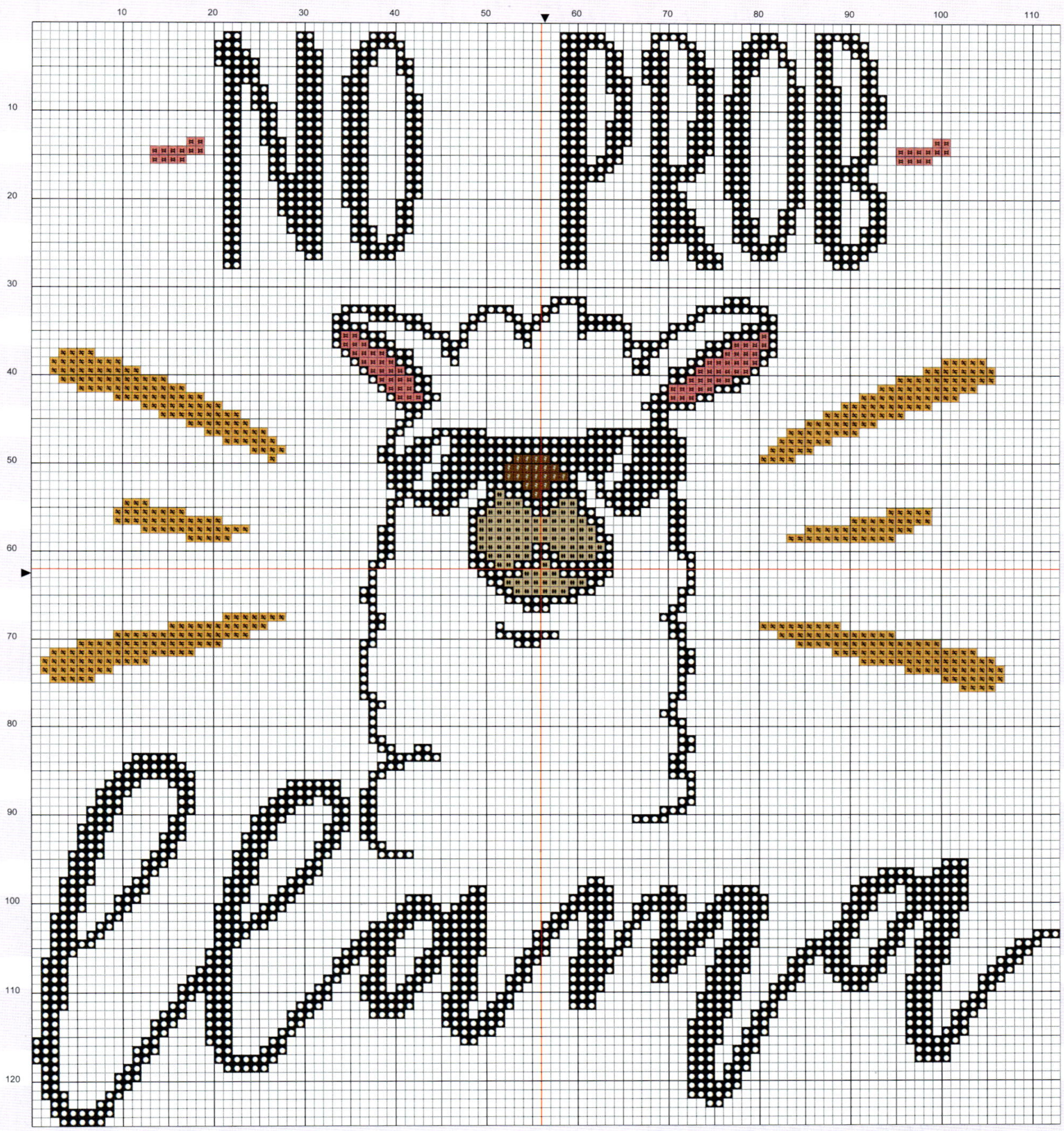

Design size:

112w x 125h stitches (8" x 8.9")

Instructions:

Following the general instructions on pages 13–19, stitch in 2 strands according to the chart. Allow yourself a little extra fabric around the edges if you intend to frame your design.

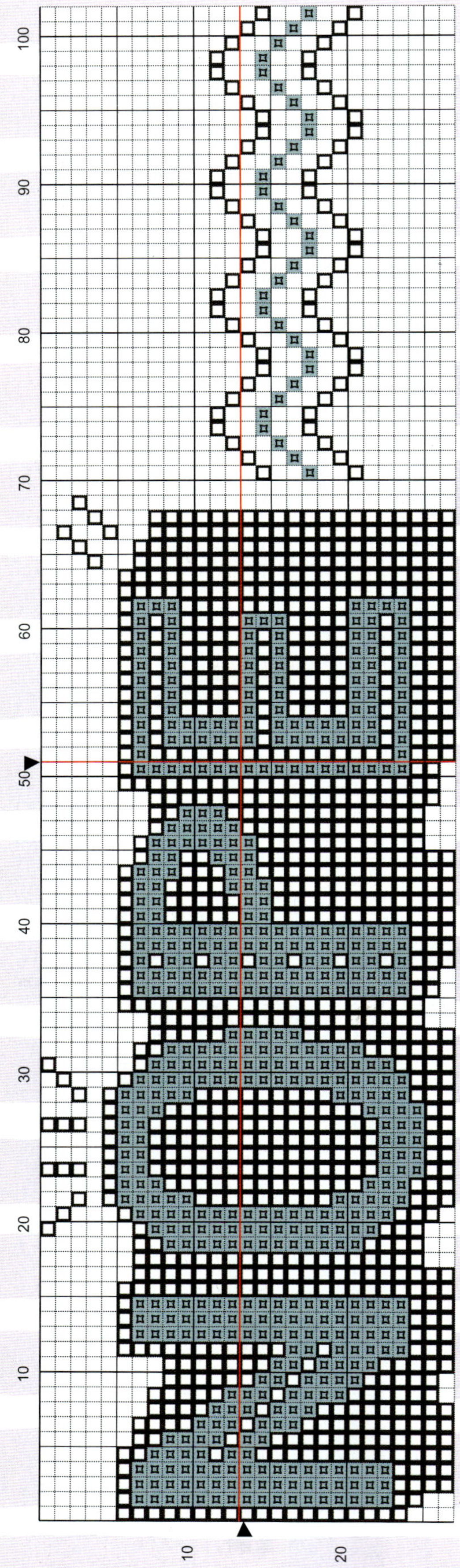

Design size:

102w x 27h stitches (7.3" x 1.9")

Instructions:

Following the general instructions on pages 13–19, stitch in 2 strands according to the chart. Refer to page 11 for ways to increase the stability of your piece to use it as a bookmark.

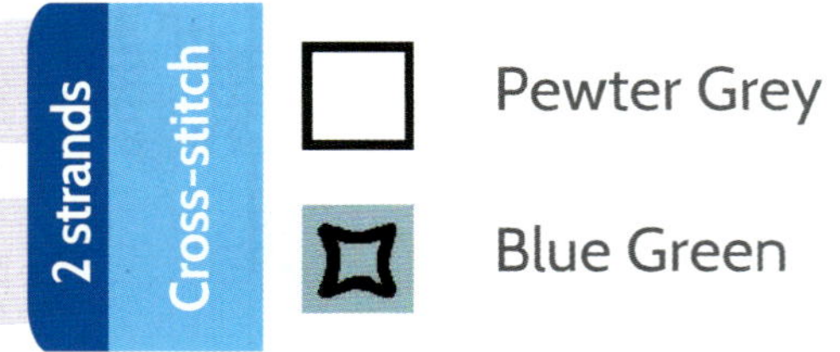

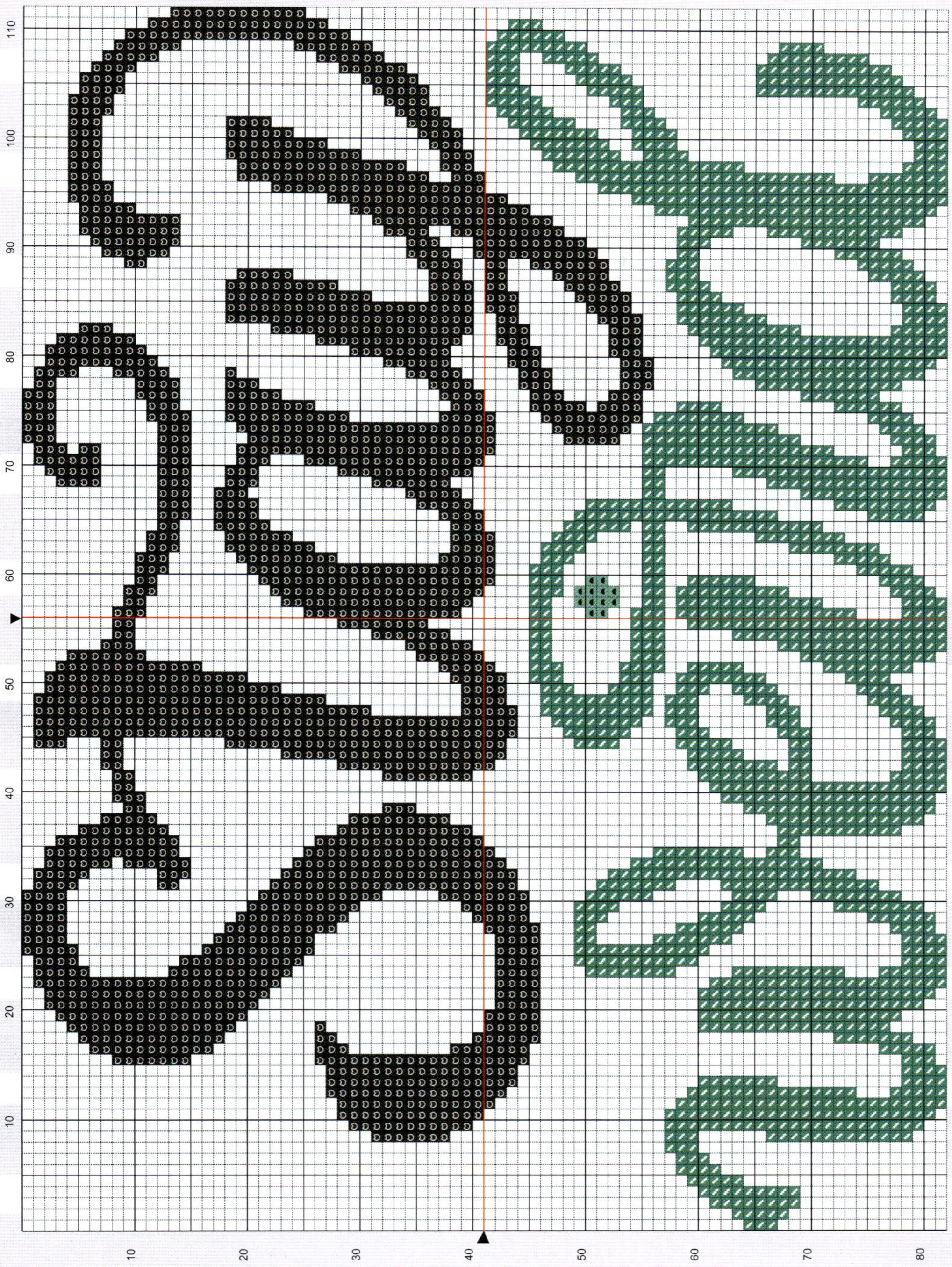

Design size:
112w x 82h stitches (8" x 5.9")

Instructions:
Following the general instructions on pages 13–19, stitch in 2 strands according to the chart. Allow yourself a little extra fabric around the edges if you intend to frame your design.

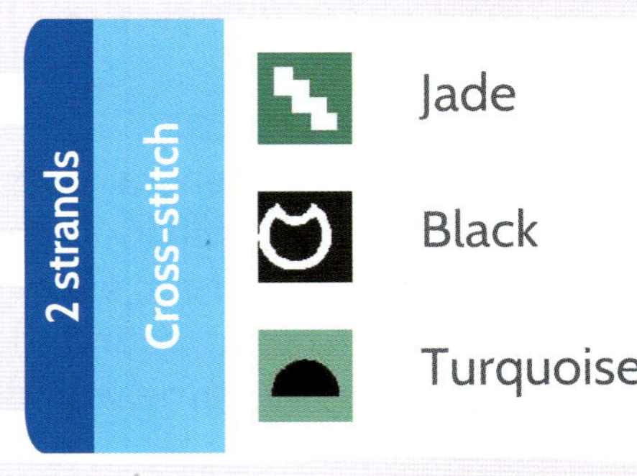

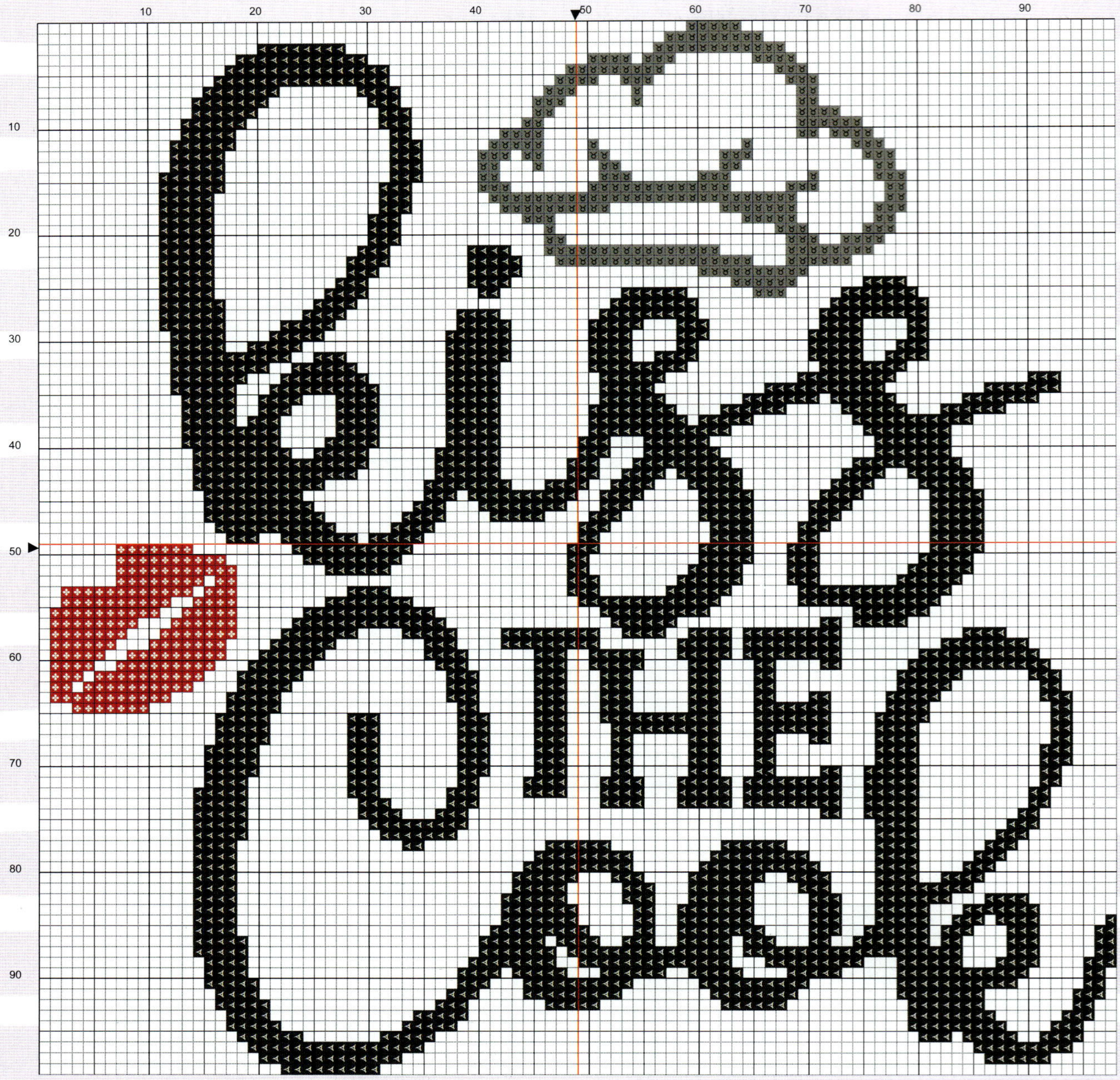

Design size:

98w x 99h stitches (7" x 7.1")

Instructions:

Following the general instructions on pages 13–19, stitch in 2 strands according to the chart. Allow yourself a little extra fabric around the edges if you intend to frame your design.

2 strands

Cross-stitch

 Red

 Black

 Grey Blue

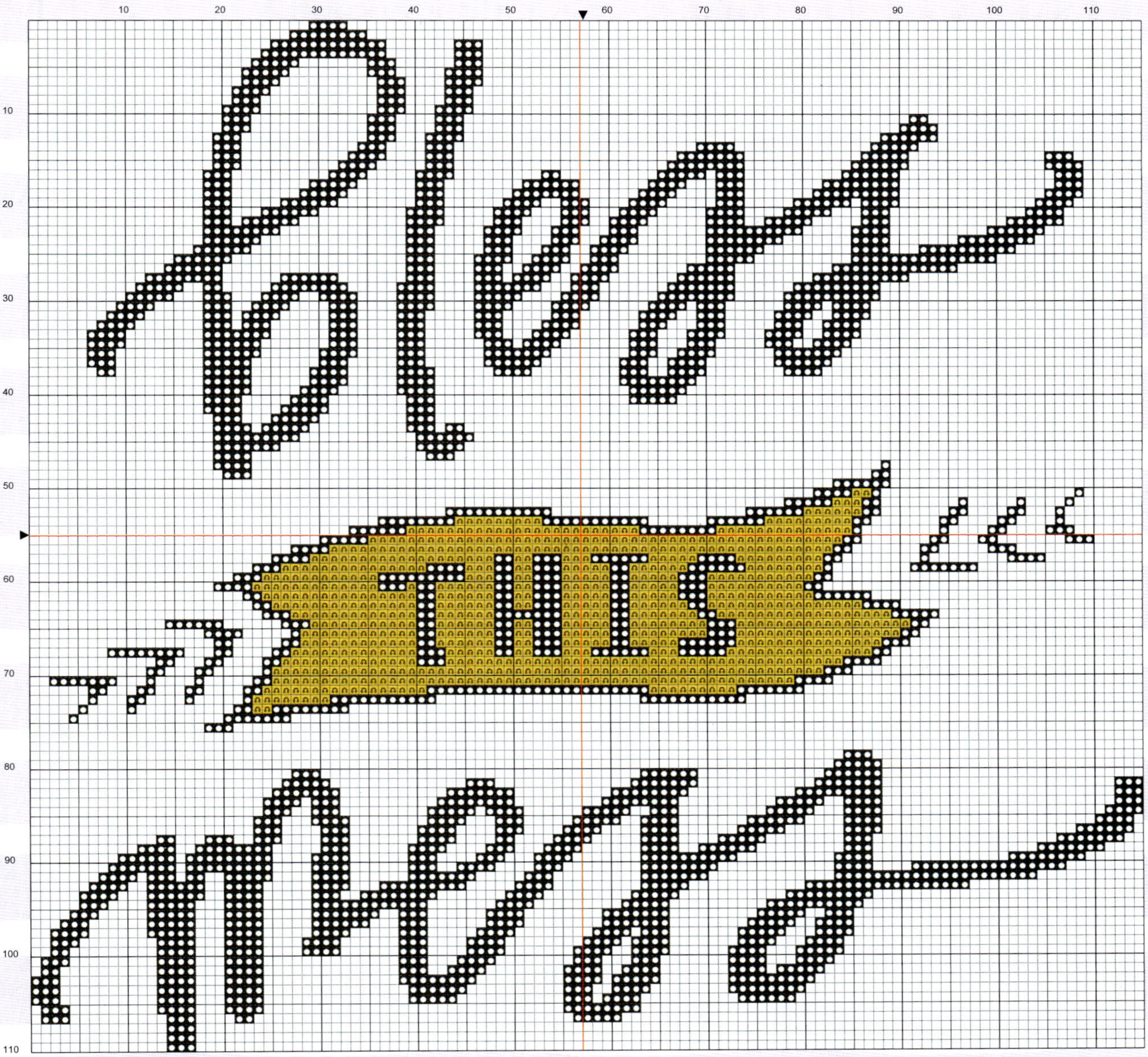

Design size:
115w x 110h stitches
(8.2" x 7.9")

Instructions:
Following the general instructions on pages 13–19, stitch in 2 strands according to the chart. Allow yourself a little extra fabric around the edges if you intend to frame your design.

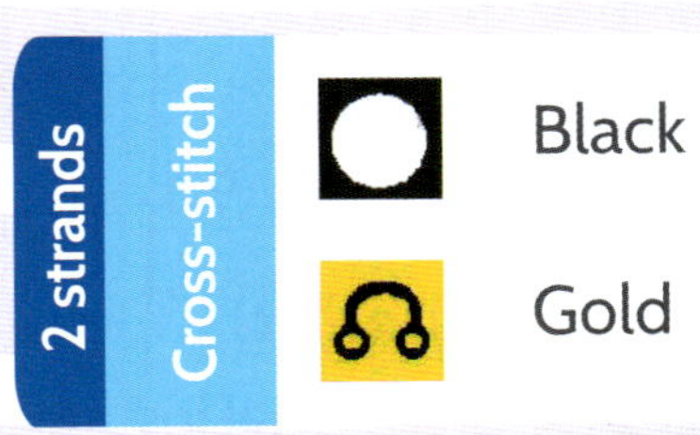

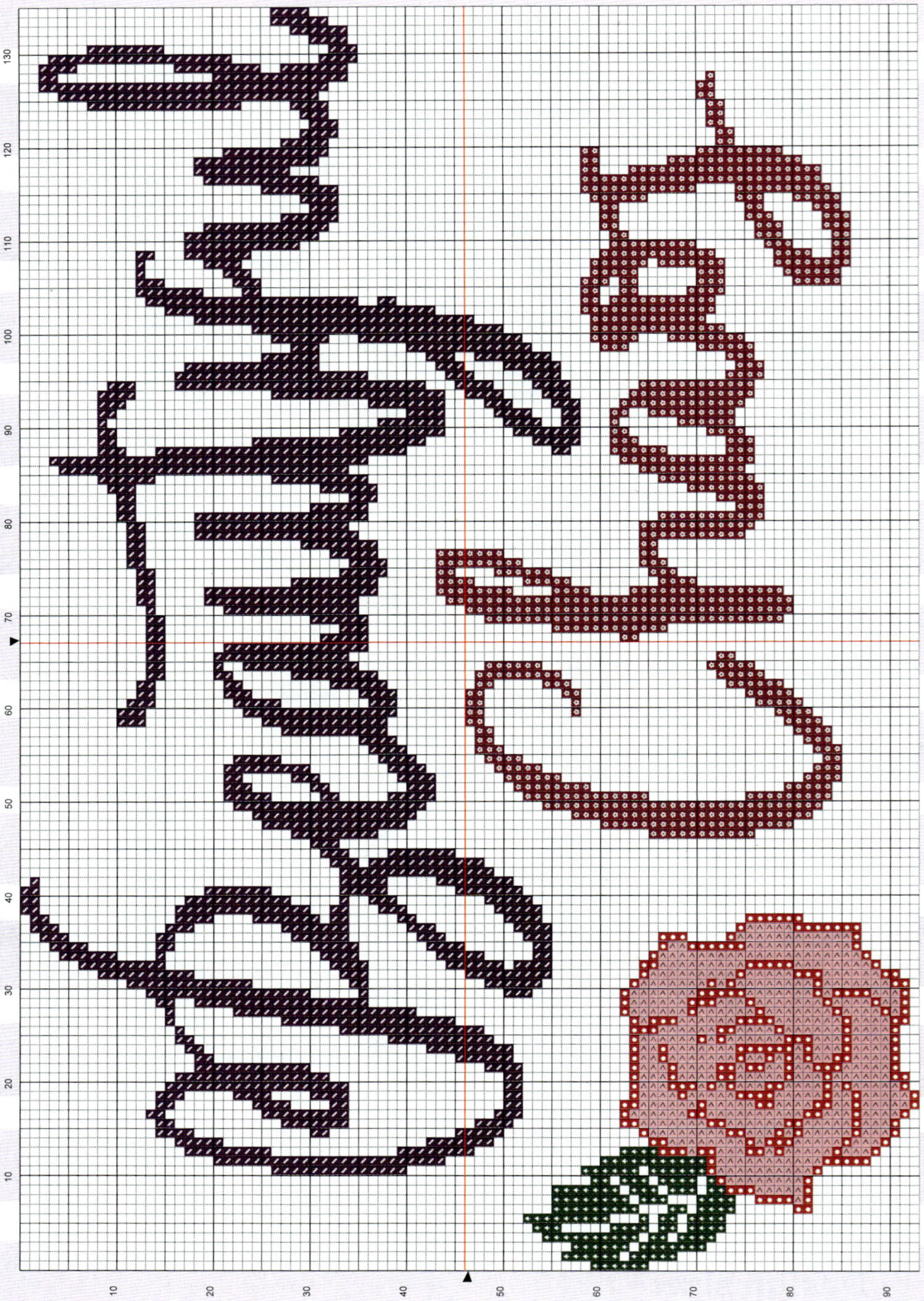

Design size:
135w x 93h stitches (9.6" x 6.6")

Instructions:
Following the general instructions on pages 13–19, stitch in 2 strands according to the chart. Allow yourself a little extra fabric around the edges if you intend to frame your design.

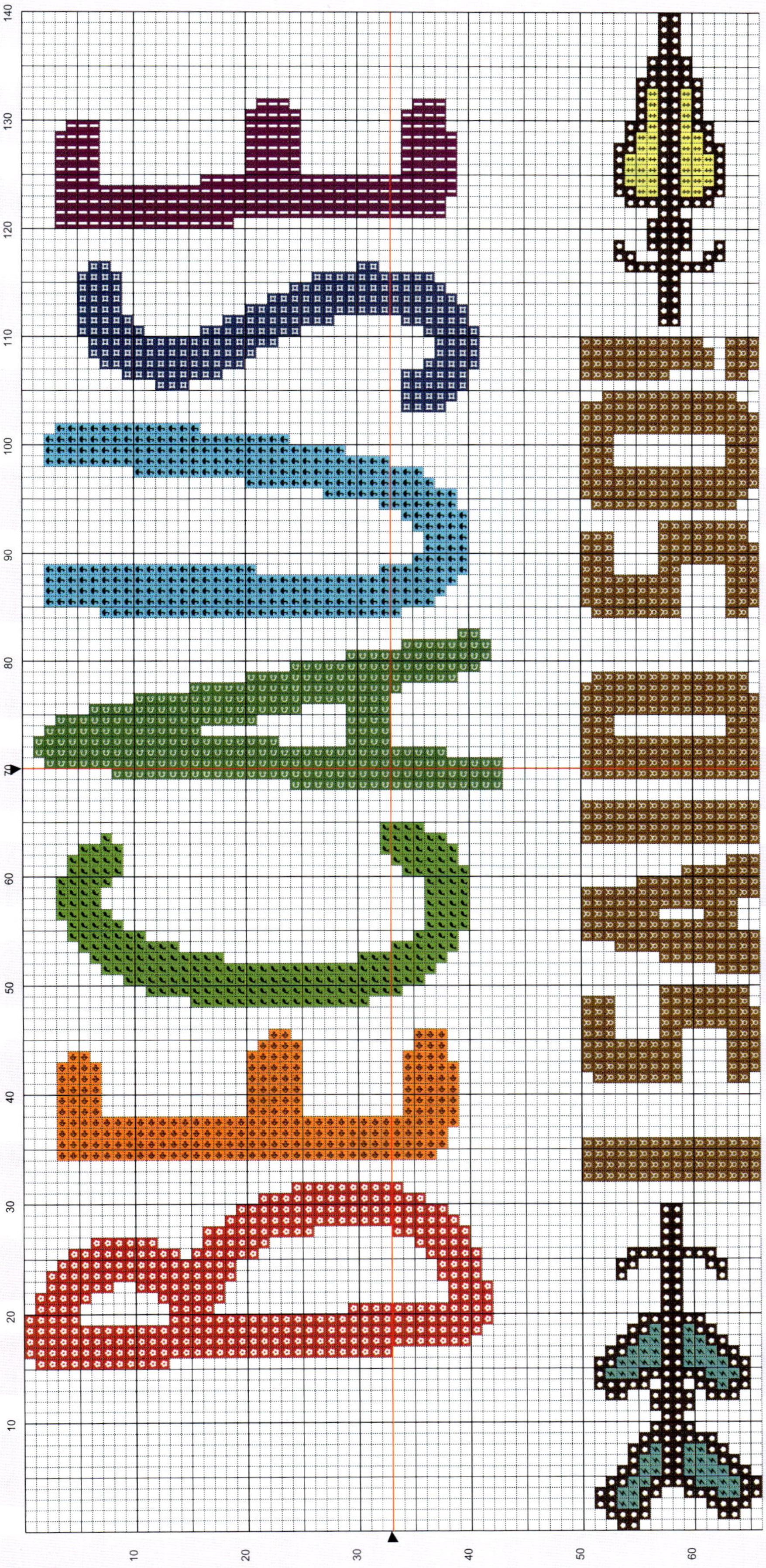

Design size:

140w x 66h stitches (10" x 4.7")

Instructions:

Following the general instructions on pages 13–19, stitch in 2 strands according to the chart. Allow yourself a little extra fabric around the edges if you intend to frame your design.

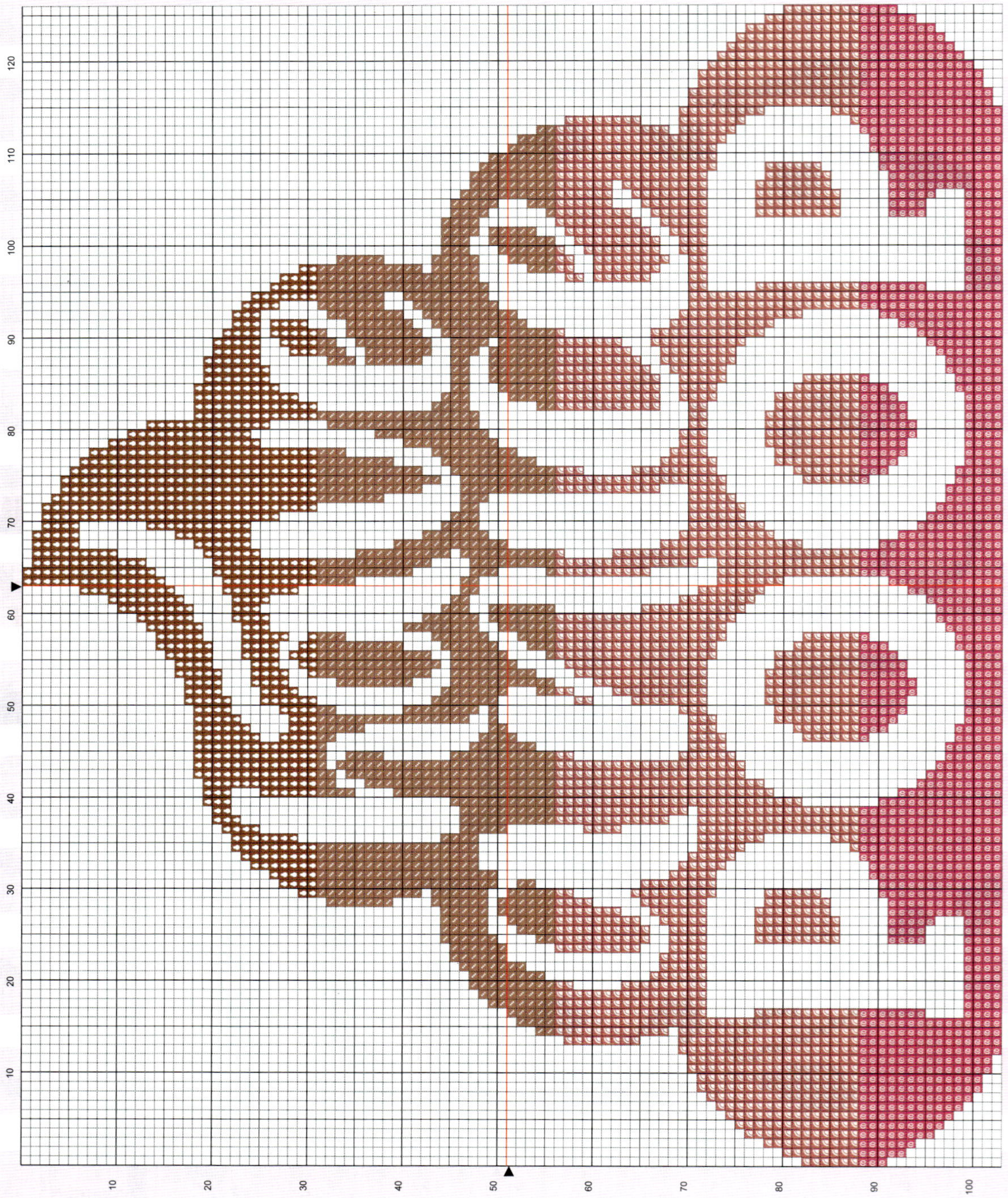

Design size:
126w x 103h stitches (9" x 7.4")

Instructions:
Following the general instructions on pages 13–19, stitch in 2 strands according to the chart. Allow yourself a little extra fabric around the edges if you intend to frame your design.

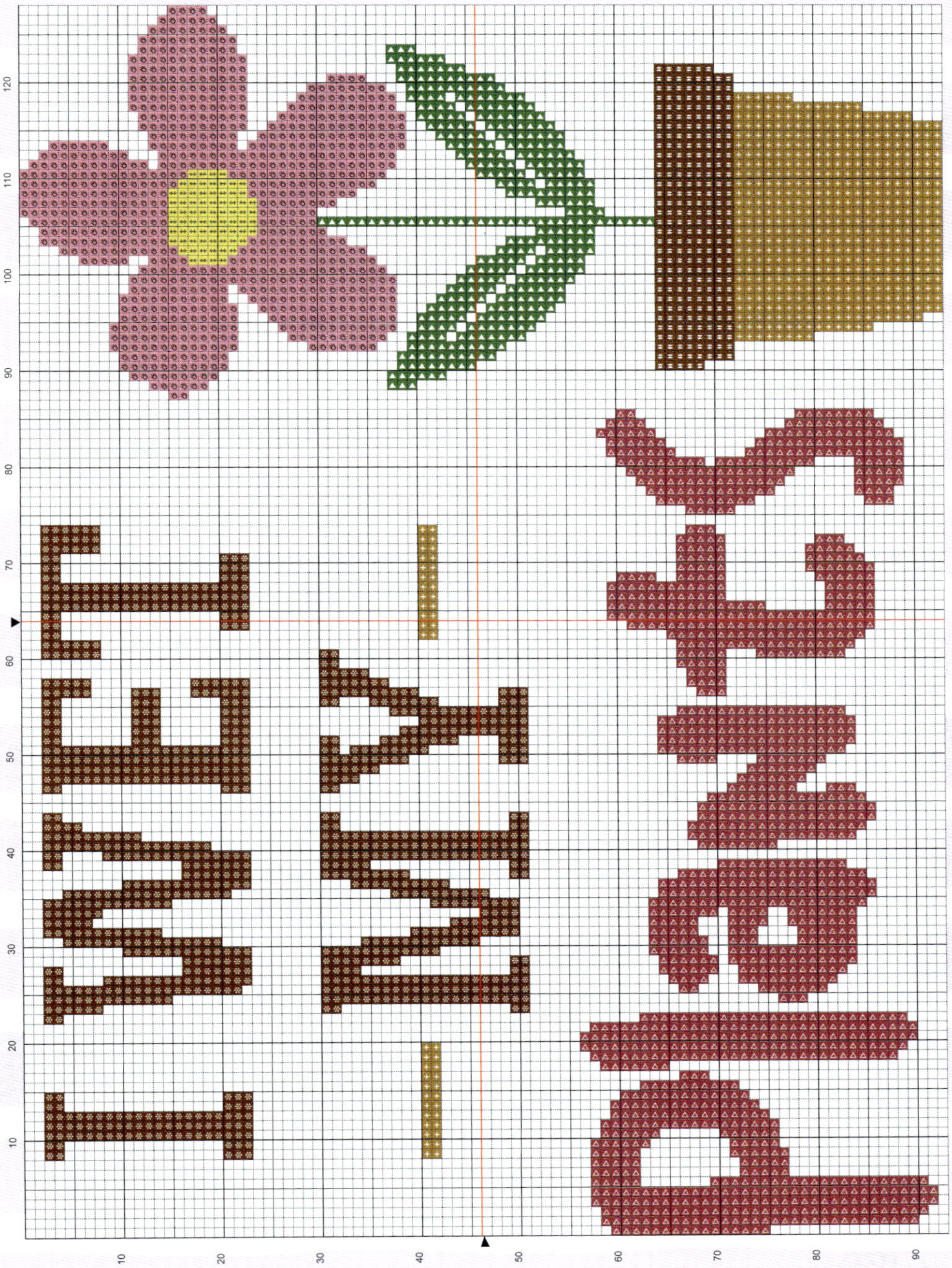

Design size:

128w x 93h stitches (9.1" x 6.6")

Instructions:

Following the general instructions on pages 13–19, stitch in 2 strands according to the chart. Allow yourself a little extra fabric around the edges if you intend to frame your design.

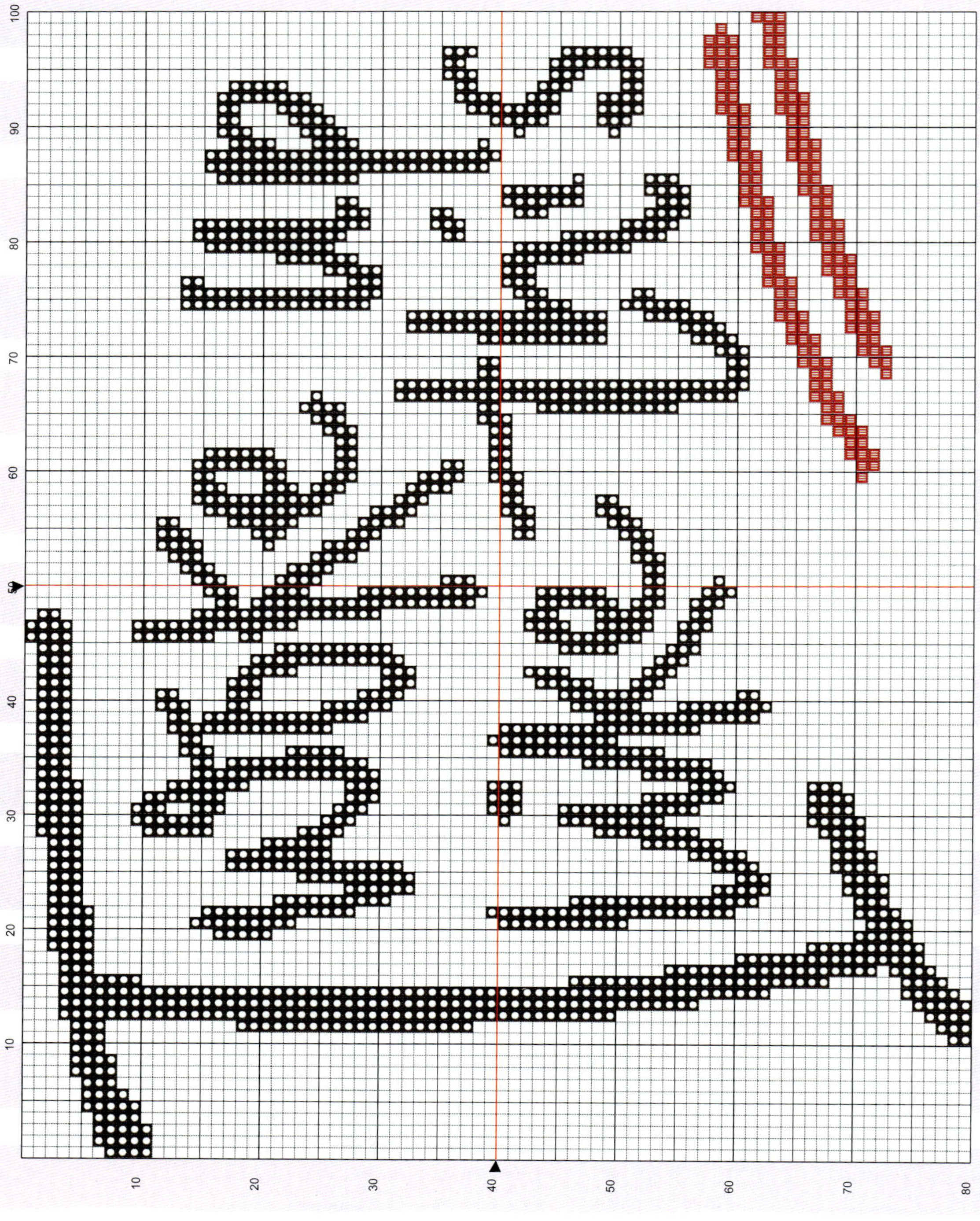

Design size:
100w x 80h stitches (7.1" x 5.7")

Instructions:
Following the general instructions on pages 13–19, stitch in 2 strands according to the chart. Allow yourself a little extra fabric around the edges if you intend to frame your design.

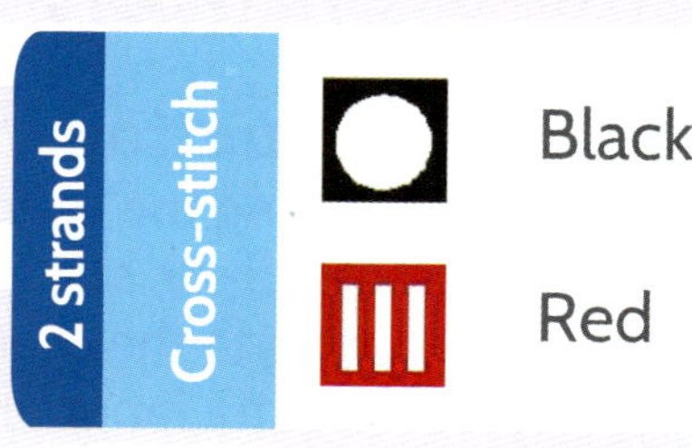

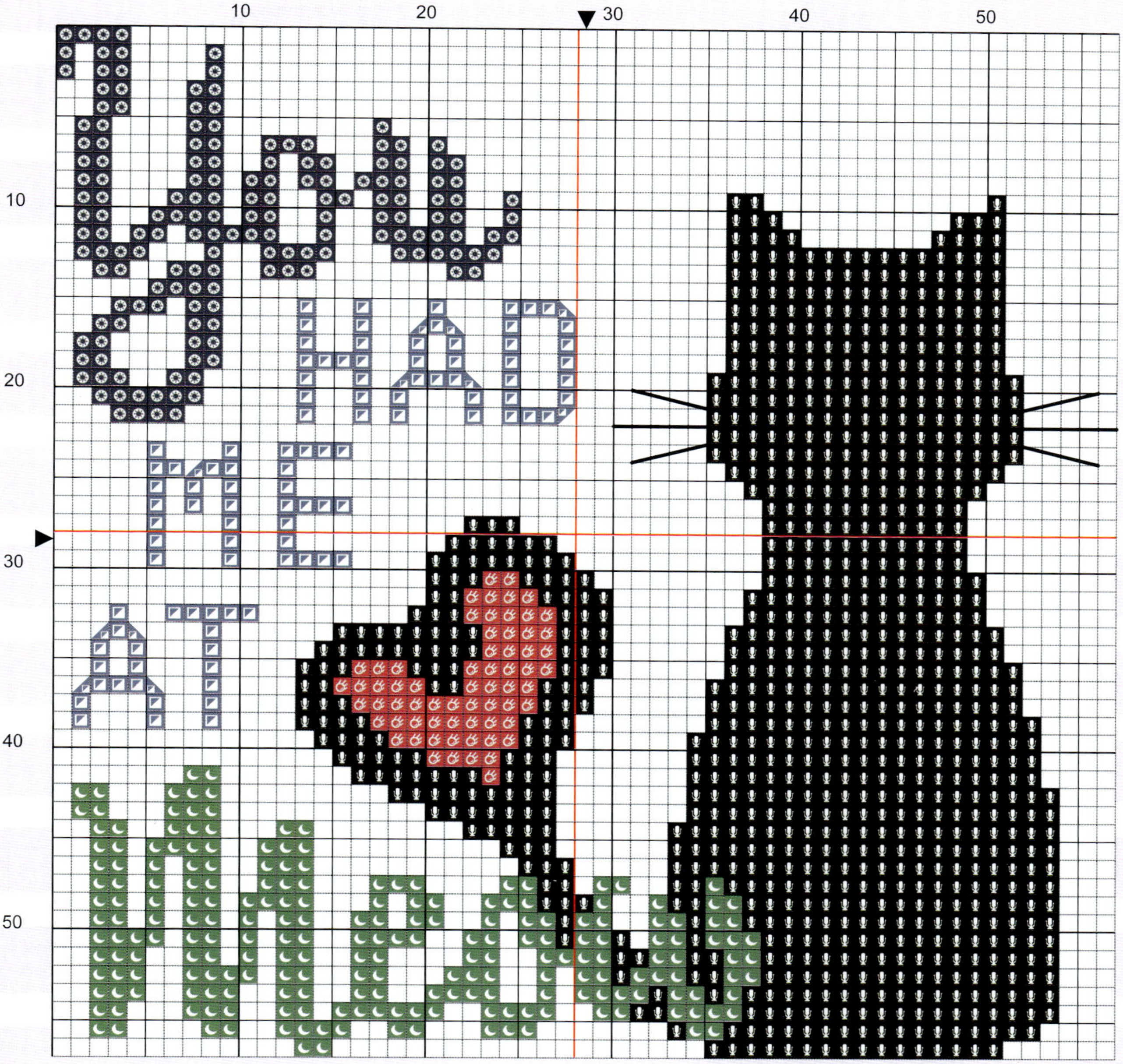

Design size:

57w x 57h stitches (4.1" x 4.1")

Instructions:

Following the general instructions on pages 13–19, stitch in 2 strands according to the chart. Squares in the chart that are only half filled use a half stitch. Once all cross-stitching is done, backstitch the cat's whiskers in black floss. Allow yourself a little extra fabric around the edges if you intend to frame your design.

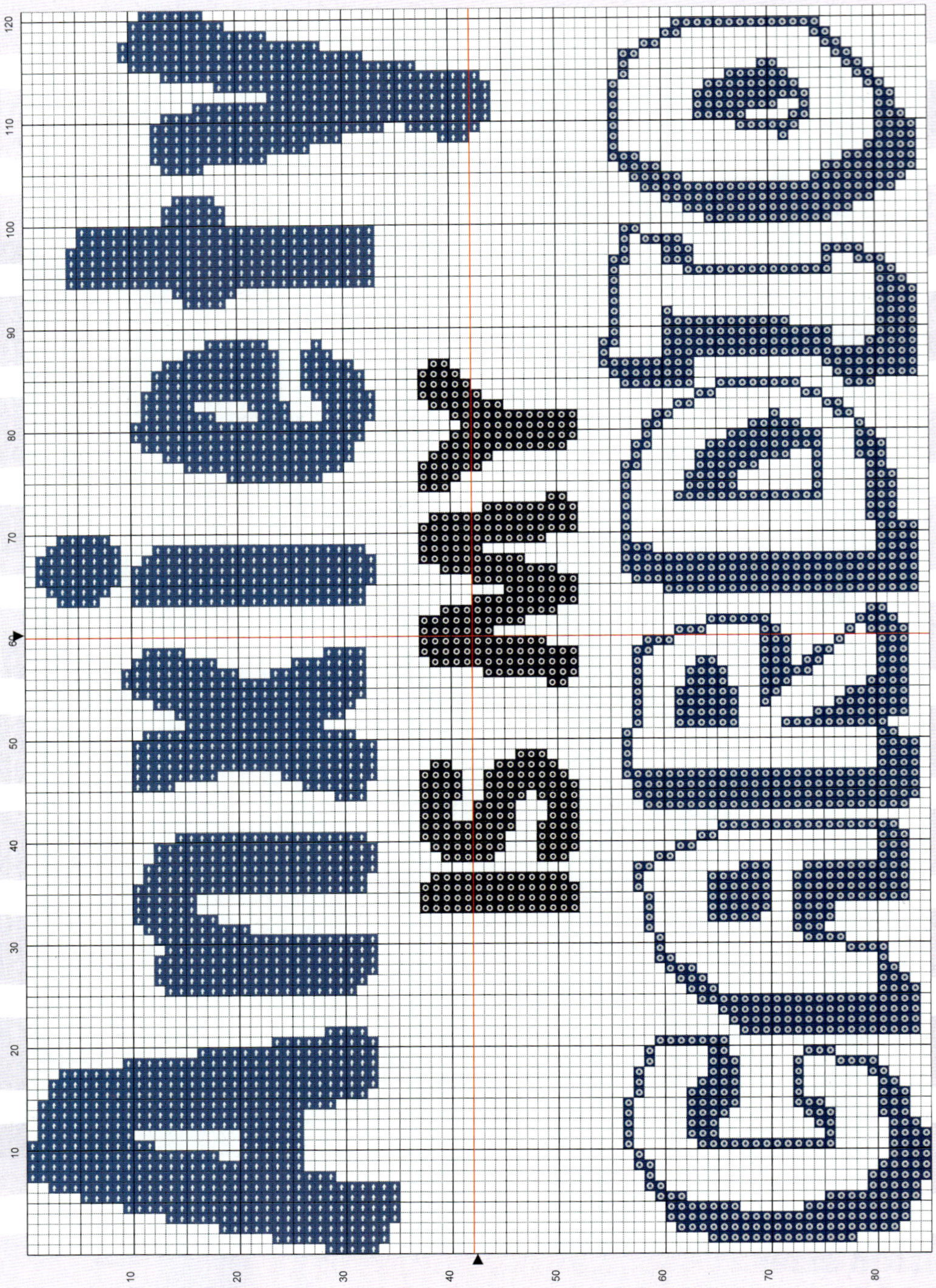

Design size:
121w x 85h stitches (8.6" x 6.1")

Instructions:
Following the general instructions on pages 13–19, stitch in 2 strands according to the chart. Allow yourself a little extra fabric around the edges if you intend to frame your design.

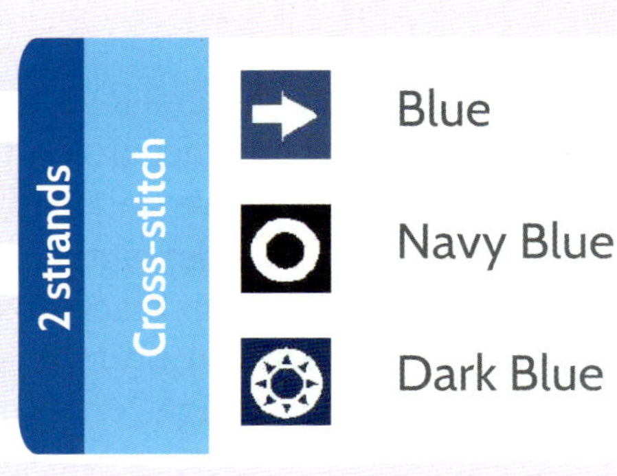

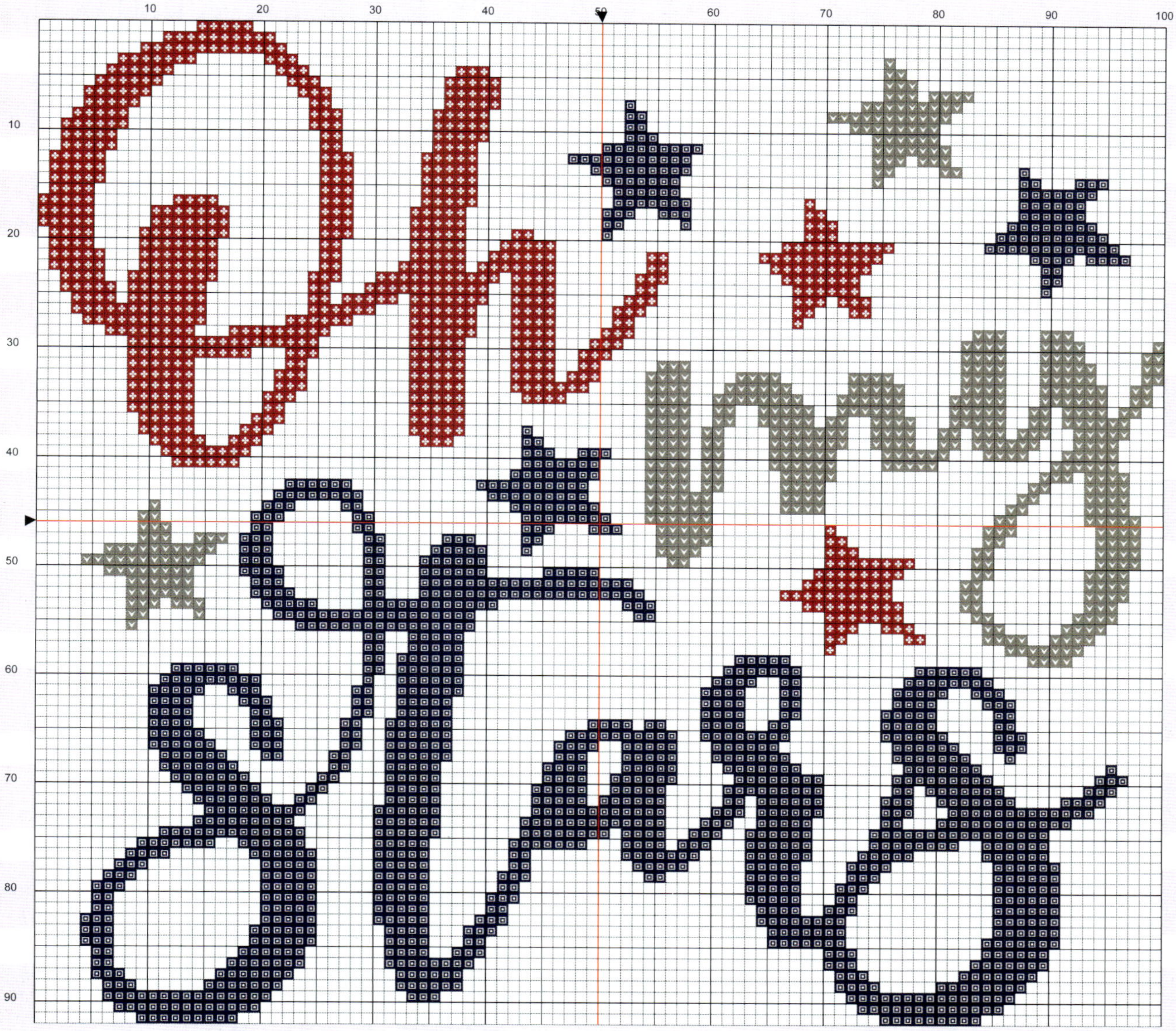

Design size:
100w x 92h stitches
(7.1" x 6.6")

Instructions:
Following the general instructions on pages 13–19, stitch in 2 strands according to the chart. Allow yourself a little extra fabric around the edges if you intend to frame your design.

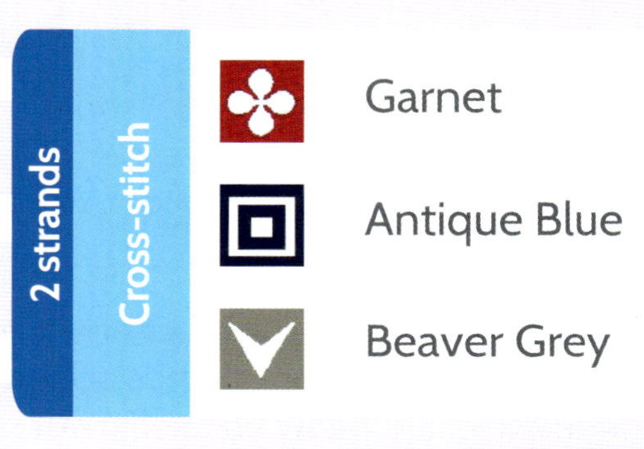

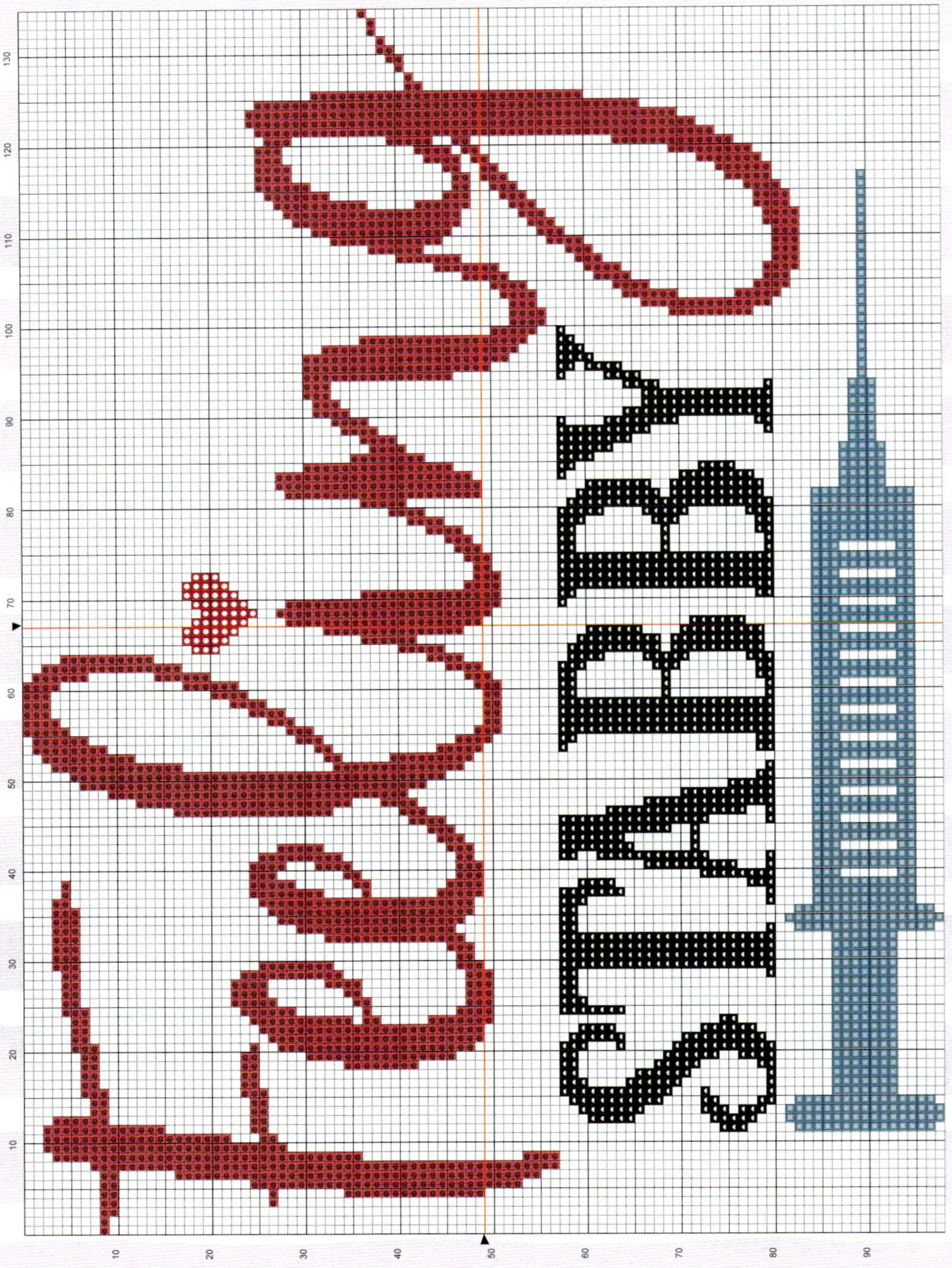

Design size:

135w x 98h stitches (9.6" x 7")

Instructions:

Following the general instructions on pages 13–19, stitch in 2 strands according to the chart. Allow yourself a little extra fabric around the edges if you intend to frame your design.

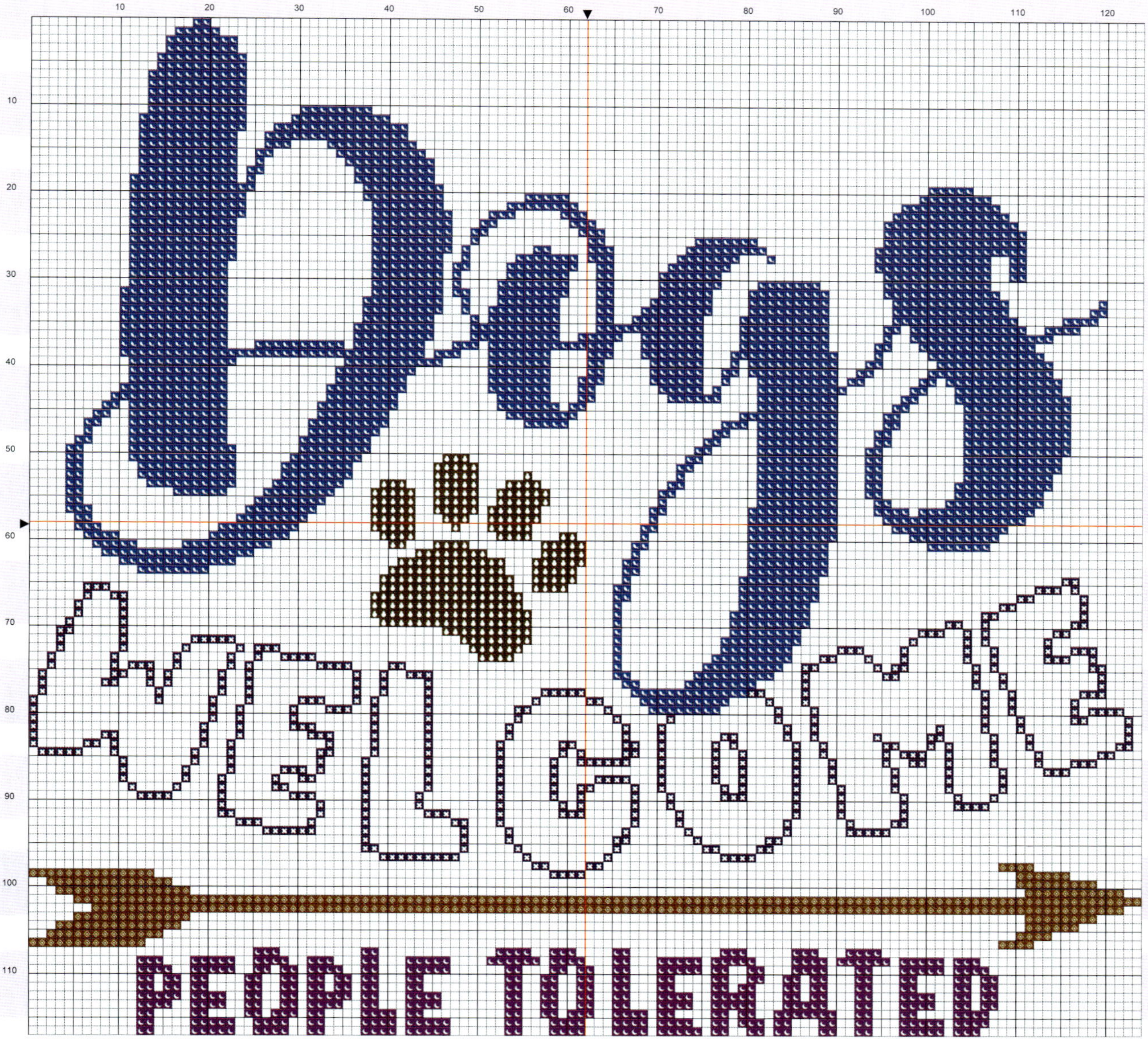

Design size:
124w x 117h stitches
(8.9" x 8.4")

Instructions:
Following the general instructions on pages 13–19, stitch in 2 strands according to the chart. Allow yourself a little extra fabric around the edges if you intend to frame your design.

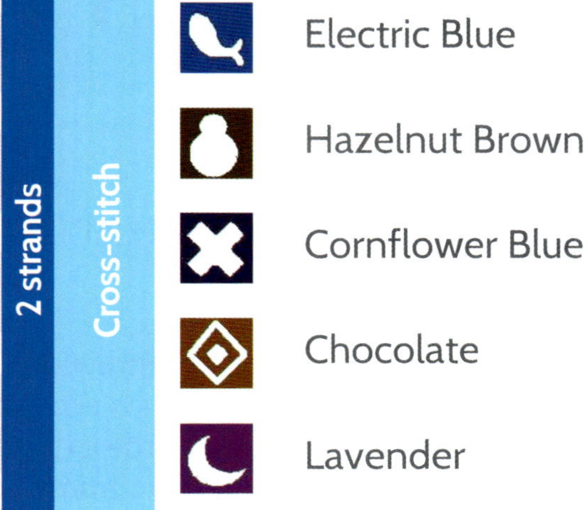

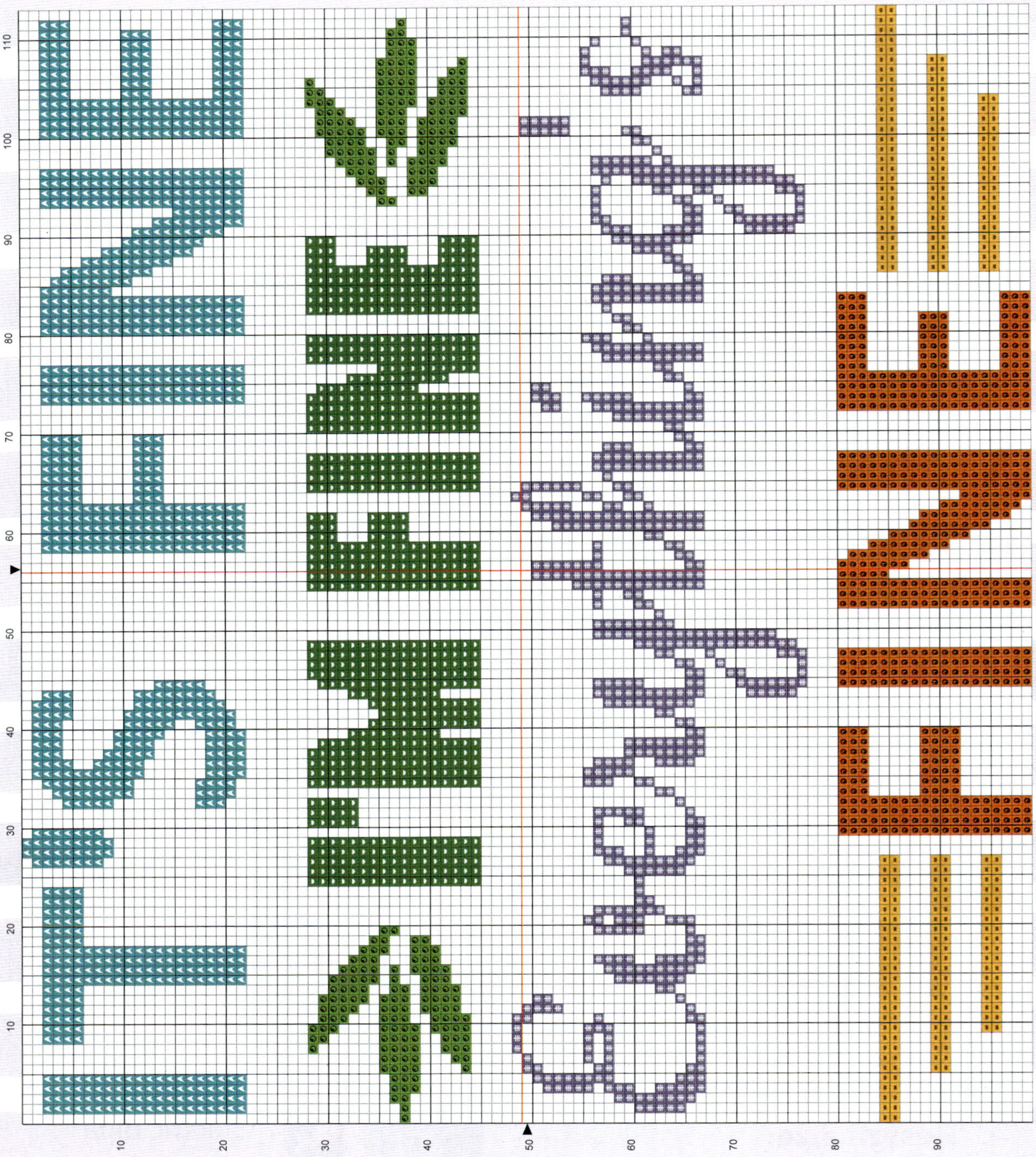

Design size:

113w x 99h stitches (8.1" x 7.1")

Instructions:

Following the general instructions on pages 13–19, stitch in 2 strands according to the chart. Allow yourself a little extra fabric around the edges if you intend to frame your design.

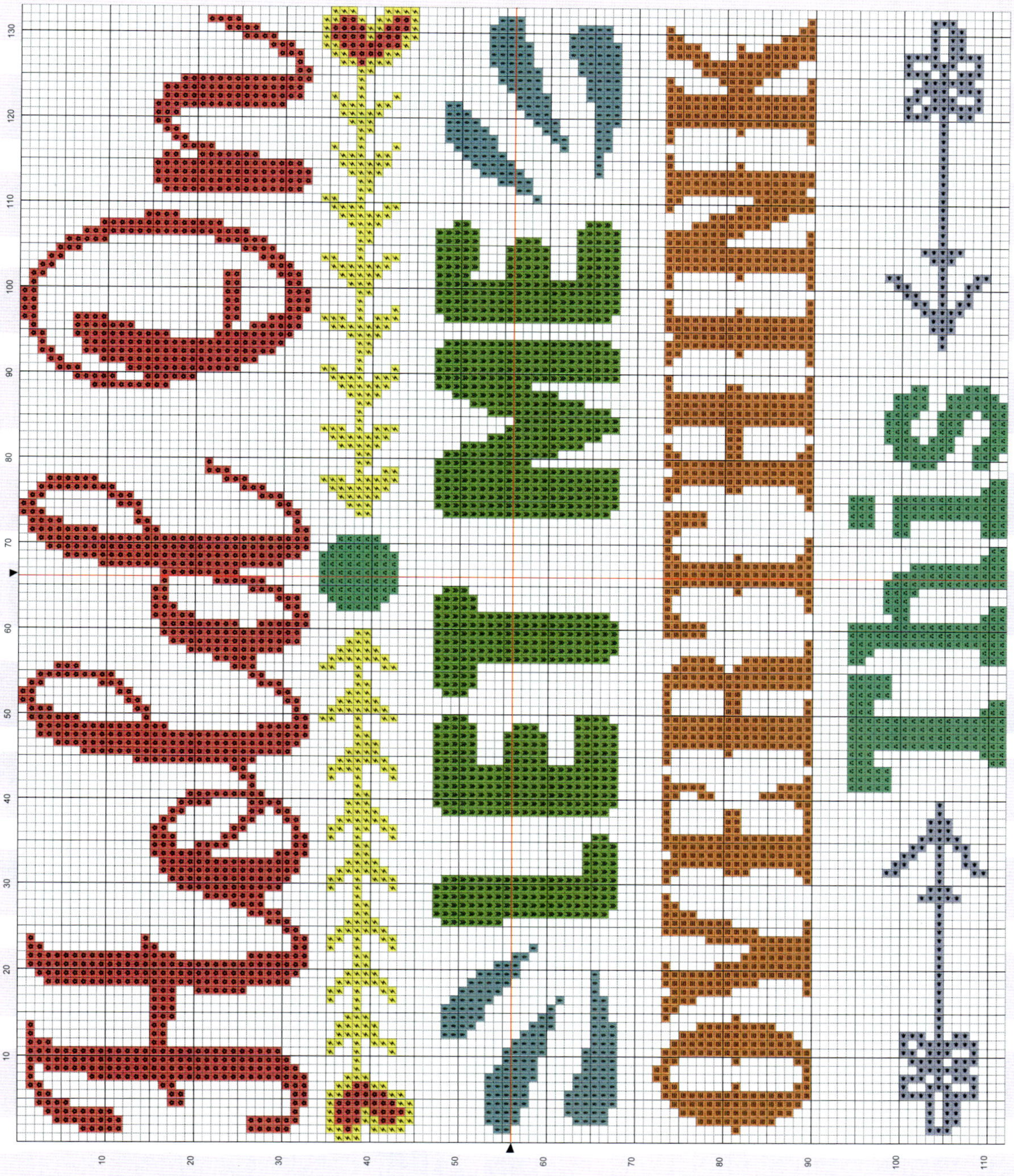

Design size:

133w x 112h stitches (9.5" x 8")

Instructions:

Following the general instructions on pages 13–19, stitch in 2 strands according to the chart. Allow yourself a little extra fabric around the edges if you intend to frame your design.

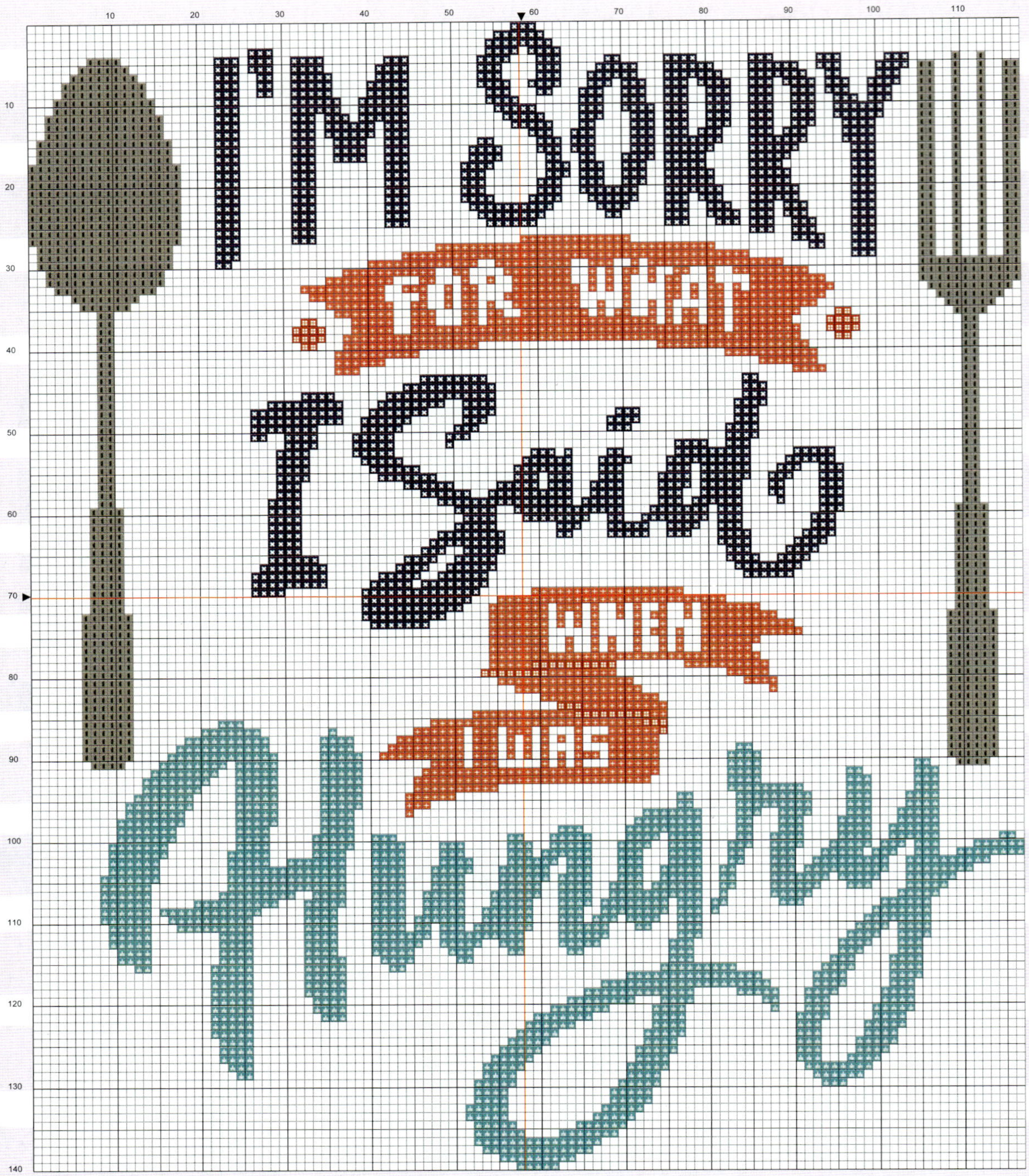

Design size:

117w x 140h stitches (8.4" x 10")

Instructions:

Following the general instructions on pages 13–19, stitch in 2 strands according to the chart. Allow yourself a little extra fabric around the edges if you intend to frame your design.

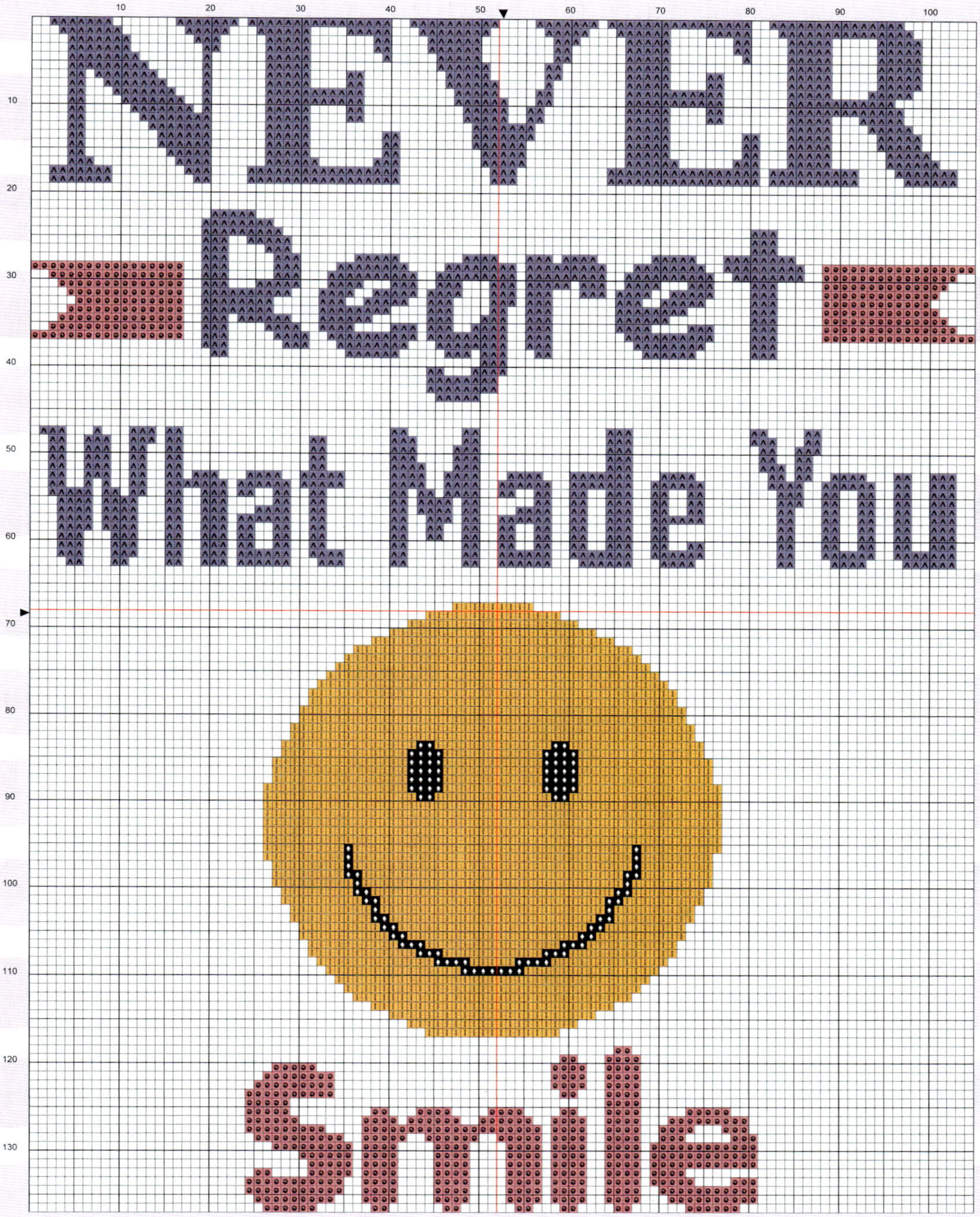

Design size:
105w x 137h stitches (7.5" x 9.8")

Instructions:
Following the general instructions on pages 13–19, stitch in 2 strands according to the chart. Allow yourself a little extra fabric around the edges if you intend to frame your design.

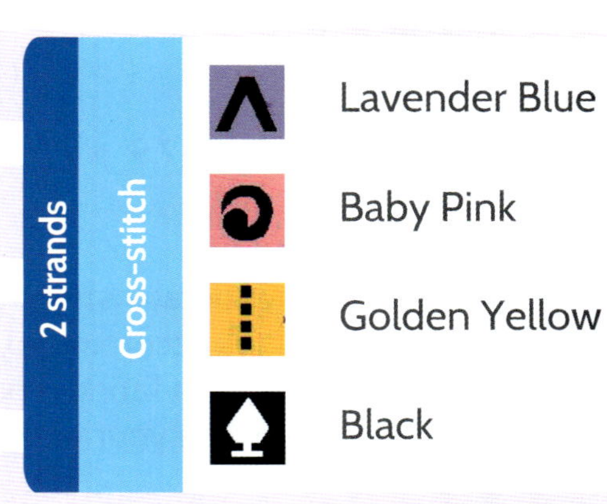

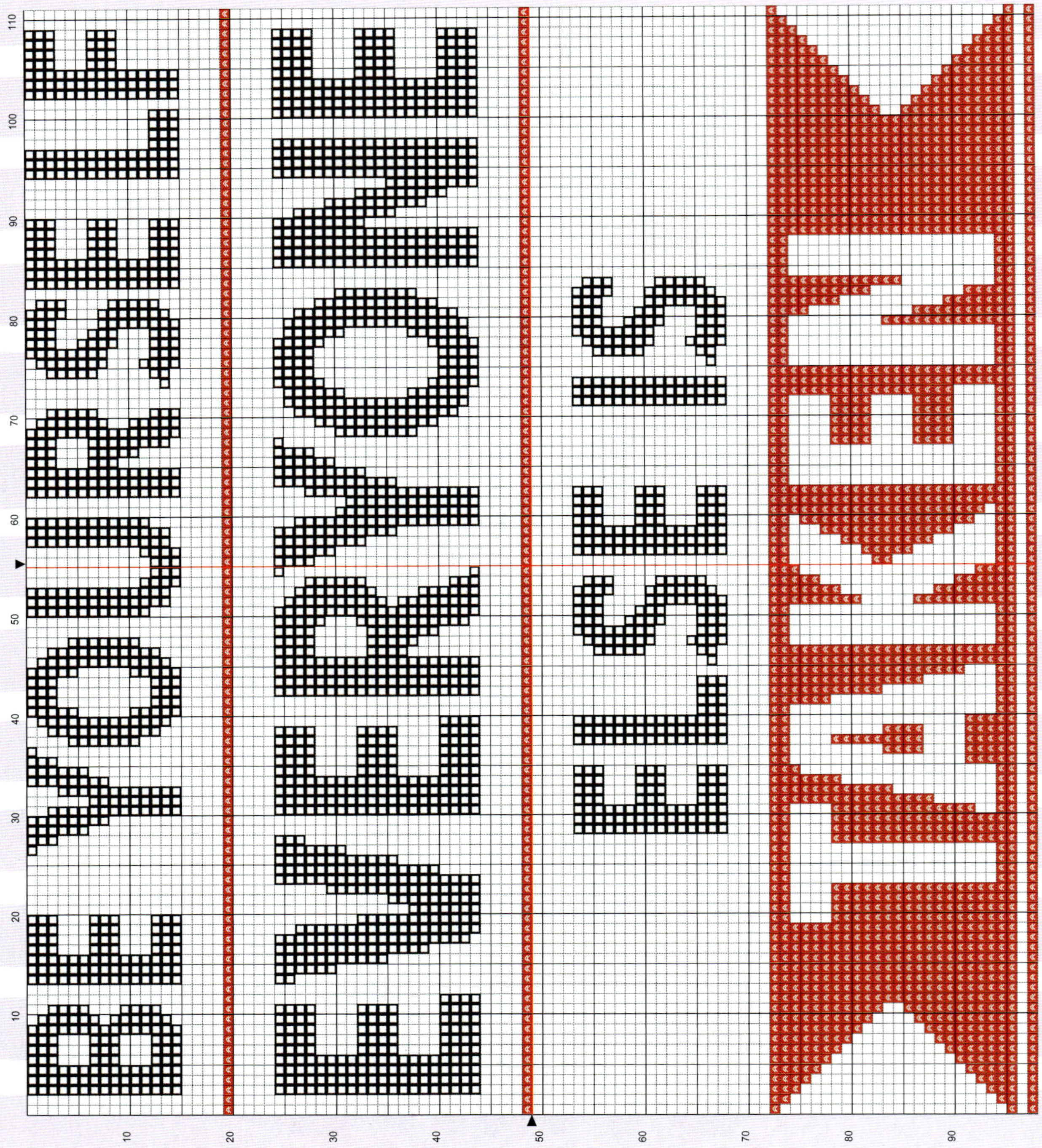

Design size:
111w x 98h stitches (7.9" x 7")

Instructions:
Following the general instructions on pages 13–19, stitch in 2 strands according to the chart. Allow yourself a little extra fabric around the edges if you intend to frame your design.

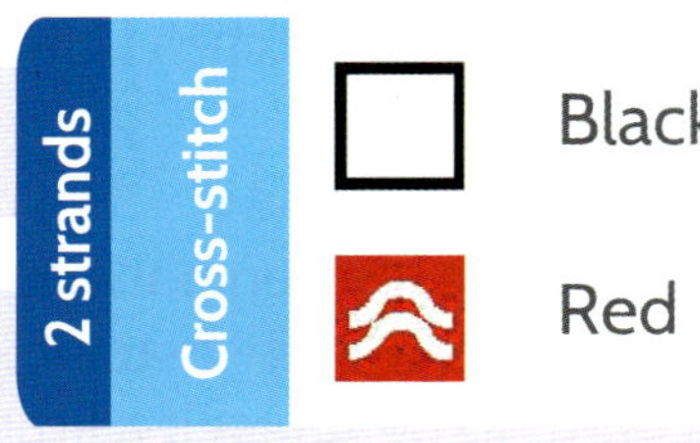

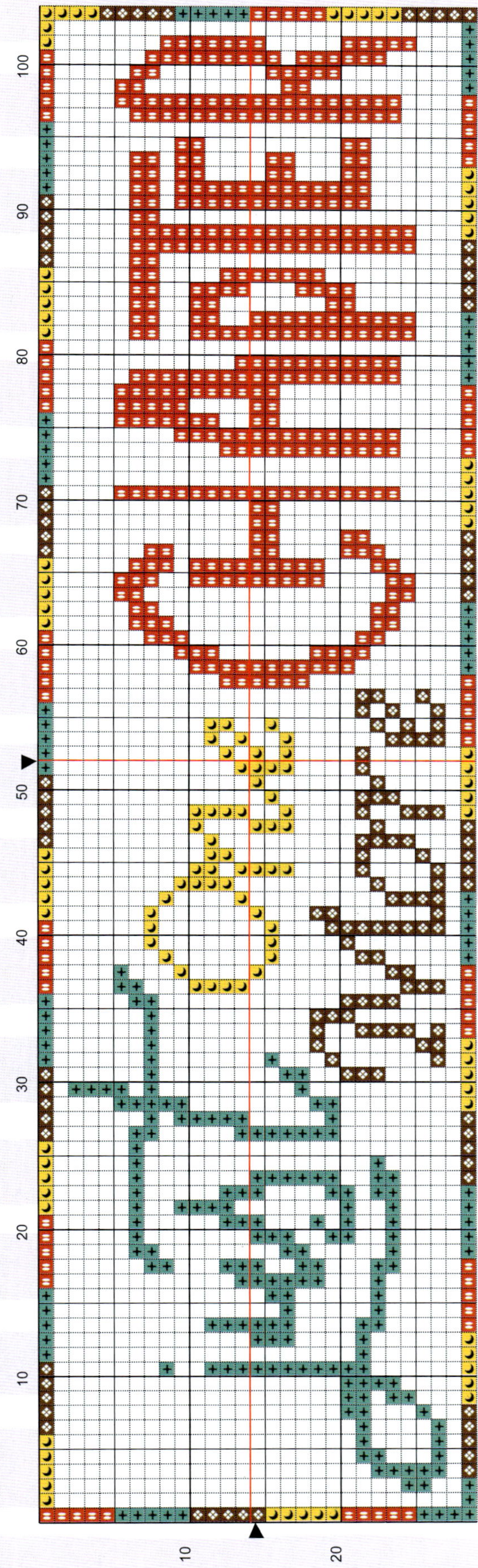

Design size:
104w x 29h stitches (7.4" x 2.1")

Instructions:
Following the general instructions on pages 13–19, stitch in 2 strands according to the chart. Refer to page 11 for ways to increase the stability of your piece to use it as a bookmark.

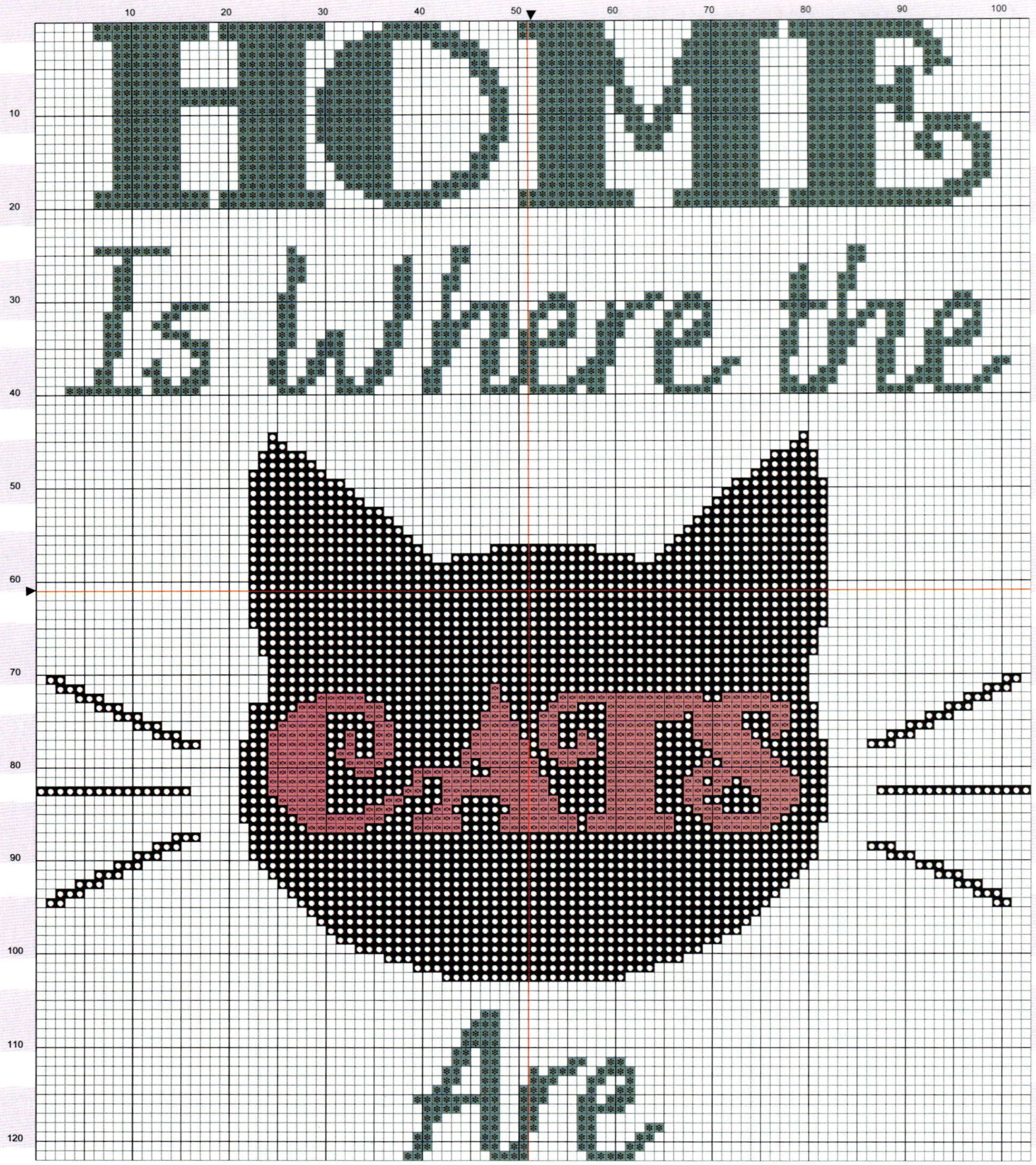

Design size:

103w x 122h stitches (7.4" x 8.7")

Instructions:

Following the general instructions on pages 13–19, stitch in 2 strands according to the chart. Allow yourself a little extra fabric around the edges if you intend to frame your design.

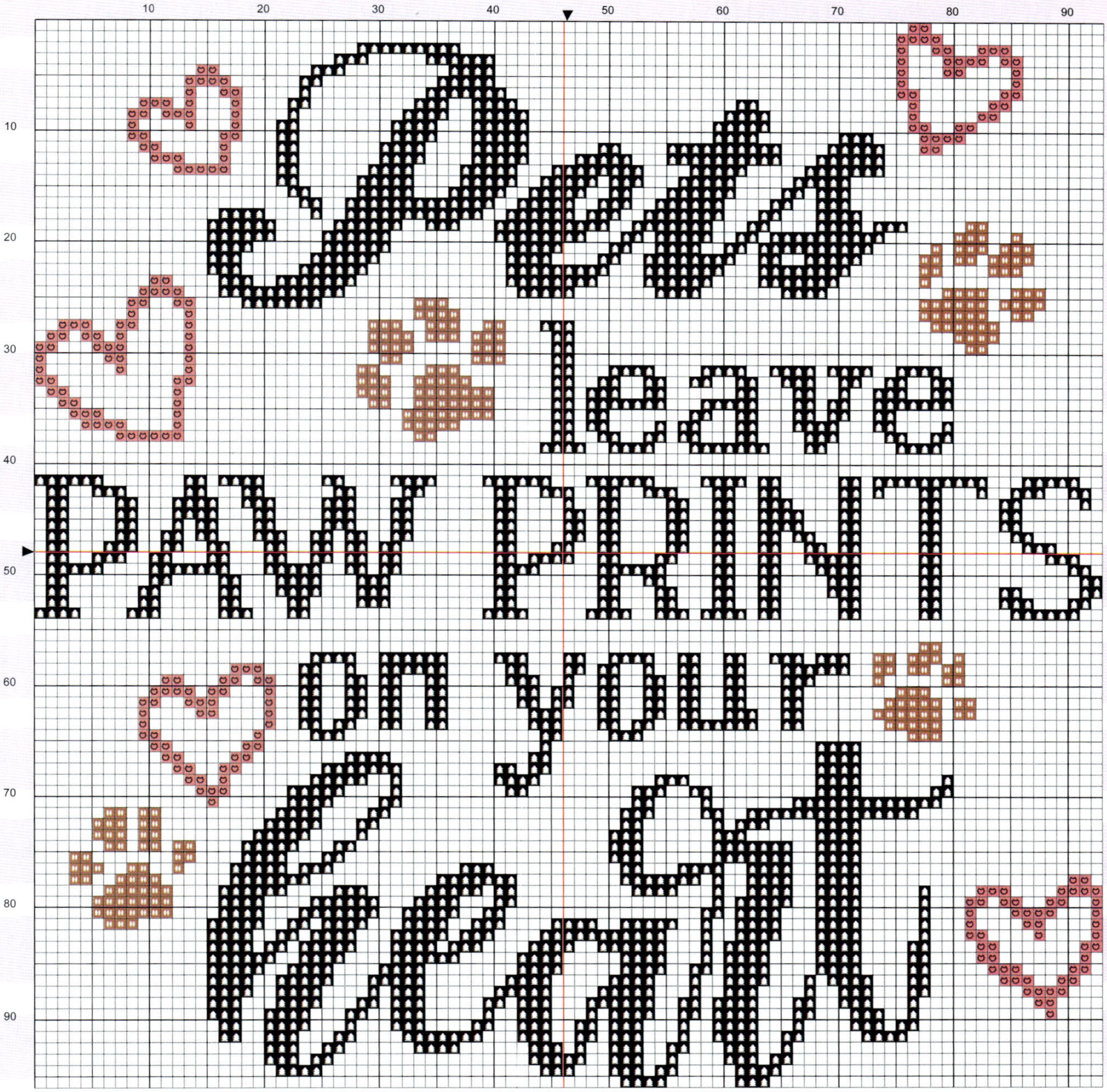

Design size:
93w x 96h stitches (6.6" x 6.9")

Instructions:
Following the general instructions on pages 13–19, stitch in 2 strands according to the chart. Allow yourself a little extra fabric around the edges if you intend to frame your design.

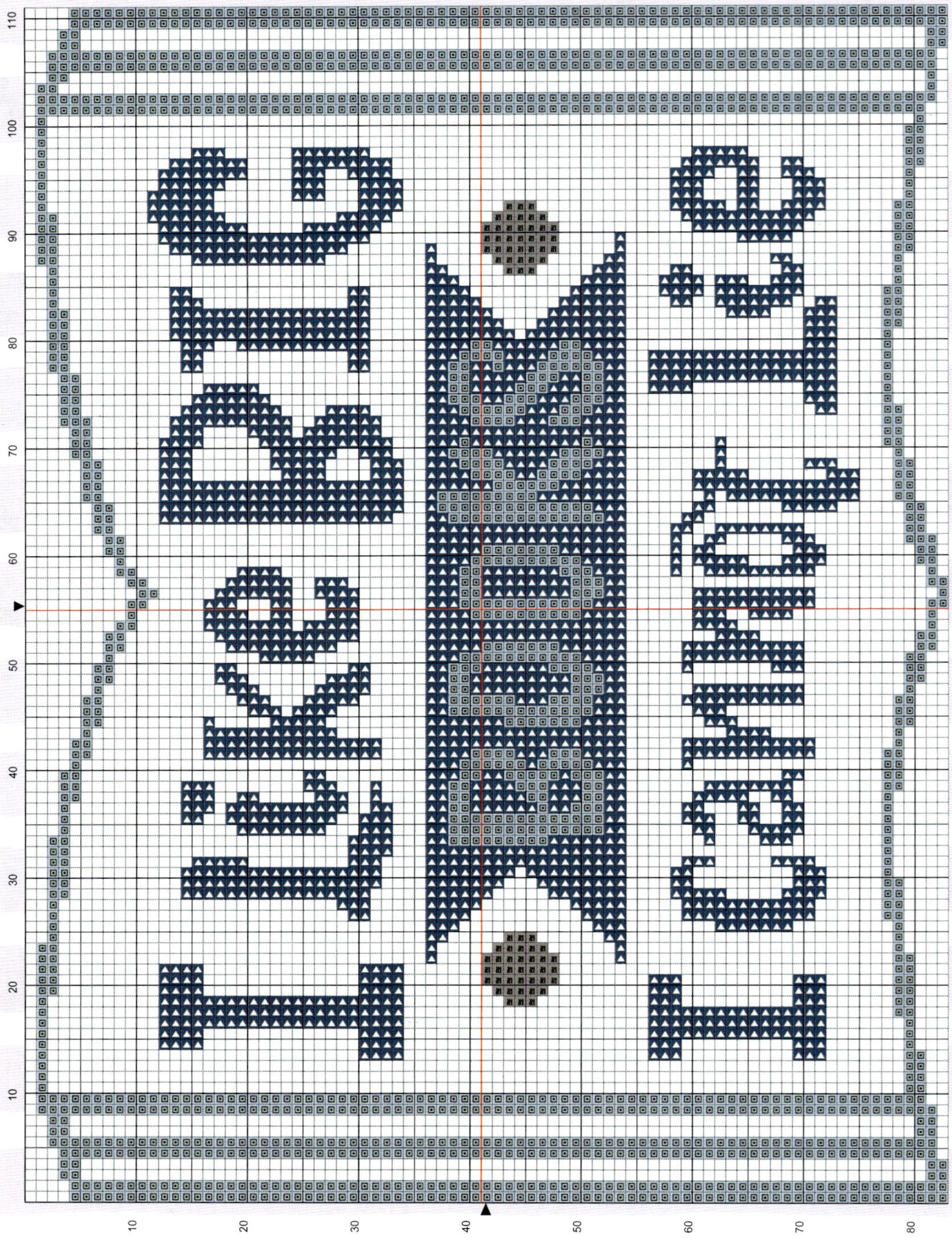

Design size:
111w x 83h stitches (7.9" x 5.9")

Instructions:
Following the general instructions on pages 13–19, stitch in 2 strands according to the chart. Allow yourself a little extra fabric around the edges if you intend to frame your design.

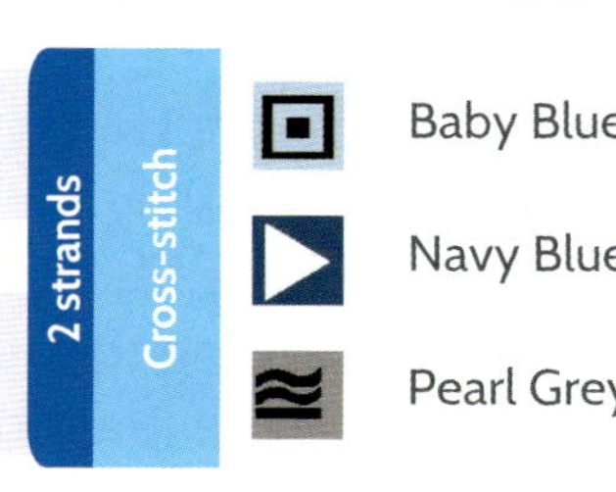

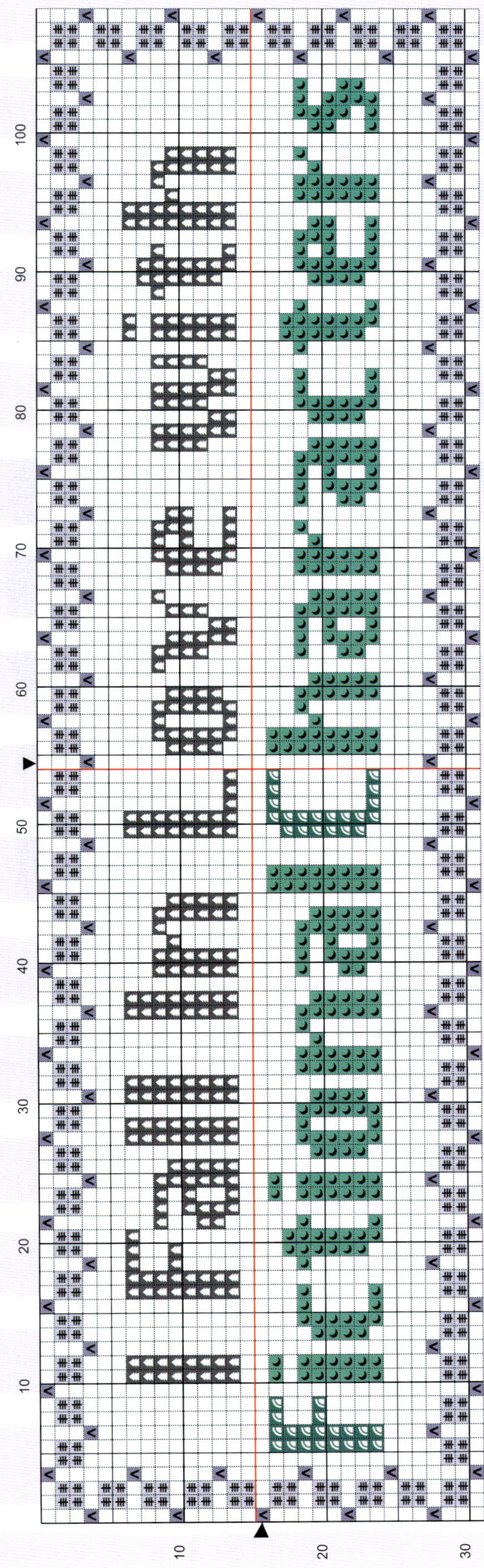

Design size:
109w x 31h stitches (7.8" x 2.2")

Instructions:
Following the general instructions on pages 13–19, stitch in 2 strands according to the chart. Refer to page 11 for ways to increase the stability of your piece to use it as a bookmark.

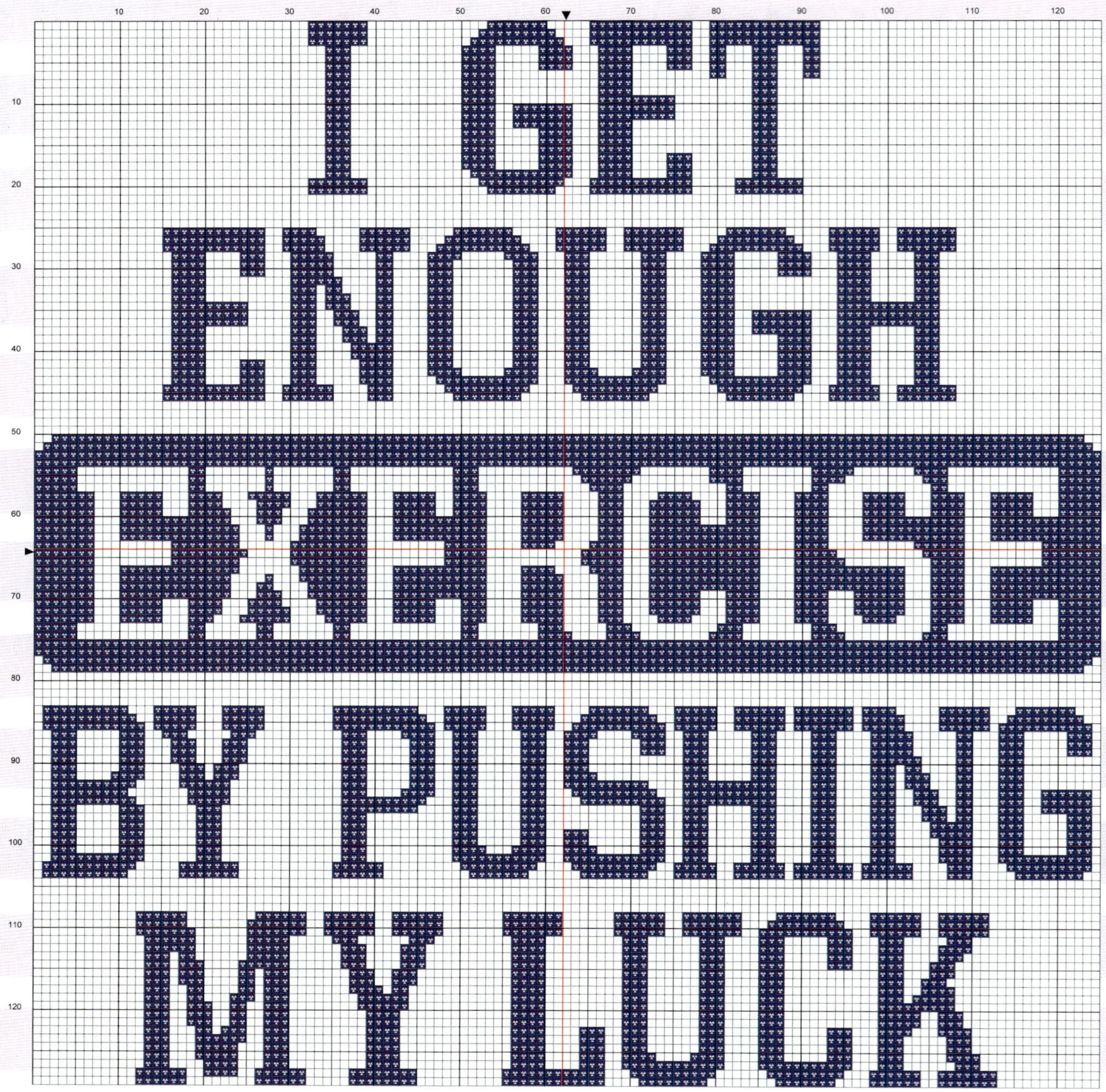

Design size:
125w x 129h stitches (8.9" x 9.2")

Instructions:
Following the general instructions on pages 13–19, stitch in 2 strands according to the chart. Allow yourself a little extra fabric around the edges if you intend to frame your design.

Royal Blue

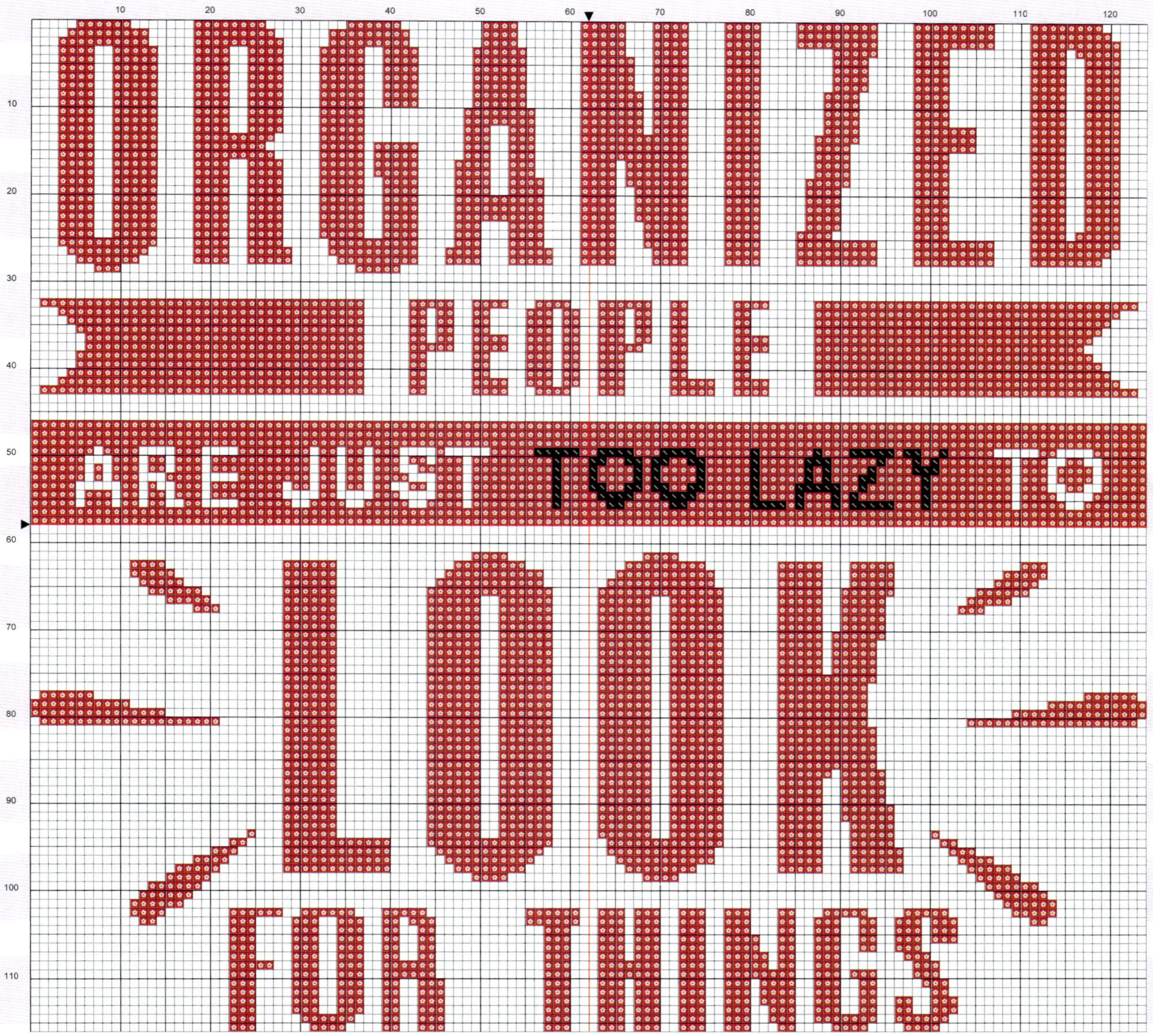

Design size:
124w x 116h stitches (8.9" x 8.3")

Instructions:
Following the general instructions on pages 13–19, stitch in 2 strands according to the chart. Allow yourself a little extra fabric around the edges if you intend to frame your design.

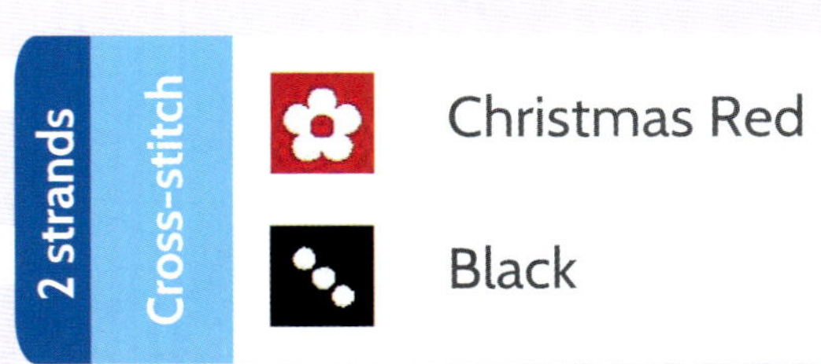

Snarky
Please Leave
by 9 pm

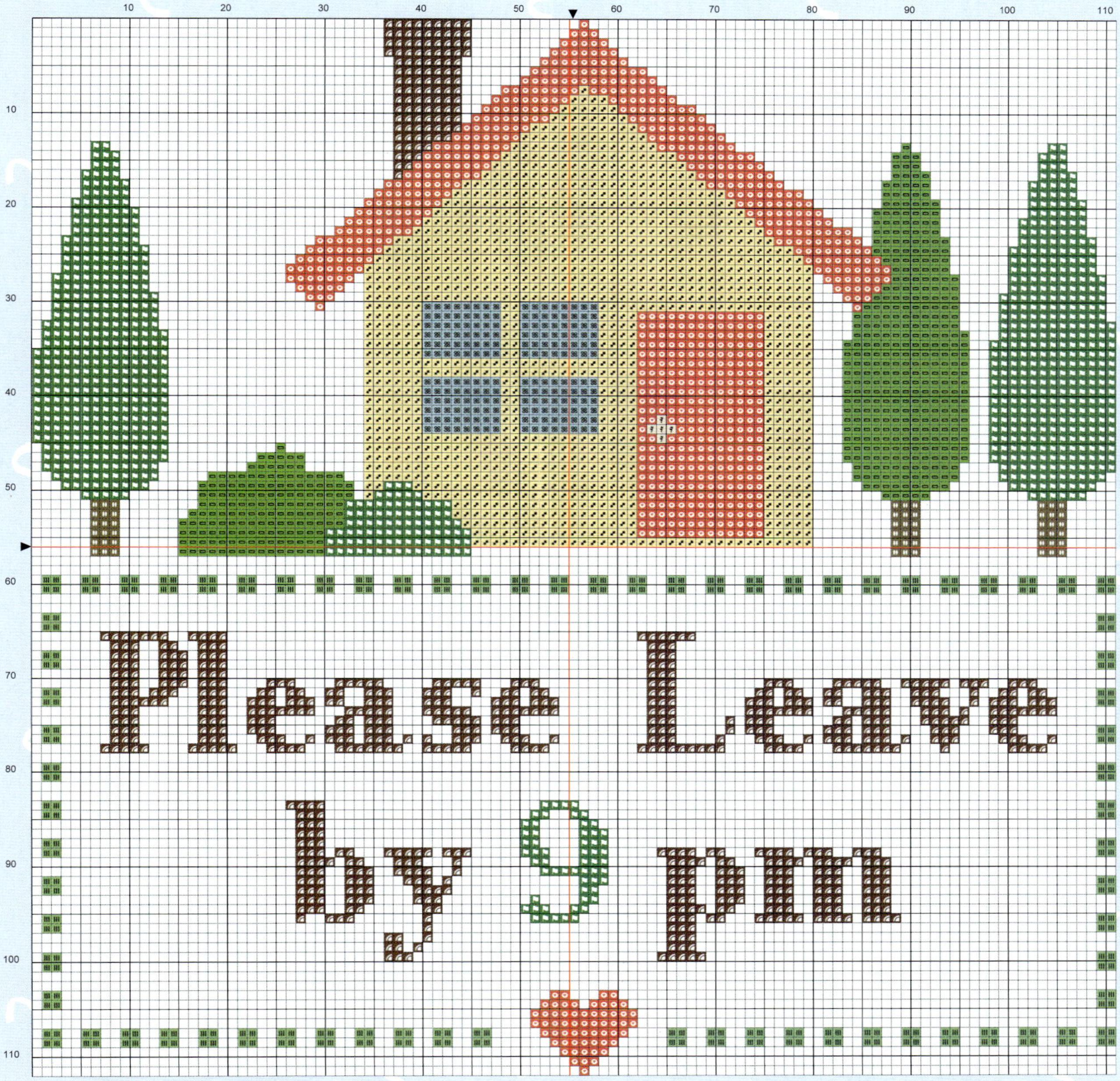

Design size:
111w x 112h stitches (7.9" x 8")

Instructions:
Following the general instructions on pages 13–19, stitch in 2 strands according to the chart. Allow yourself a little extra fabric around the edges if you intend to frame your design.

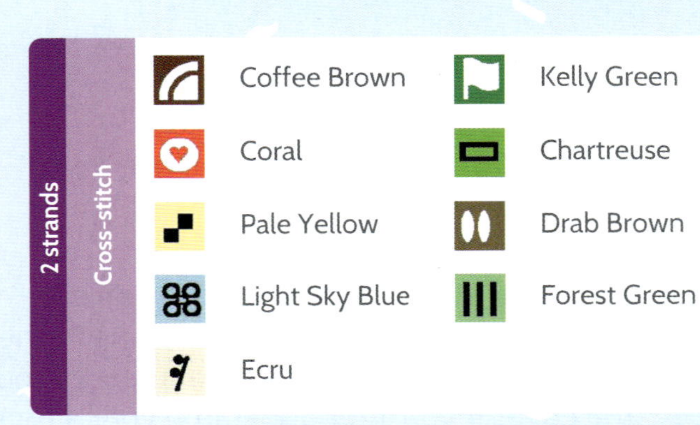

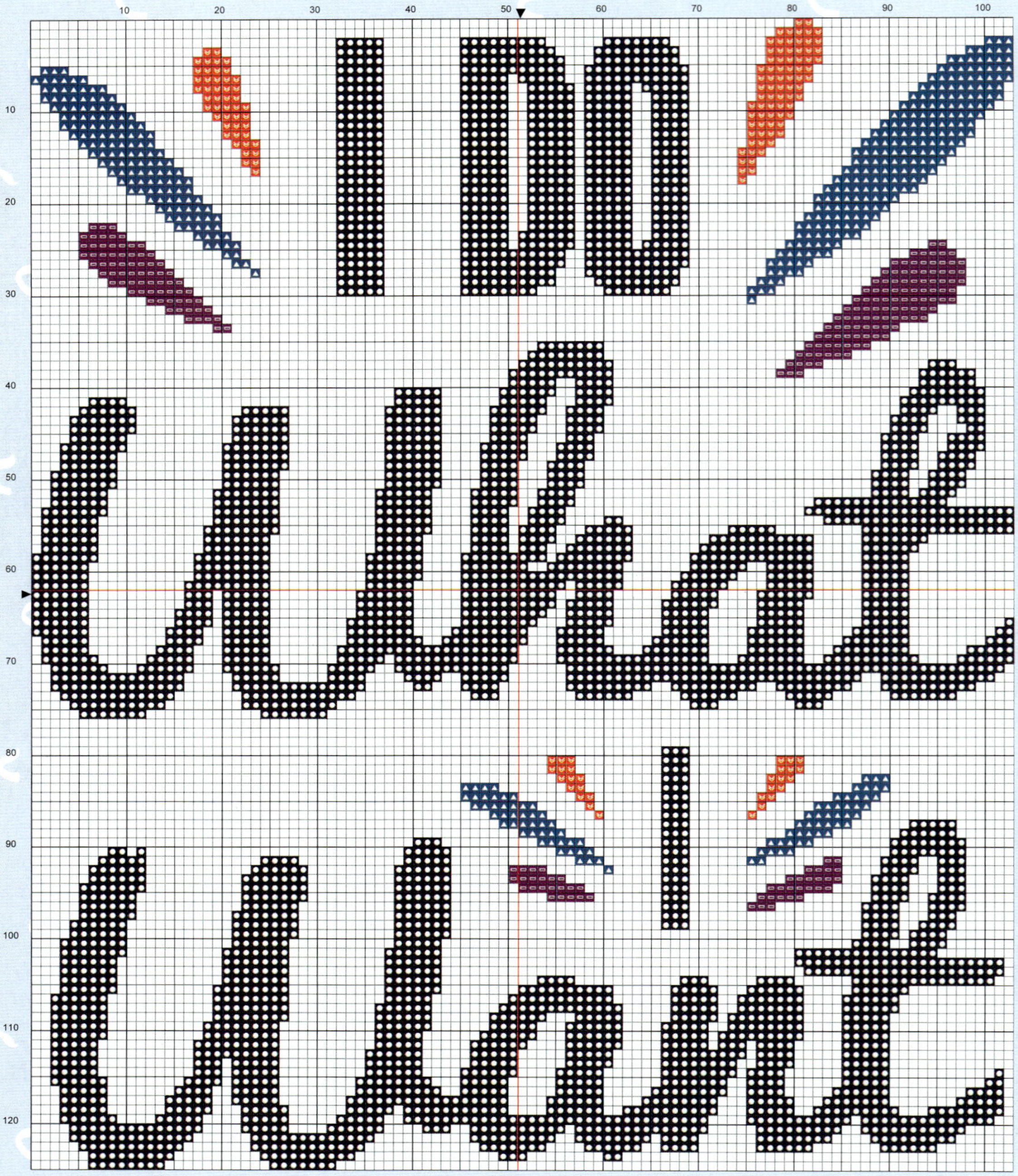

Design size:
103w x 125h stitches (7.4" x 8.9")

Instructions:
Following the general instructions on pages 13–19, stitch in 2 strands according to the chart. Allow yourself a little extra fabric around the edges if you intend to frame your design.

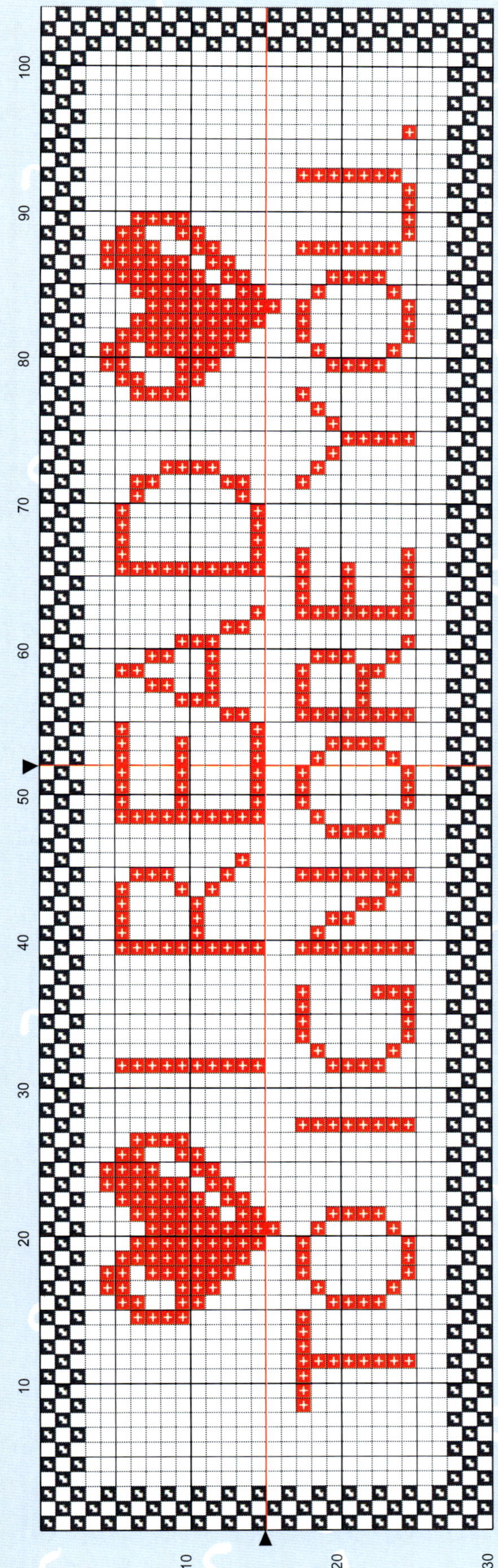

Design size:

104w x 30h stitches (7.4" x 2.1")

Instructions:

Following the general instructions on pages 13–19, stitch in 2 strands according to the chart. Refer to page 11 for ways to increase the stability of your piece to use it as a bookmark.

2 strands	Cross-stitch	
		Christmas Red
		Pewter Grey

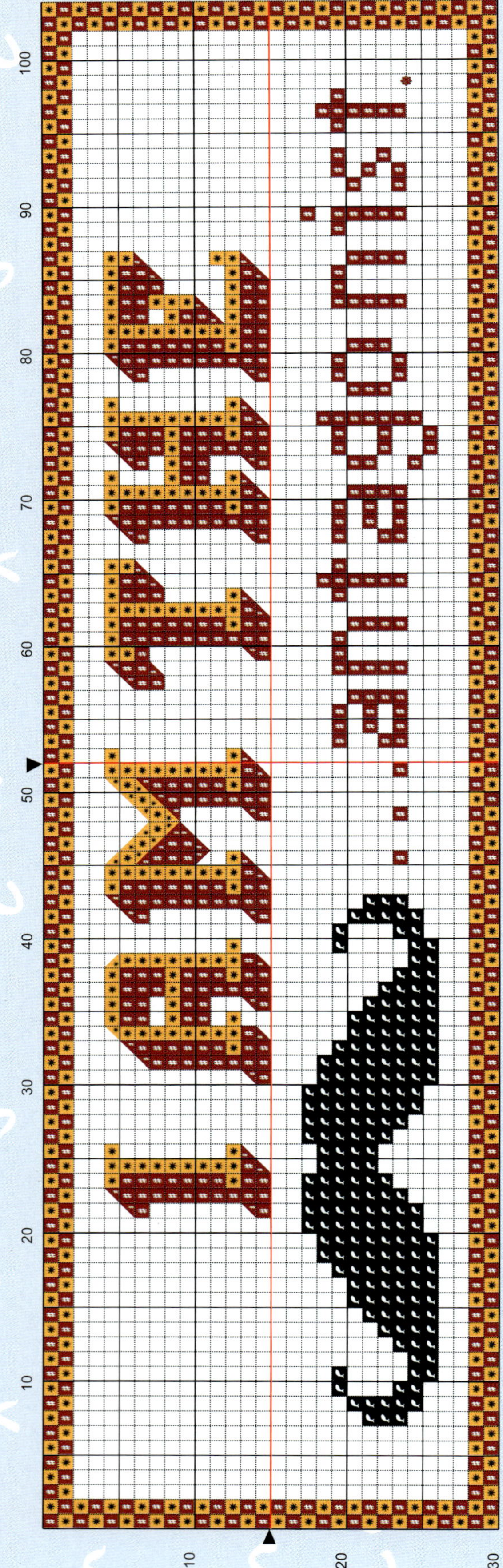

Design size:
104w x 30h stitches (7.4" x 2.1")

Instructions:
Following the general instructions on pages 13–19, stitch in 2 strands according to the chart. Squares in the chart that are only half filled use a half stitch. Use French knots for the dots of the ellipsis. Refer to page 11 for ways to increase the stability of your piece to use it as a bookmark.

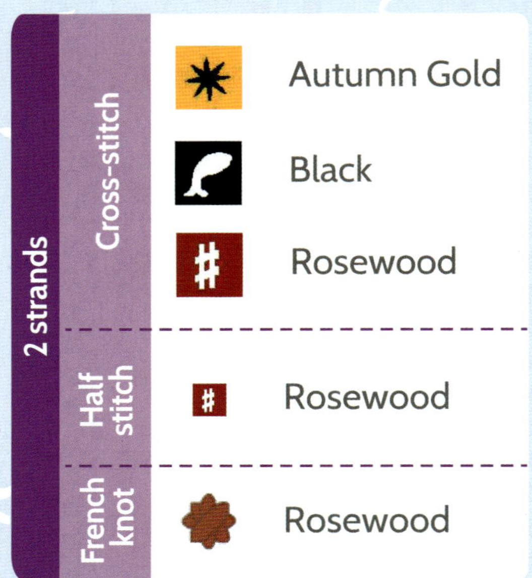

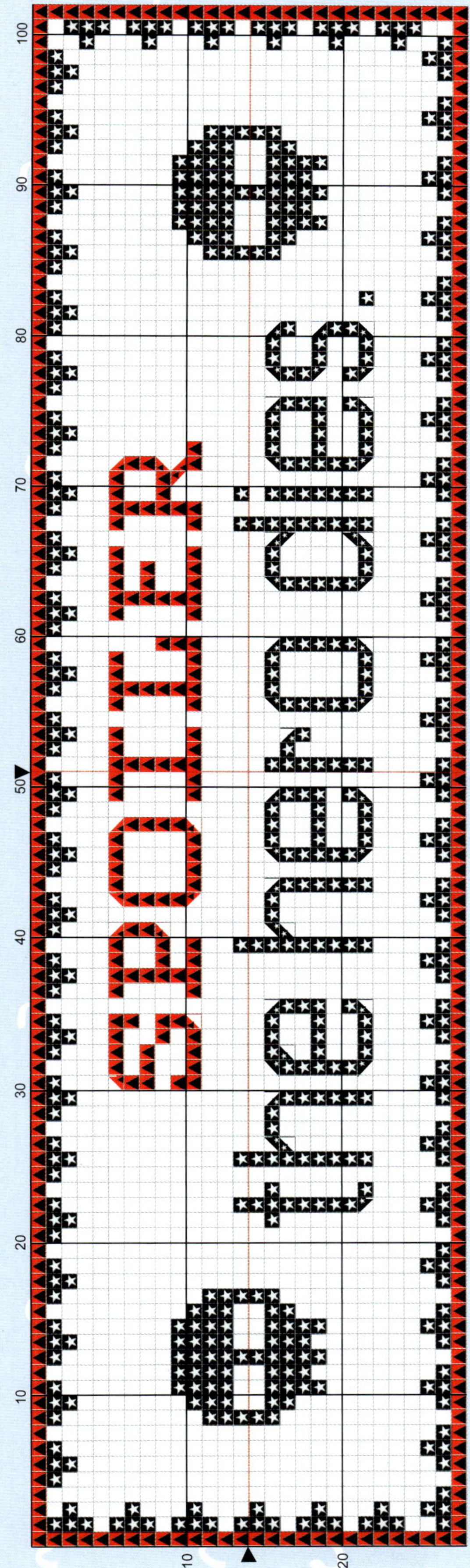

Design size:
102w x 28h stitches (7.3" x 2")

Instructions:
Following the general instructions on pages 13–19, stitch in 2 strands according to the chart. Squares in the chart that are only half filled use a half stitch. Refer to page 11 for ways to increase the stability of your piece to use it as a bookmark.

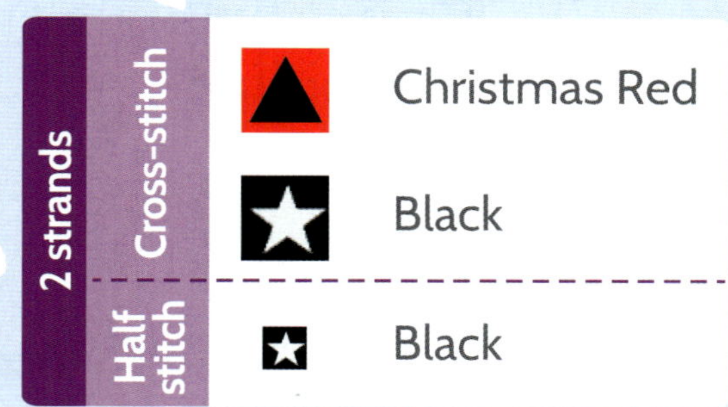

Design size:
79w x 99h stitches (5.6" x 7.1")

Instructions:
Following the general instructions on pages 13–19, stitch in 2 strands according to the chart. Allow yourself a little extra fabric around the edges if you intend to frame your design.

2 strands | Cross-stitch

- Royal Blue
- Black
- Lemon
- Mahogany

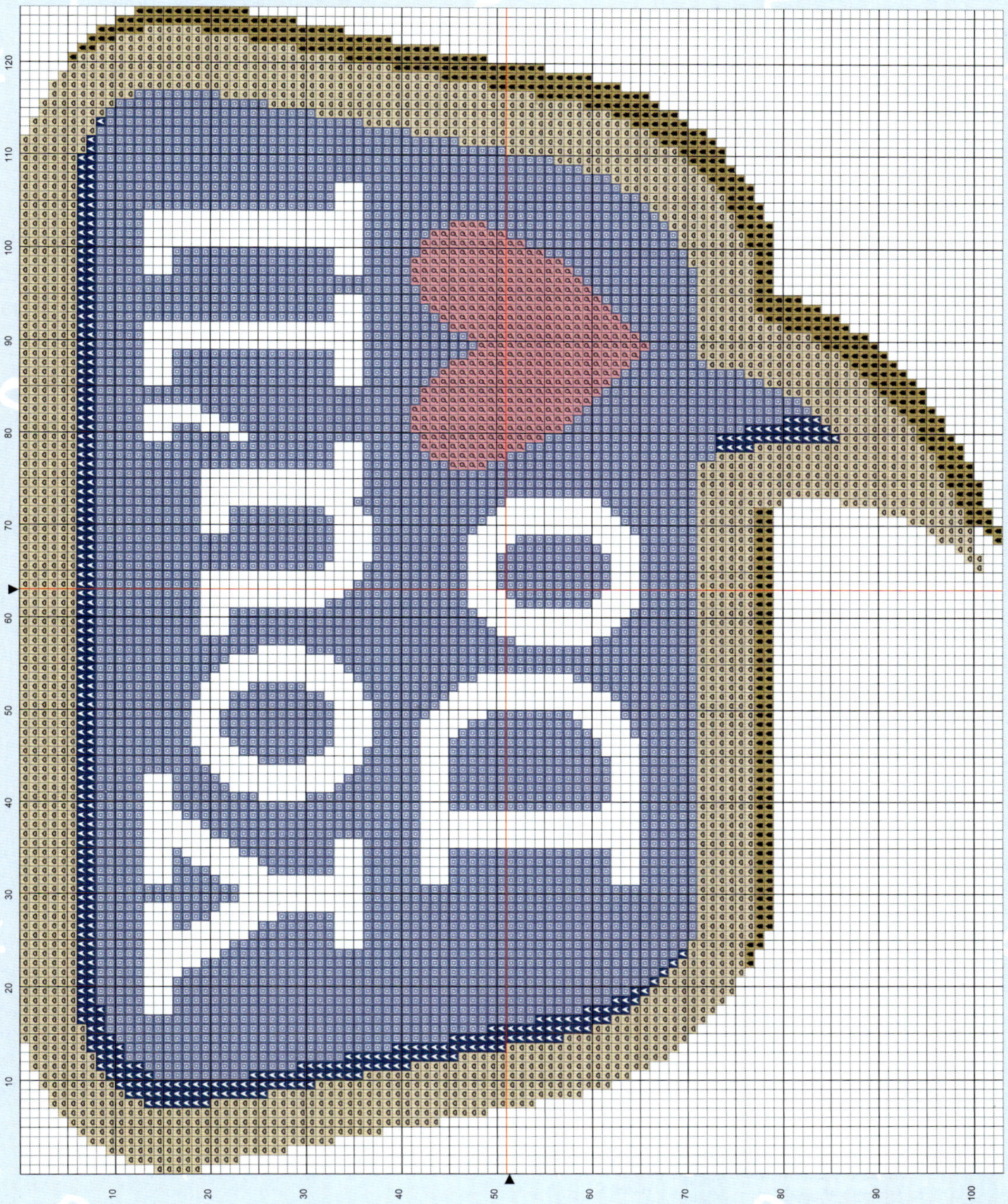

Design size:
126w x 103h stitches (9'' x 7.4'')

Instructions:
Following the general instructions on pages 13–19, stitch in 2 strands according to the chart. Allow yourself a little extra fabric around the edges if you intend to frame your design.

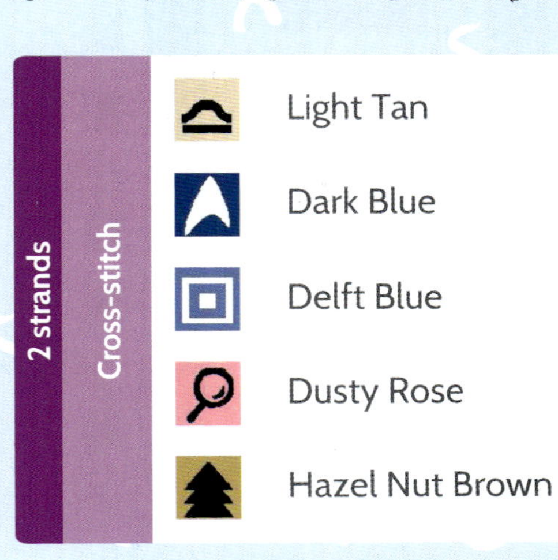

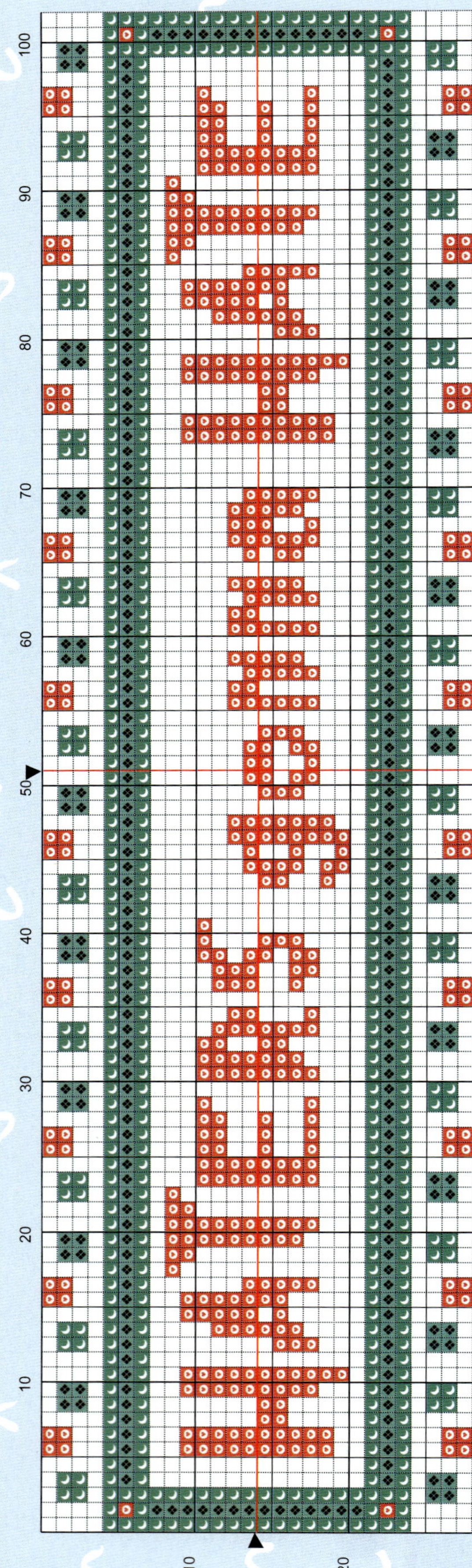

Design size:
102w x 28h stitches (7.3" x 2")

Instructions:
Following the general instructions on pages 13–19, stitch in 2 strands according to the chart. Refer to page 11 for ways to increase the stability of your piece to use it as a bookmark.

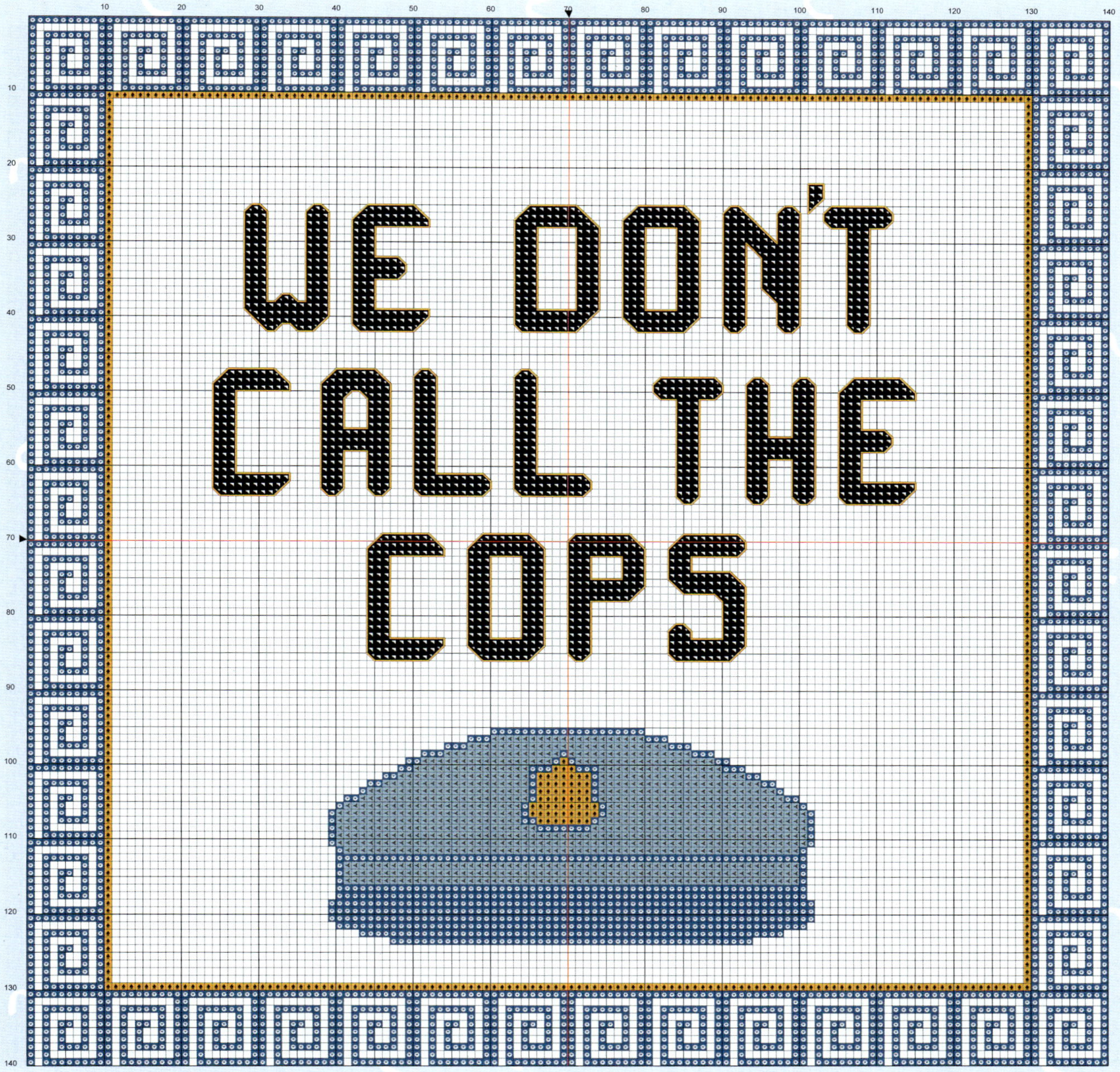

Design size:
140w x 140h stitches (10" x 10")

Instructions:
Following the general instructions on pages 13–19, stitch in 2 strands according to the chart. Squares in the chart that are only half filled use a half stitch. When all cross-stitching is done, backstitch the outline of the border in medium gold.

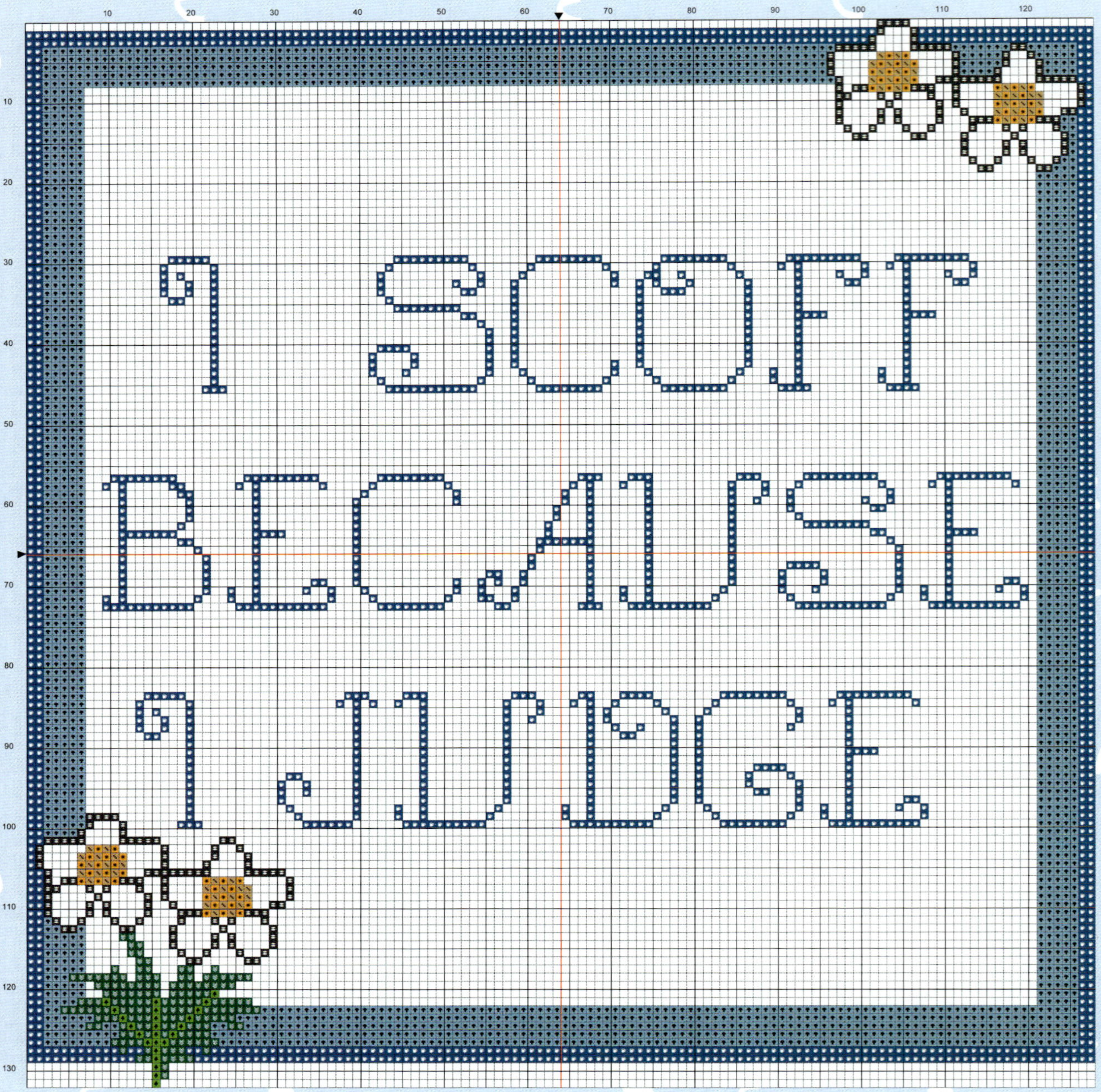

Design size:
128w x 130h stitches (9.1" x 9.4")

Instructions:
Following the general instructions on pages 13–19, stitch in 2 strands according to the chart. Allow yourself a little extra fabric around the edges if you intend to frame your design.

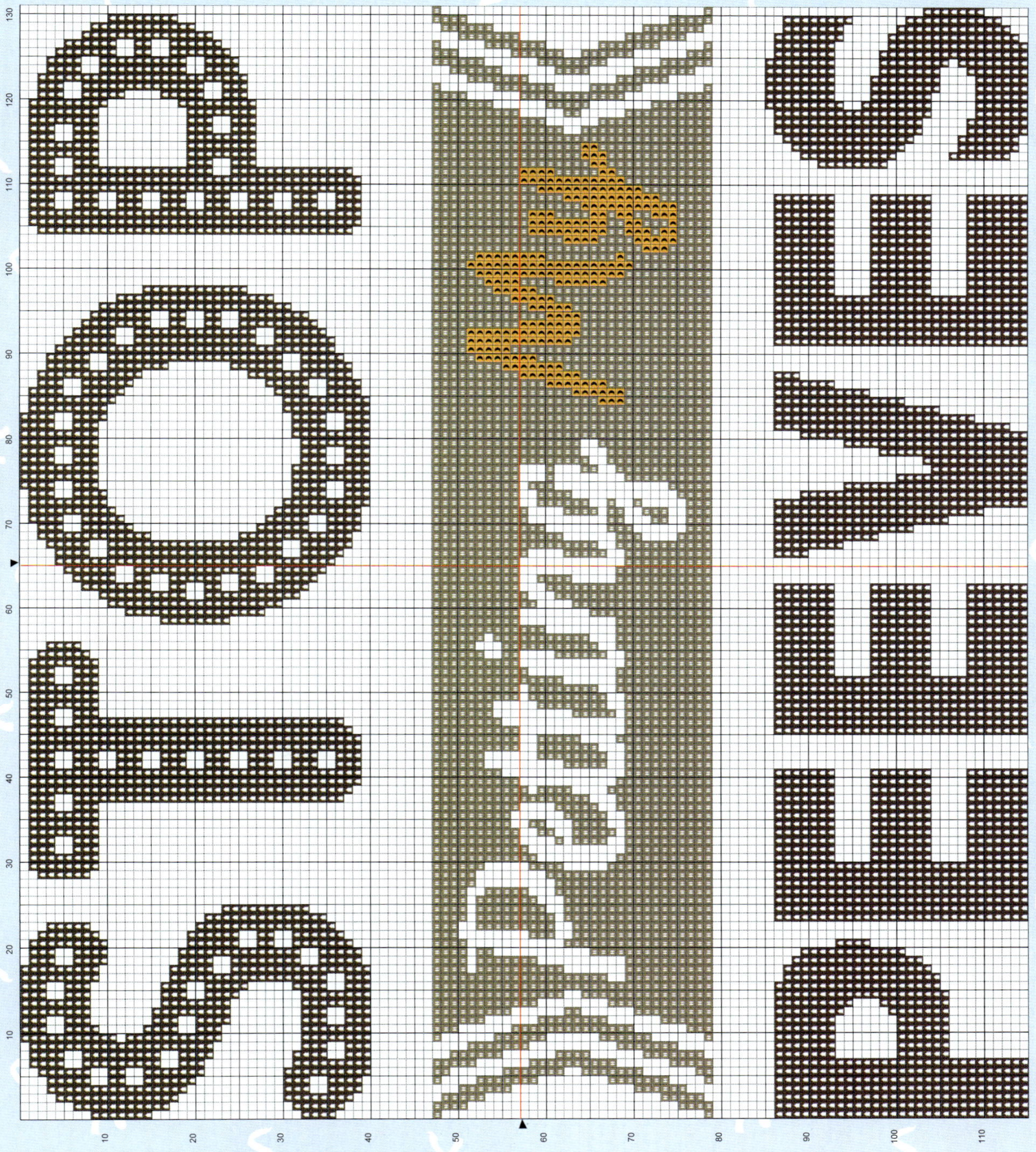

Design size:

131w x 115h stitches (9.4" x 8.2")

Instructions:

Following the general instructions on pages 13–19, stitch in 2 strands according to the chart. Allow yourself a little extra fabric around the edges if you intend to frame your design.

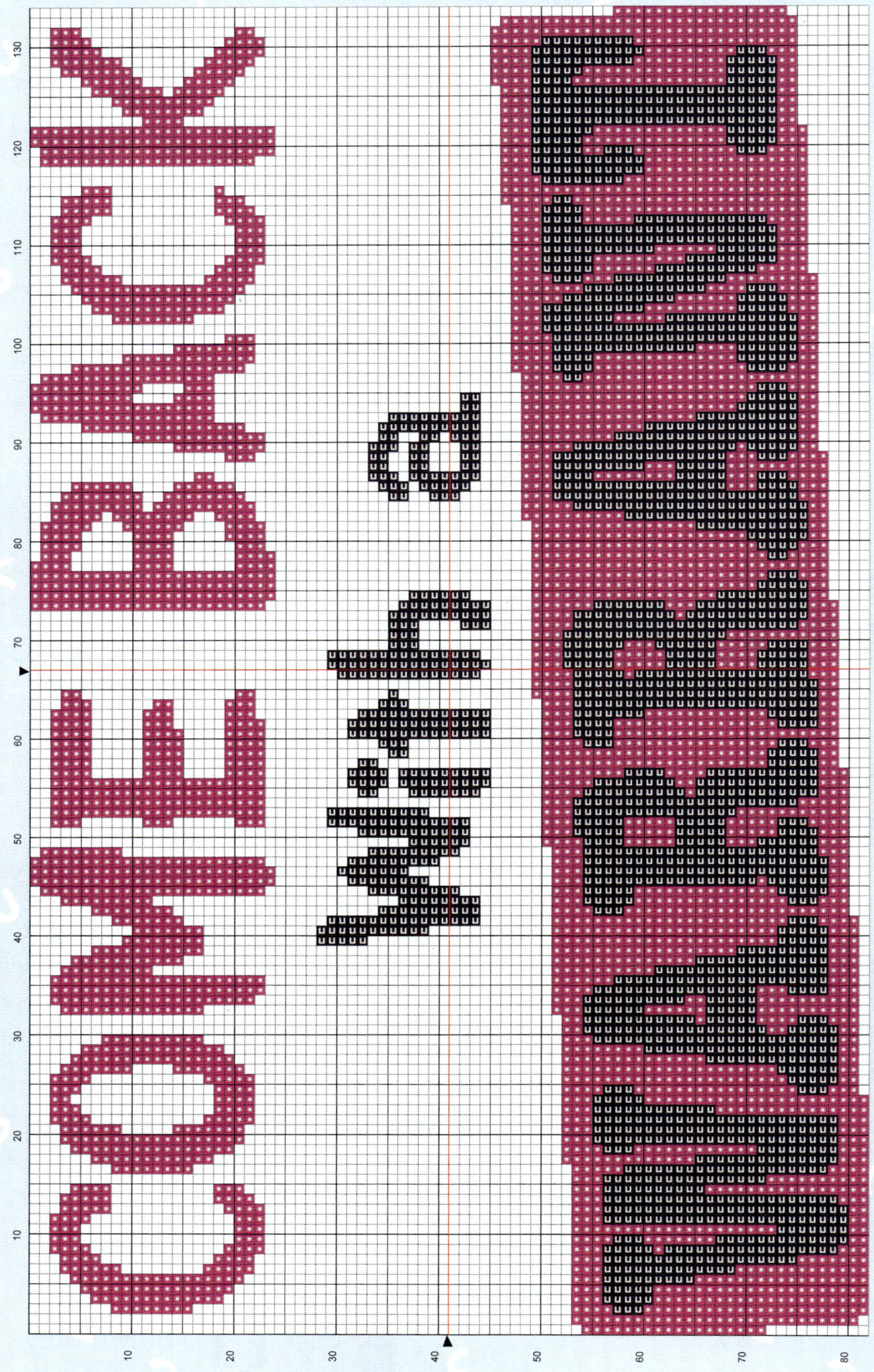

Design size:
134w x 82h stitches (9.6" x 5.9")

Instructions:
Following the general instructions on pages 13–19, stitch in 2 strands according to the chart. Allow yourself a little extra fabric around the edges if you intend to frame your design.

2 strands	Cross-stitch	
	✱	Plum
	▣	Navy Blue

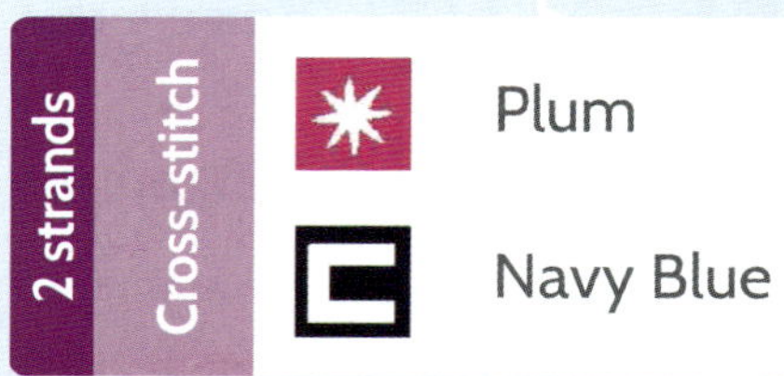

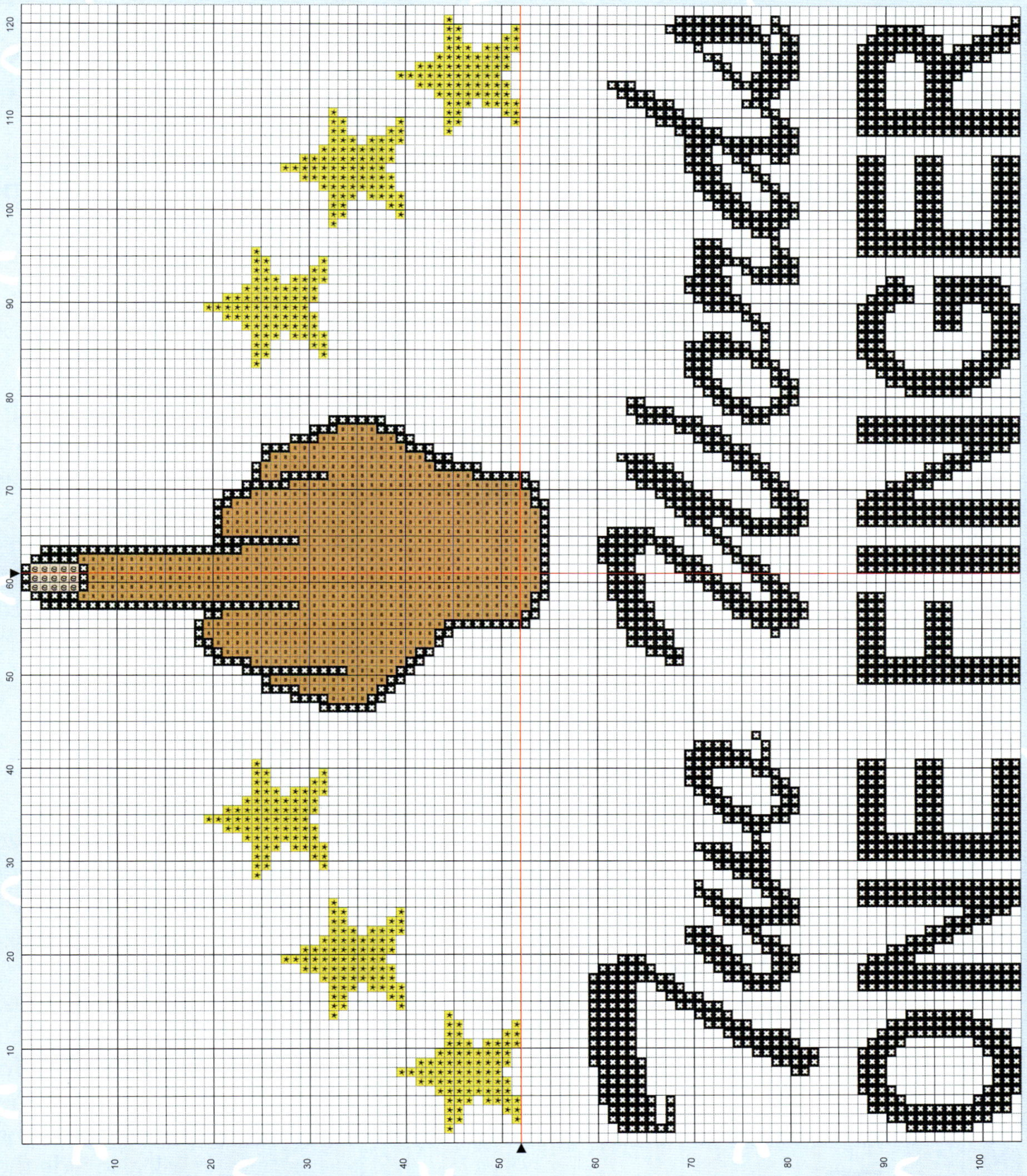

Design size:
122w x 104h stitches (8.7" x 7.4")

Instructions:
Following the general instructions on pages 13–19, stitch in 2 strands according to the chart. Allow yourself a little extra fabric around the edges if you intend to frame your design.

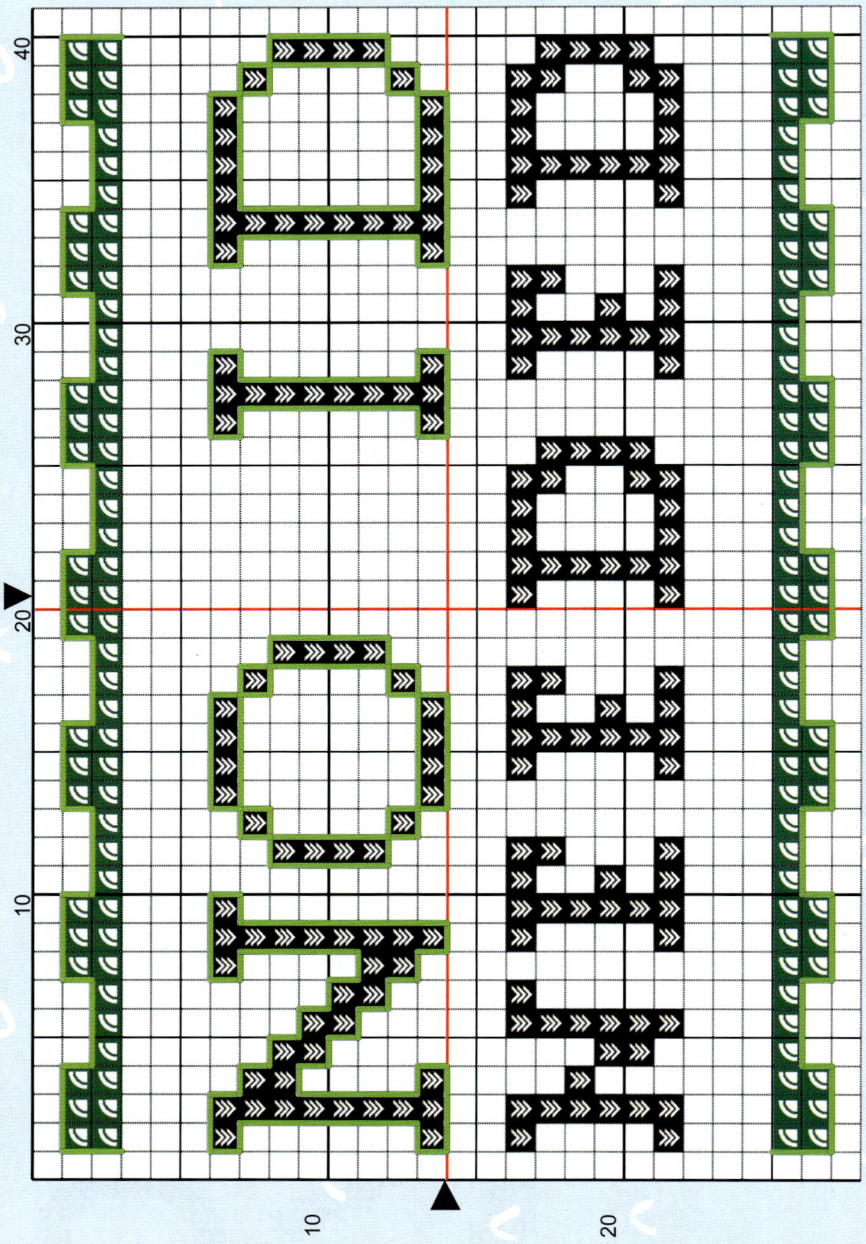

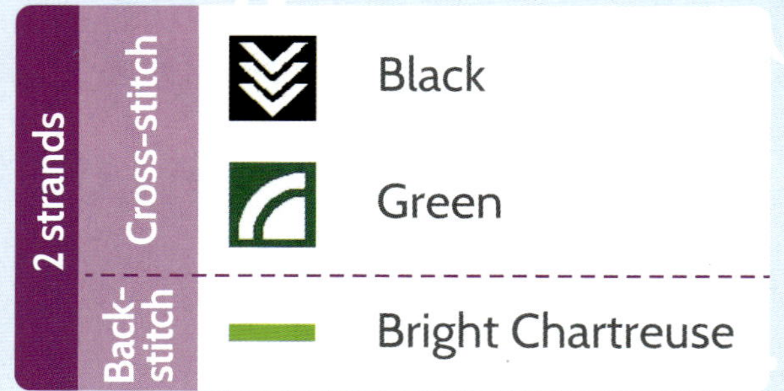

Design size:

41w x 28h stitches (2.9" x 2")

Instructions:

Following the general instructions on pages 13–19, stitch in 2 strands according to the chart. When all cross-stitching is done, backstitch the outline of No I.D. and the outline of the outer borders in light green.

Tip:

This design is a good size for a luggage tag. Trim the finished piece to fit inside a blank luggage tag case. If your case is visible from both sides, add your name and contact info on a card for the reverse side. This will also hide the threads on the back side of your design.

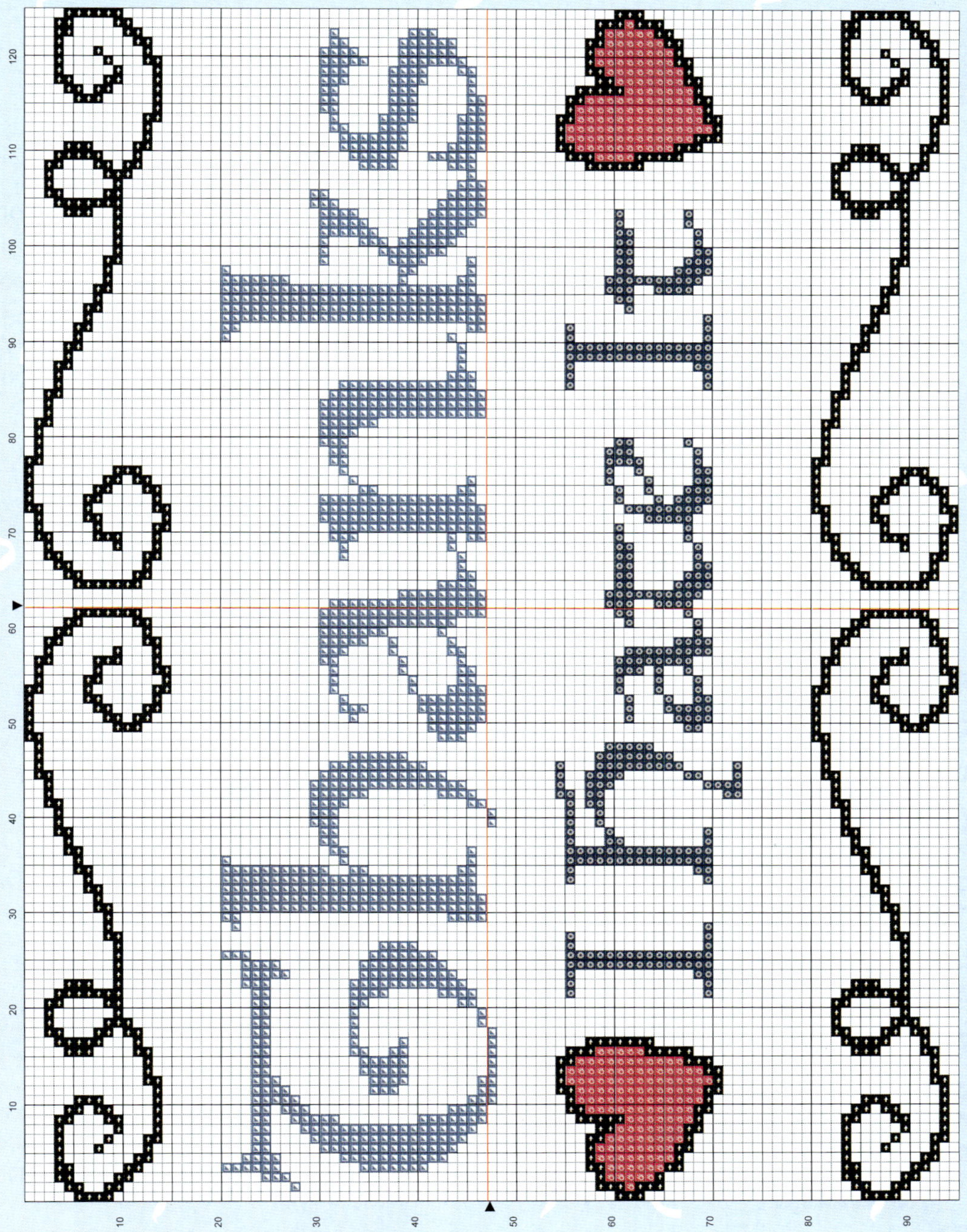

Design size:
125w x 95h stitches (8.9" x 6.8")

Instructions:
Following the general instructions on pages 13–19, stitch in 2 strands according to the chart. Allow yourself a little extra fabric around the edges if you intend to frame your design.

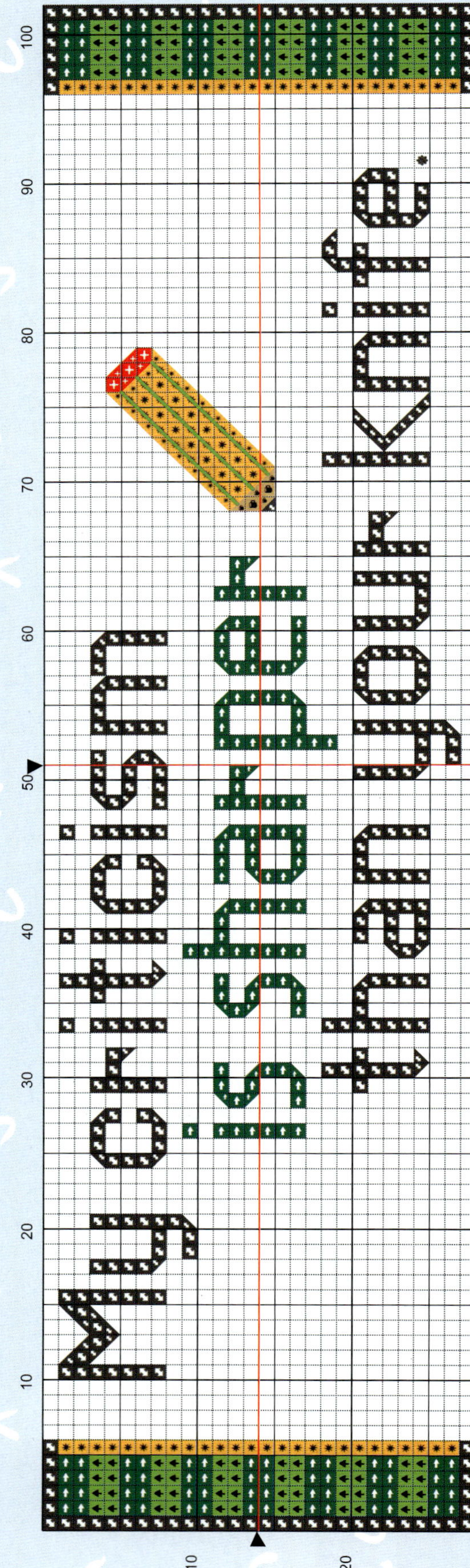

Design size:
102w x 28h stitches (7.3" x 2")

Instructions:
Following the general instructions on pages 13–19, stitch in 2 strands according to the chart. Squares in the chart that are only half filled use a half stitch. When all cross-stitching is done, backstitch the lines along the pencil in light green. Use a French knot for the period.

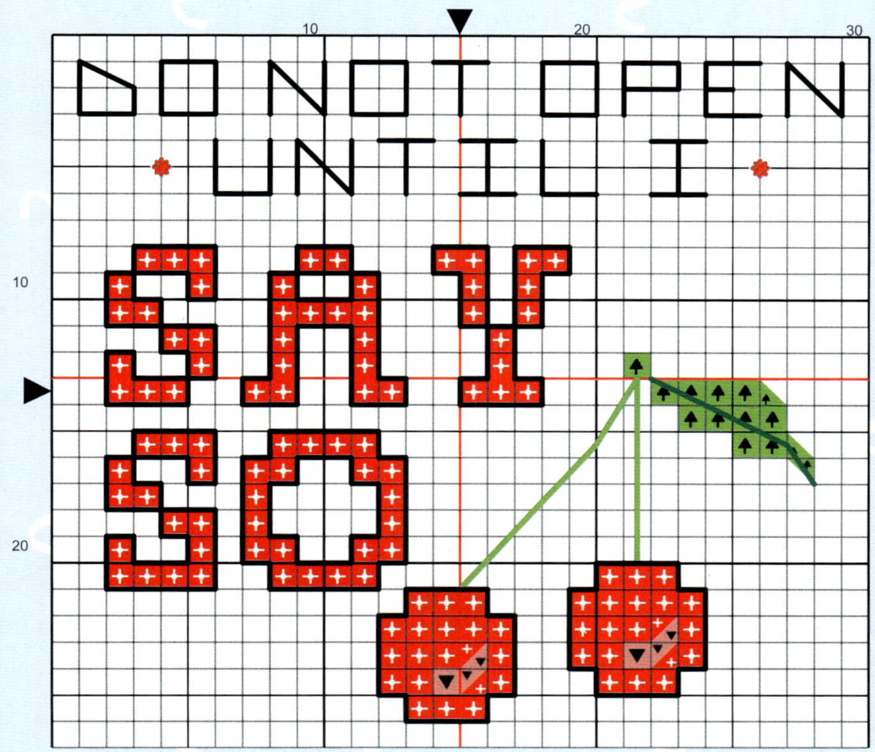

Design size:

32w x 33h stitches (2.3" x 2.4")

Instructions:

Following the general instructions on pages 13–19, stitch in 2 strands according to the chart. Squares in the chart that are only half filled use a half stitch. When all cross-stitching is done, backstitch the top two lines of text, the outline of "Say So," and the outline of the cherries in black. Backstitch the middle of the leaf in dark green. Backstitch the cherry stems in light green. Stitch the French knots on either side of the text as last, using bright red.

Tip:

This design is just the right size to use as a topper for a Mason jar. When your piece is complete, cover the top of the jar lid with your cross-stitched fabric. Secure the lid and cross-stitched piece on the jar with the outer band.

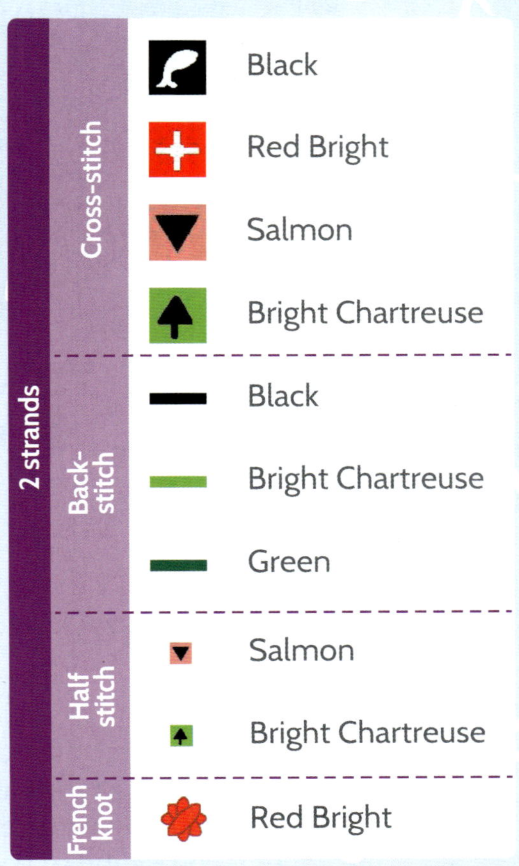

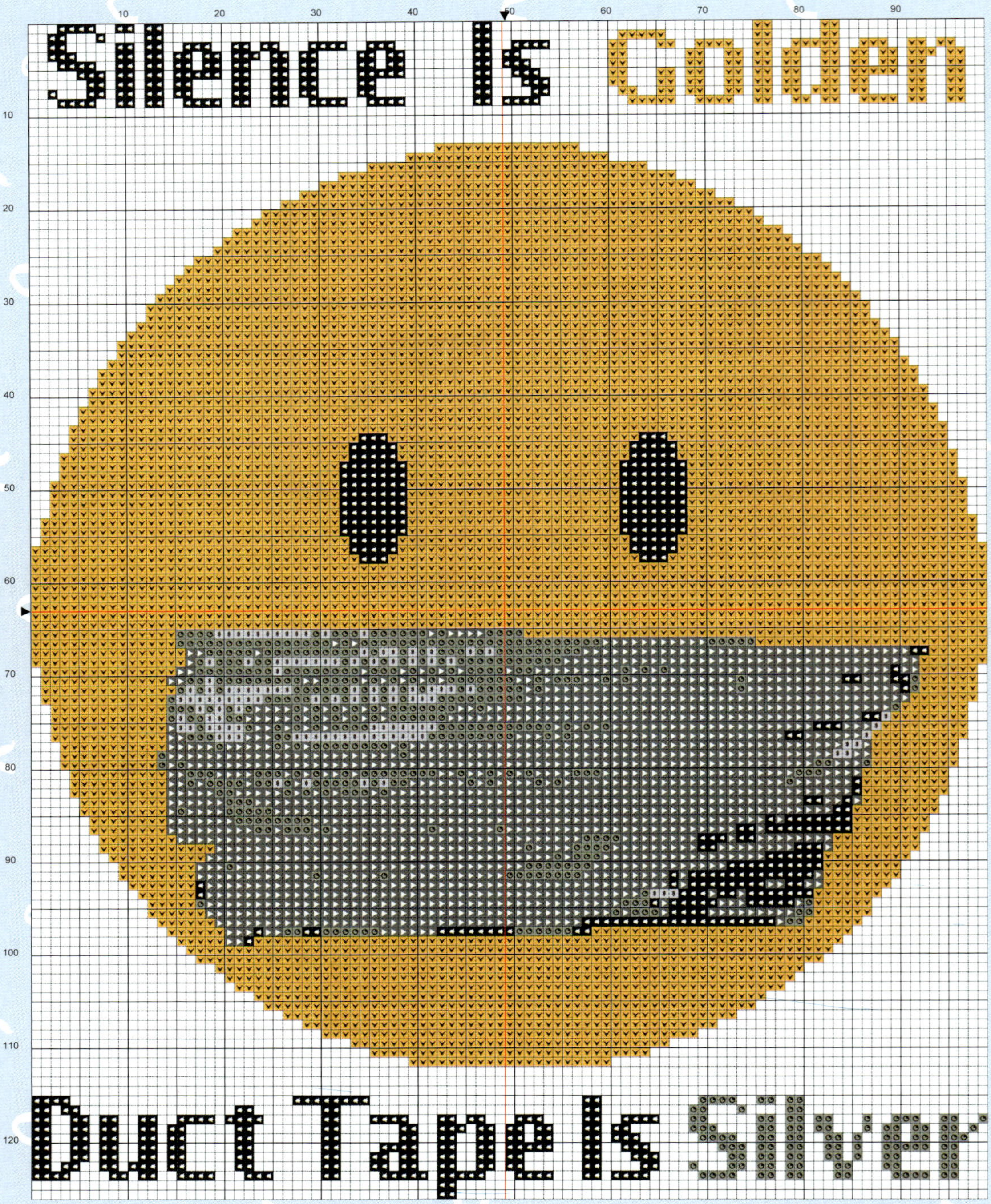

Silence Is Golden

Duct Tape Is Silver

Design size:
99w x 126h stitches (7.1" x 9")

Instructions:
Following the general instructions on pages 13–19, stitch in 2 strands according to the chart. Allow yourself a little extra fabric around the edges if you intend to frame your design.

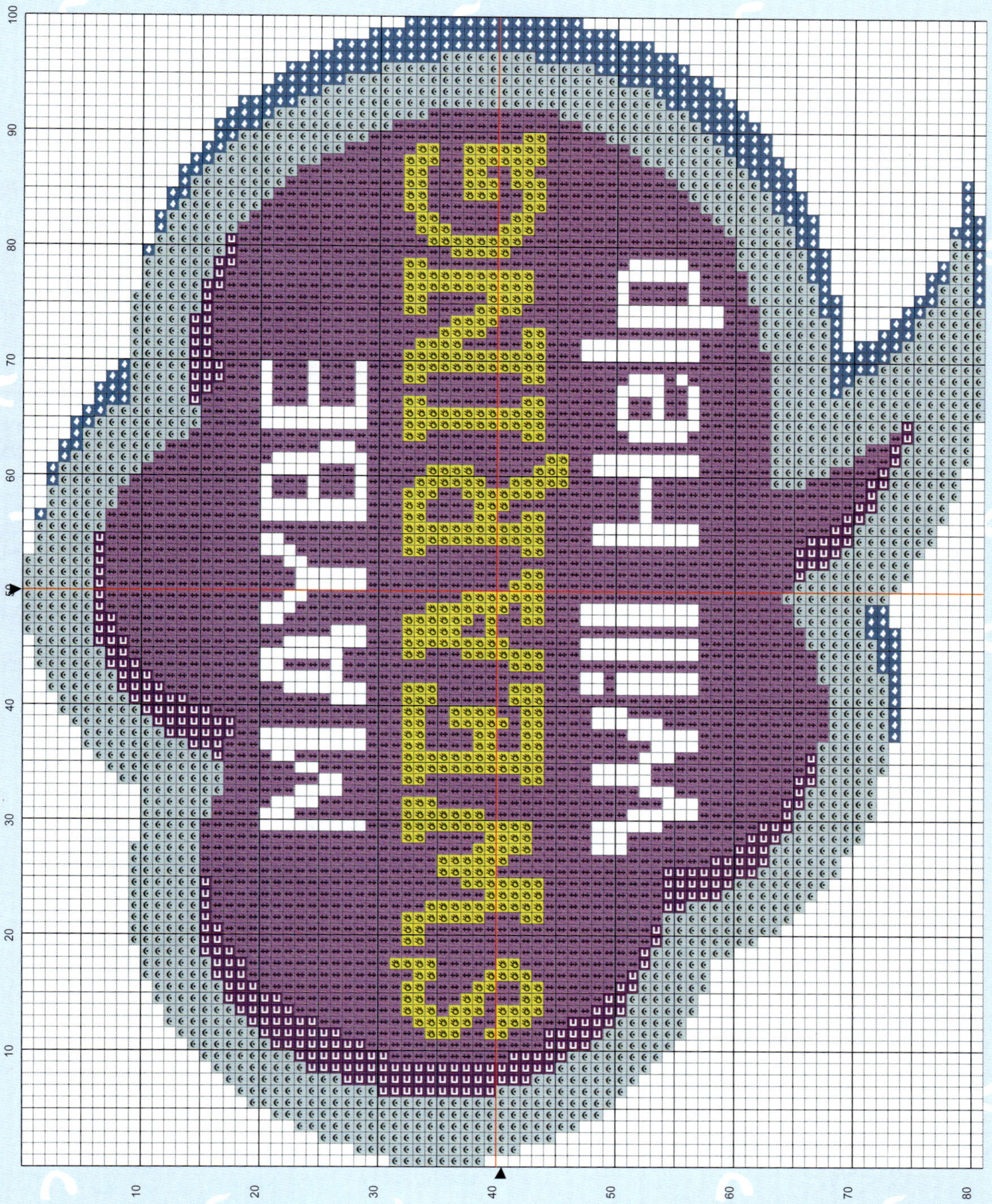

Design size:
100w x 81h stitches (7.1" x 5.8")

Instructions:
Following the general instructions on pages 13–19, stitch in 2 strands according to the chart. Allow yourself a little extra fabric around the edges if you intend to frame your design.

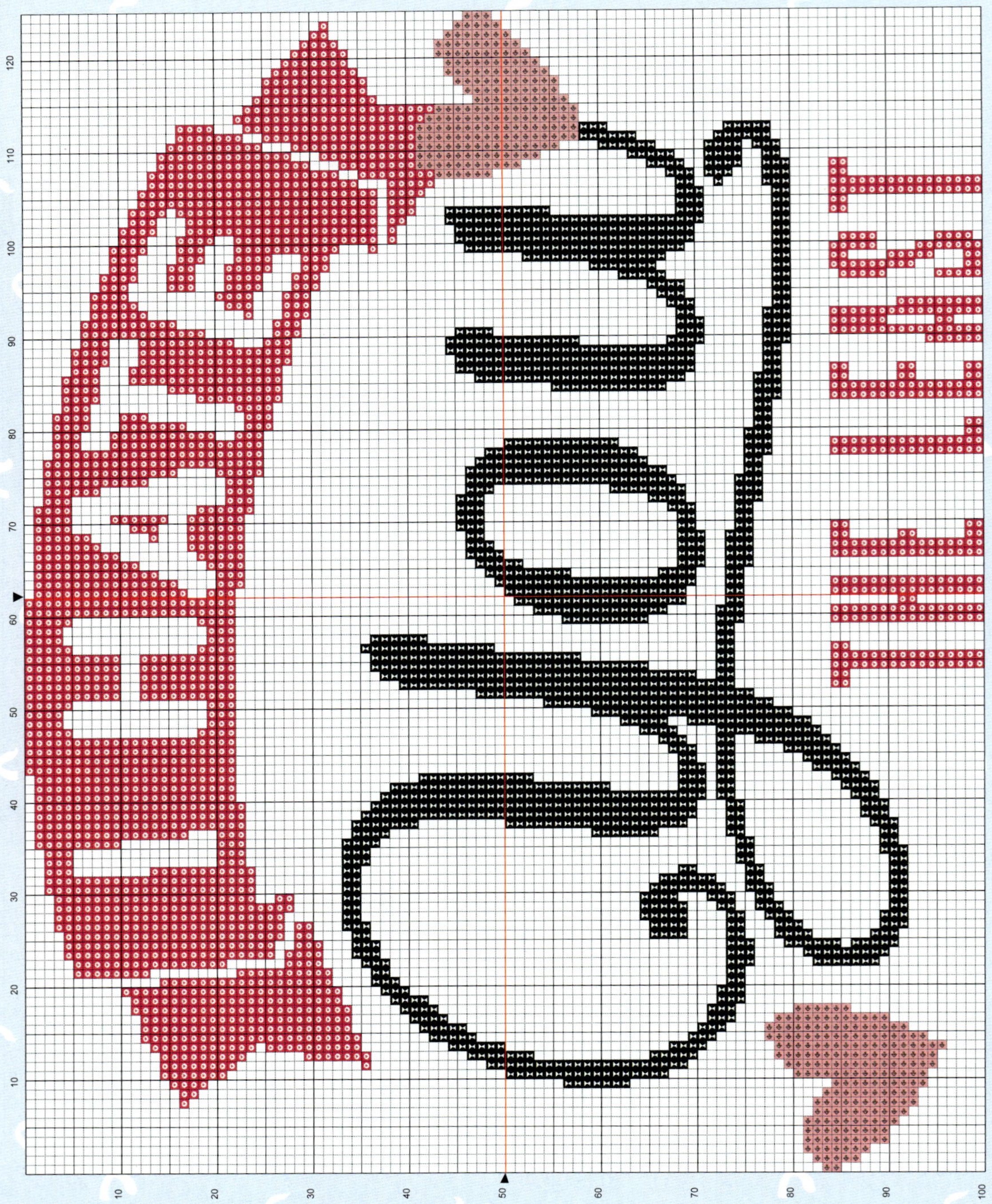

Design size:
125w x 100h stitches (8.9" x 7.1")

Instructions:
Following the general instructions on pages 13–19, stitch in 2 strands according to the chart. Allow yourself a little extra fabric around the edges if you intend to frame your design.

2 strands | Cross-stitch

Pink

Light Pink

Black

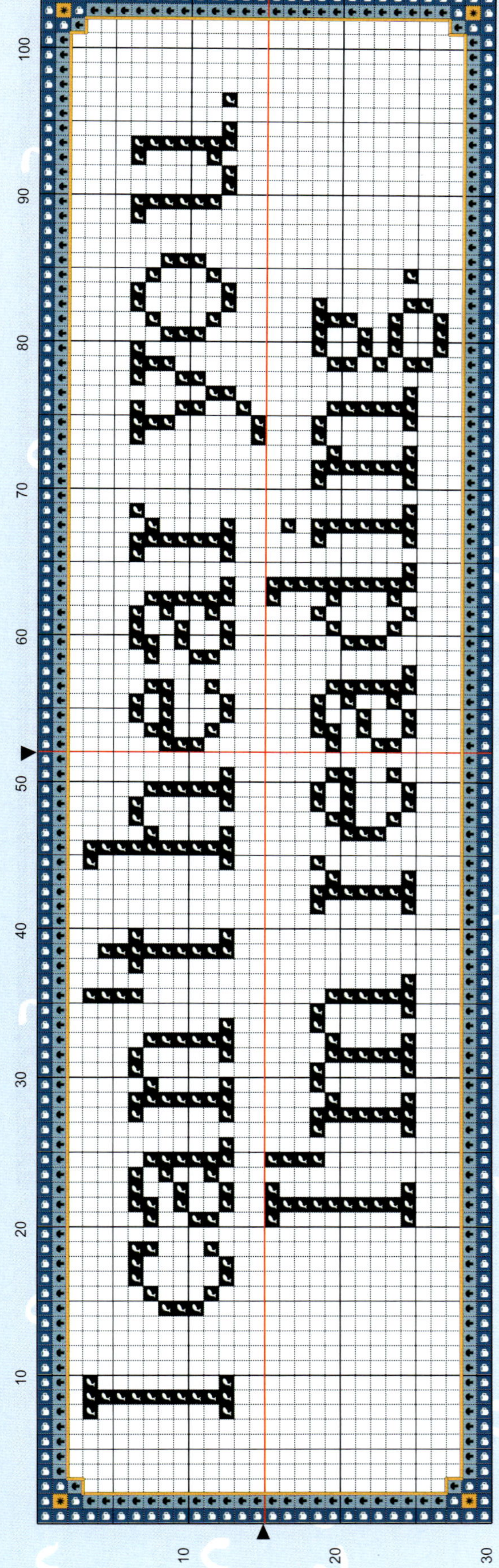

Design size:

104w x 30h stitches (7.4" x 2.1")

Instructions:

Following the general instructions on pages 13–19, stitch in 2 strands according to the chart. When all cross-stitching is done, backstitch the outline of the border in medium gold. Refer to page 11 for ways to increase the stability of your piece to use it as a bookmark.

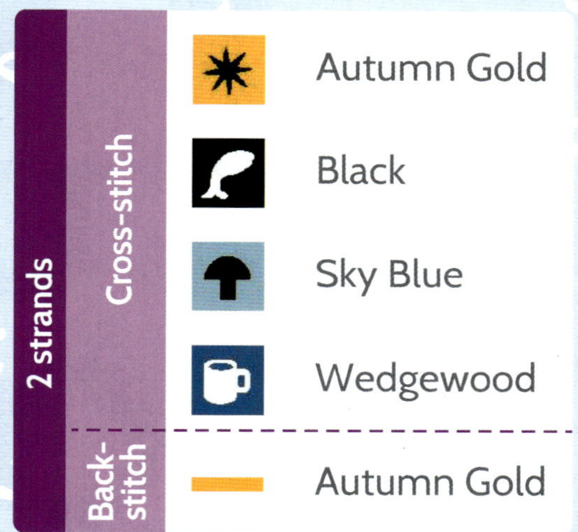

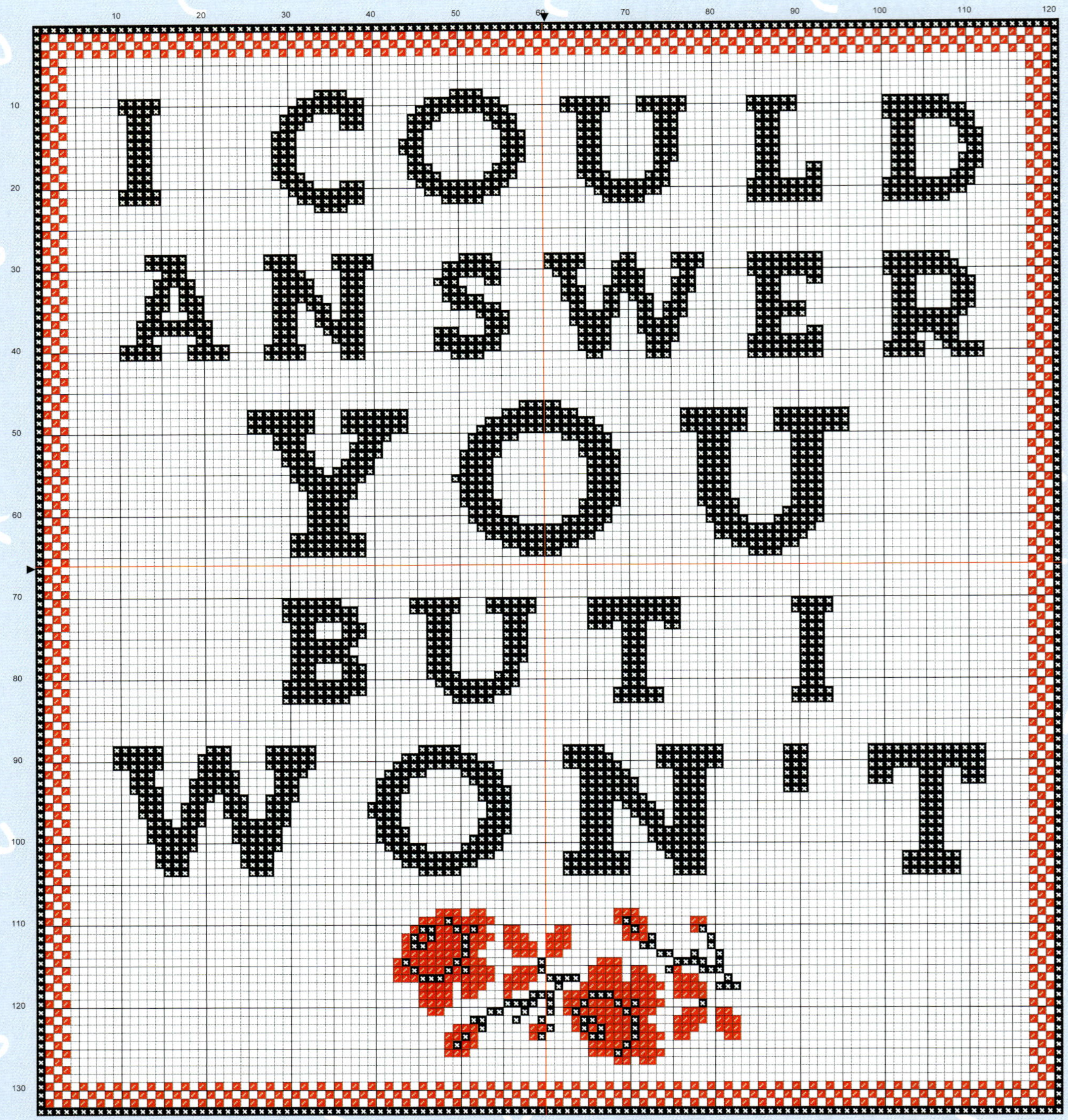

I COULD
ANSWER
YOU
BUT I
WON'T

Design size:
121w x 133h stitches (8.6" x 9.5")

Instructions:
Following the general instructions on pages 13–19, stitch in 2 strands according to the chart. Allow yourself a little extra fabric around the edges if you intend to frame your design.

2 strands
Cross-stitch

Black

Bright Red

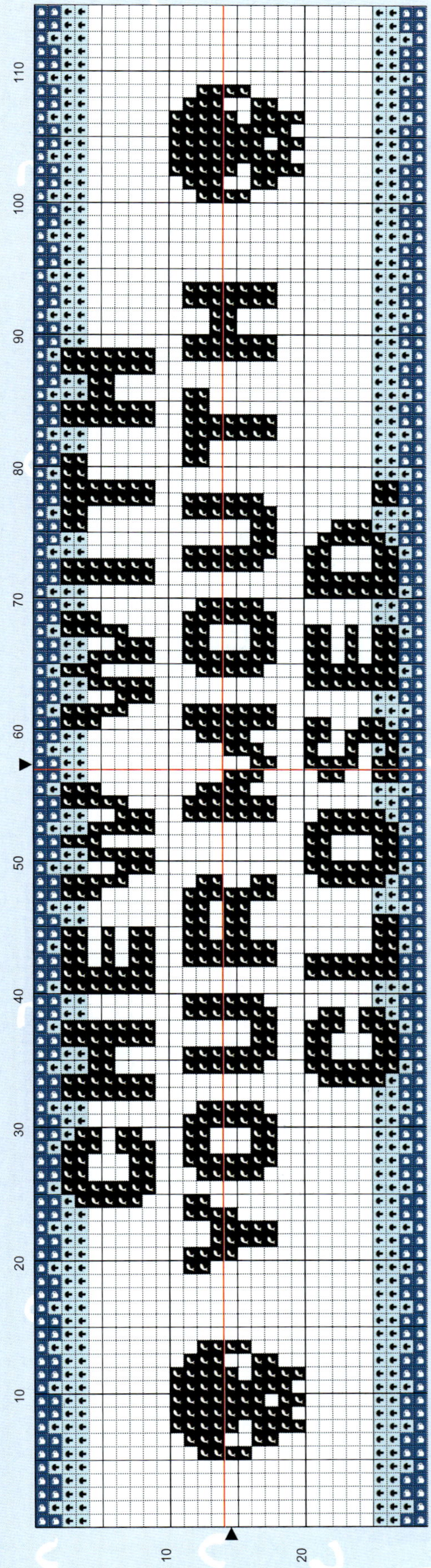

Design size:
115w x 29h stitches (8.2" x 2.1")

Instructions:
Following the general instructions on pages 13–19, stitch in 2 strands according to the chart. Allow yourself a little extra fabric around the edges if you intend to frame your design.

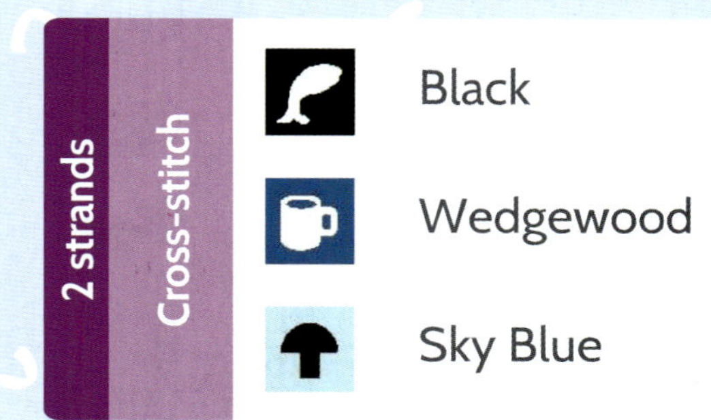

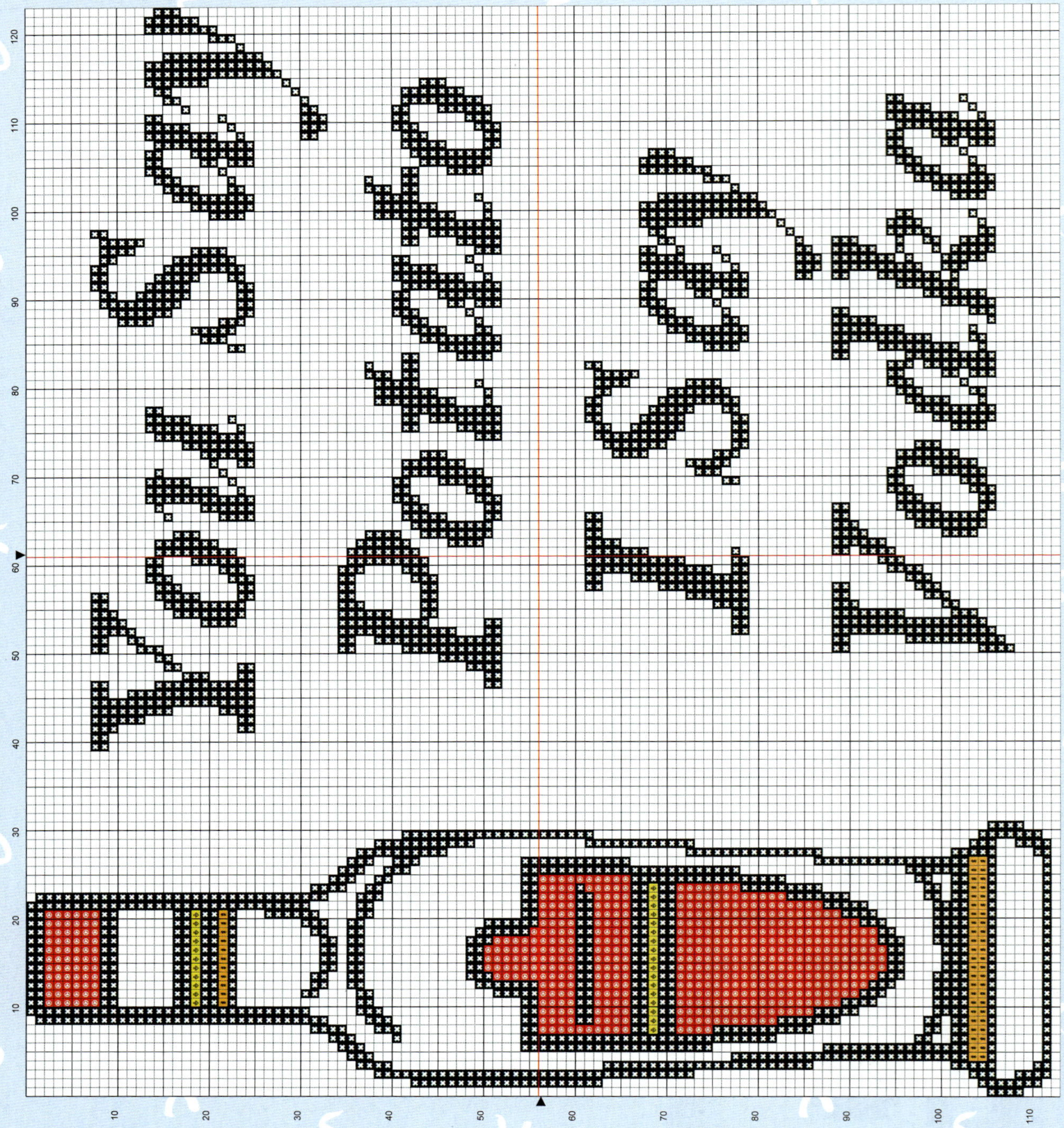

Design size:
123w x 113h stitches (8.8" x 8.1")

Instructions:
Following the general instructions on pages 13–19, stitch in 2 strands according to the chart. Allow yourself a little extra fabric around the edges if you intend to frame your design.

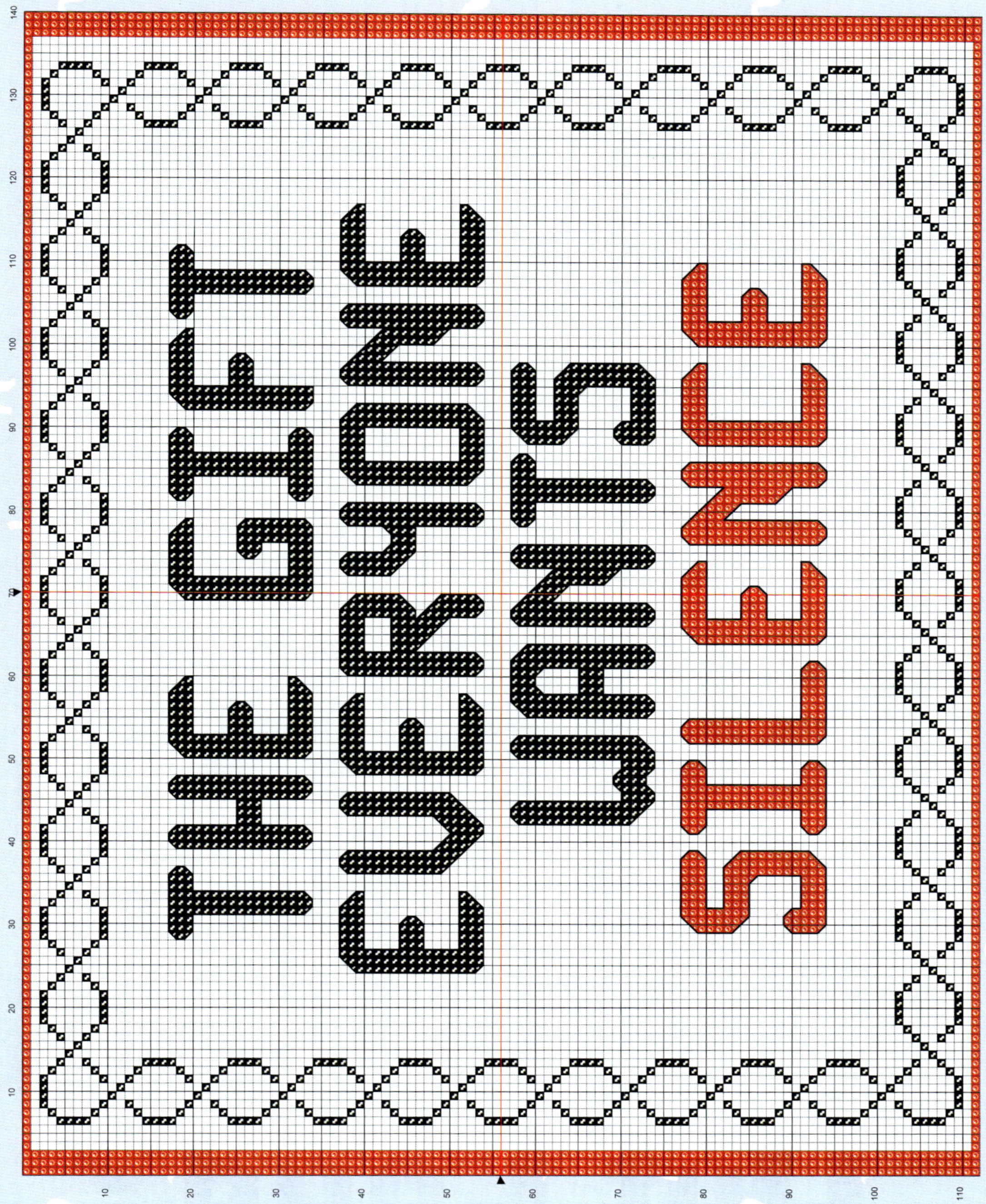

Design size:
140w x 112h stitches (10" x 8")

Instructions:
Following the general instructions on pages 13–19, stitch in 2 strands according to the chart. Squares in the chart that are only half filled use a half stitch. Allow yourself a little extra fabric around the edges if you intend to frame your design.

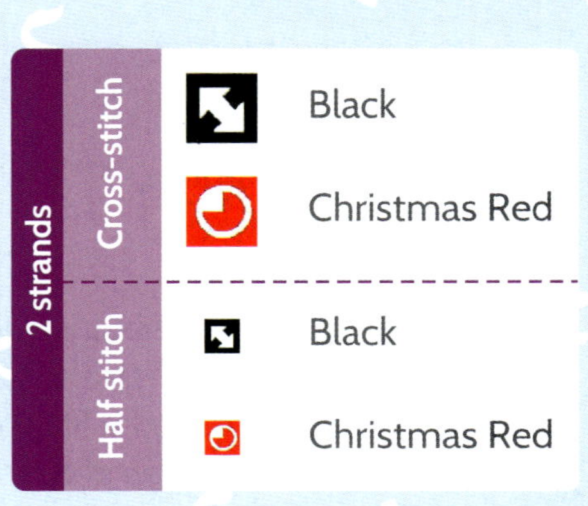

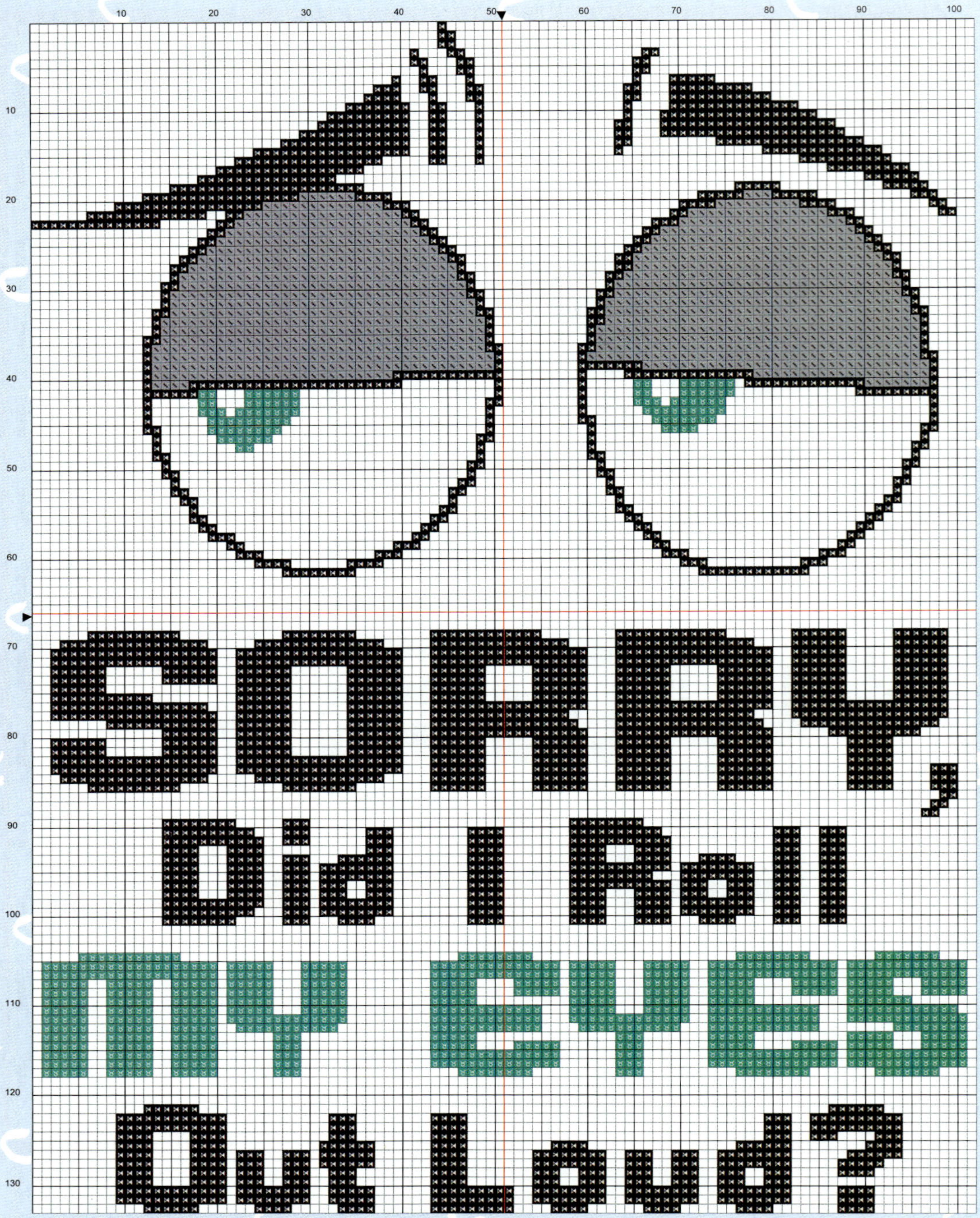

Design size:
102w x 133h stitches (7.3" x 9.5")

Instructions:
Following the general instructions on pages 13–19, stitch in 2 strands according to the chart. Allow yourself a little extra fabric around the edges if you intend to frame your design.

2 strands | Cross-stitch

	Black
	Pearl Grey
	Bright Green

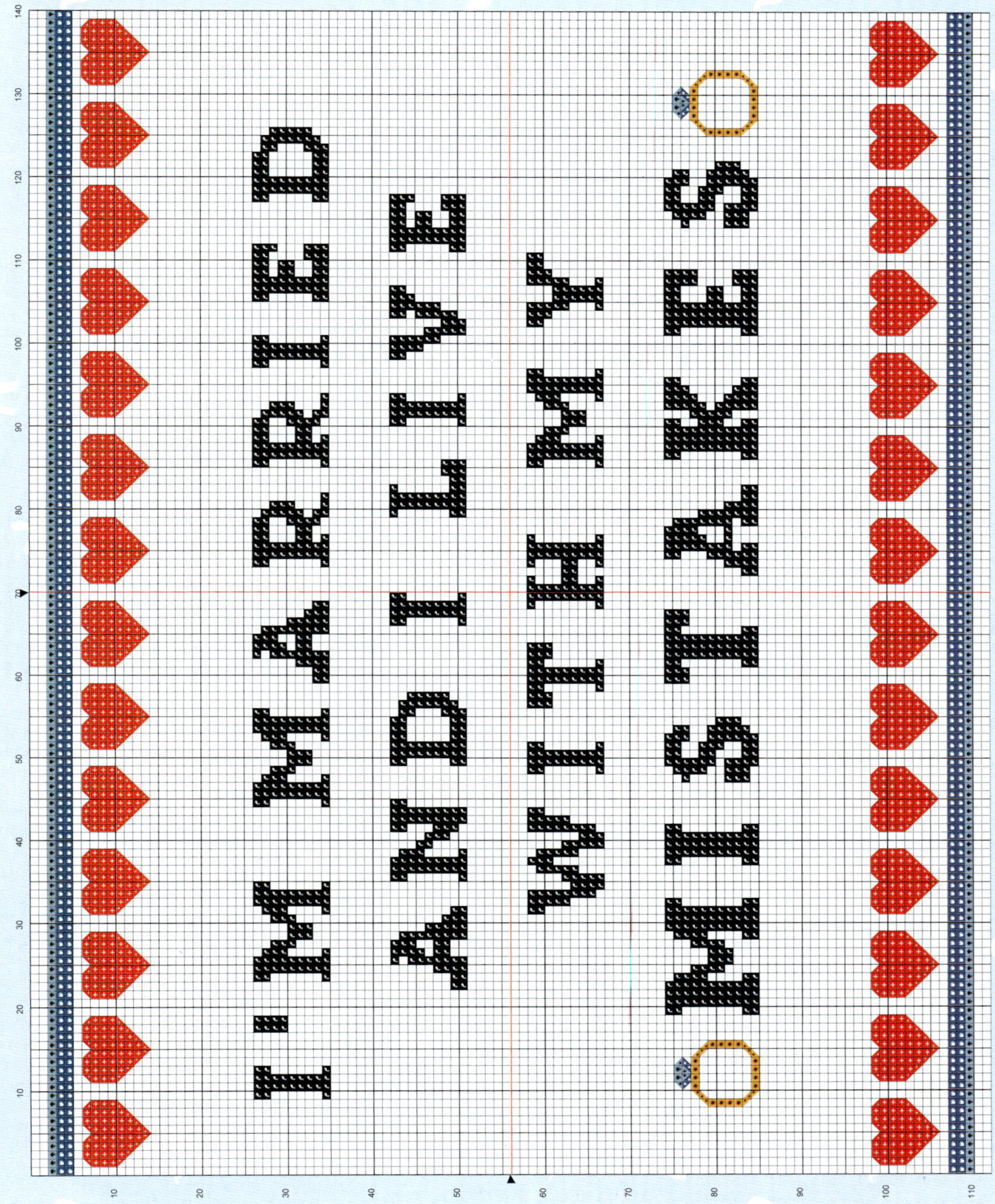

Design size:

140w x 112h stitches (10" x 8")

Instructions:

Following the general instructions on pages 13–19, stitch in 2 strands according to the chart. Squares in the chart that are only half filled use a half stitch. Allow yourself a little extra fabric around the edges if you intend to frame your design.

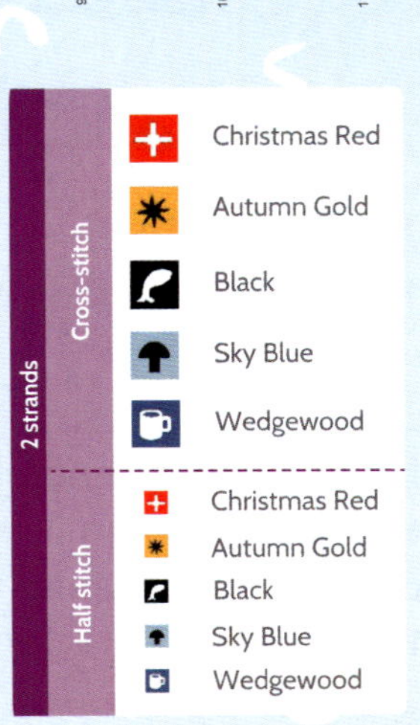

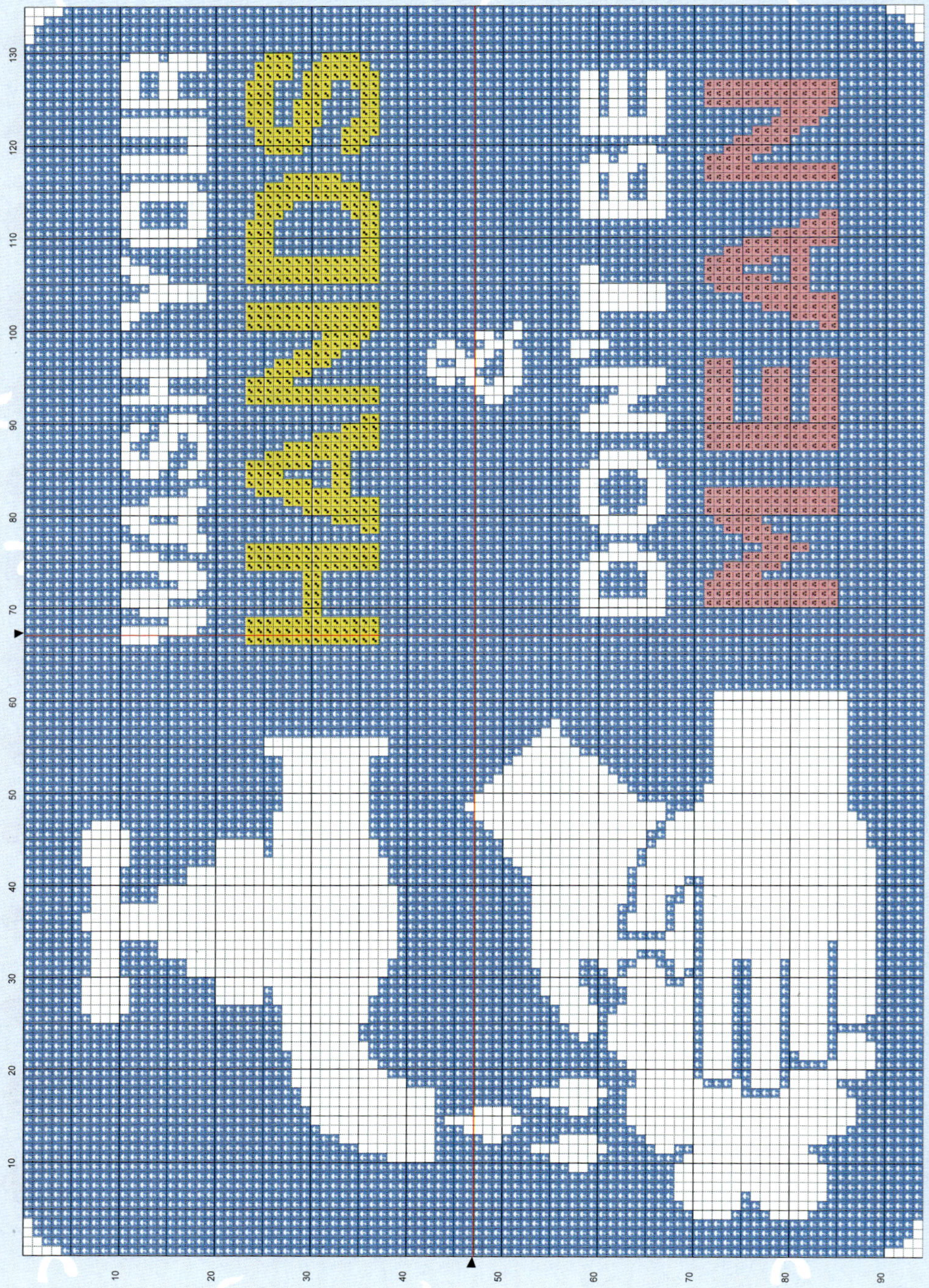

Design size:
135w x 94h stitches (9.6" x 6.7")

Instructions:
Following the general instructions on pages 13–19, stitch in 2 strands according to the chart. Allow yourself a little extra fabric around the edges if you intend to frame your design.

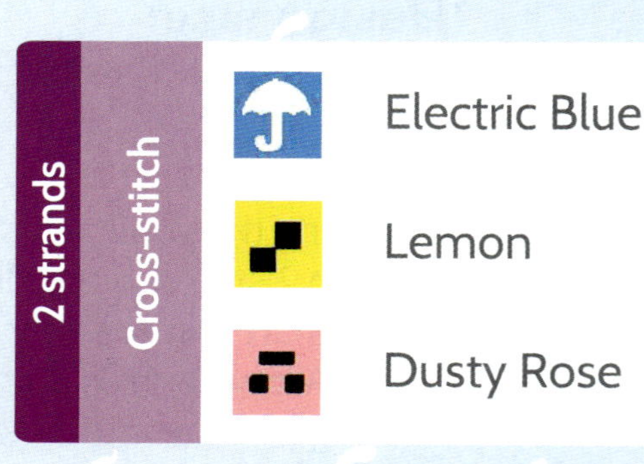

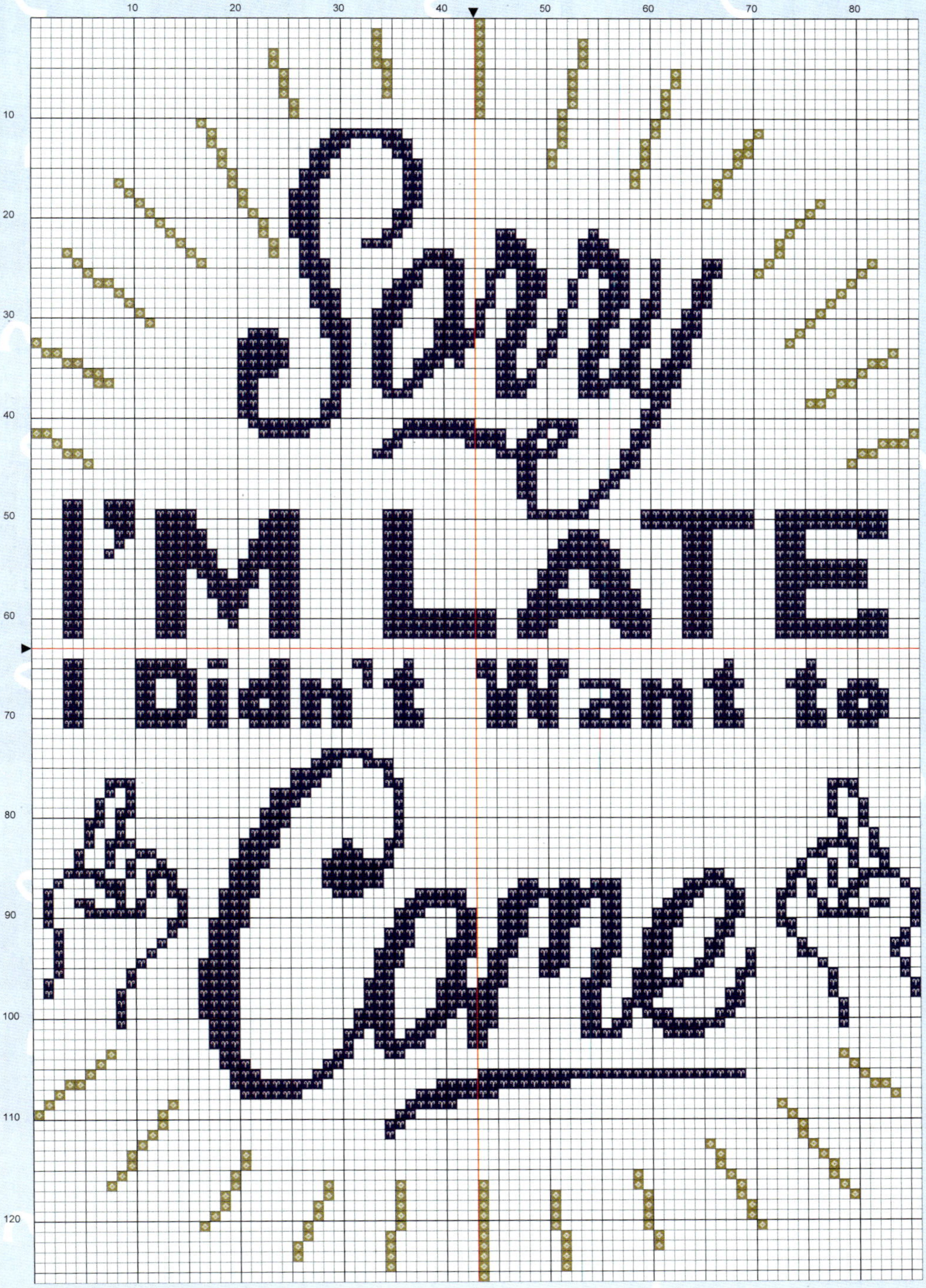

Design size:

86w x 126h stitches (6.1" x 9")

Instructions:

Following the general instructions on pages 13–19, stitch in 2 strands according to the chart. Allow yourself a little extra fabric around the edges if you intend to frame your design.

 Mustard

 Royal Blue

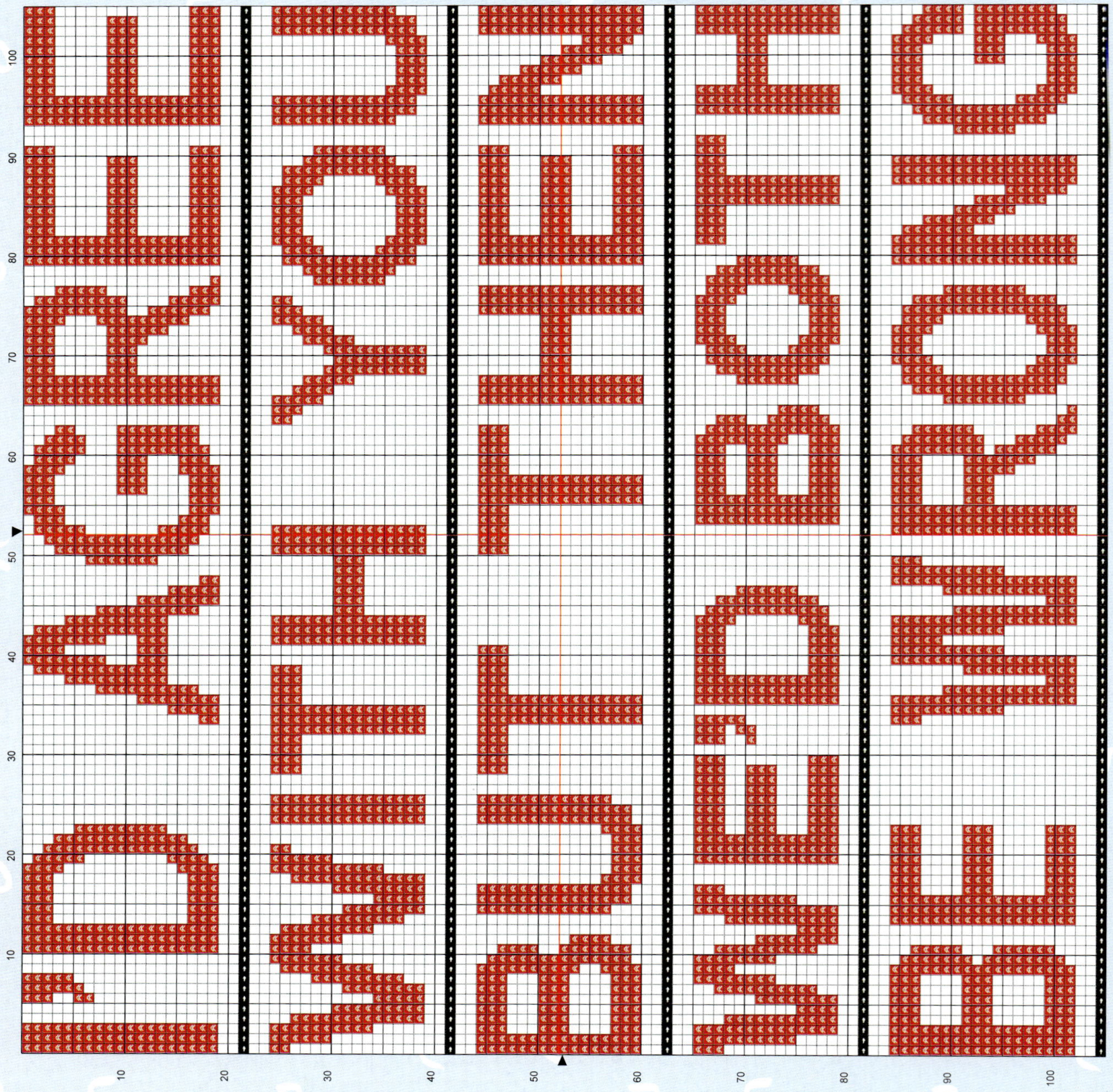

Design size:
105w x 105h stitches (7.5" x 7.5")

Instructions:
Following the general instructions on pages 13–19, stitch in 2 strands according to the chart. Allow yourself a little extra fabric around the edges if you intend to frame your design.

 Black

 Christmas Red

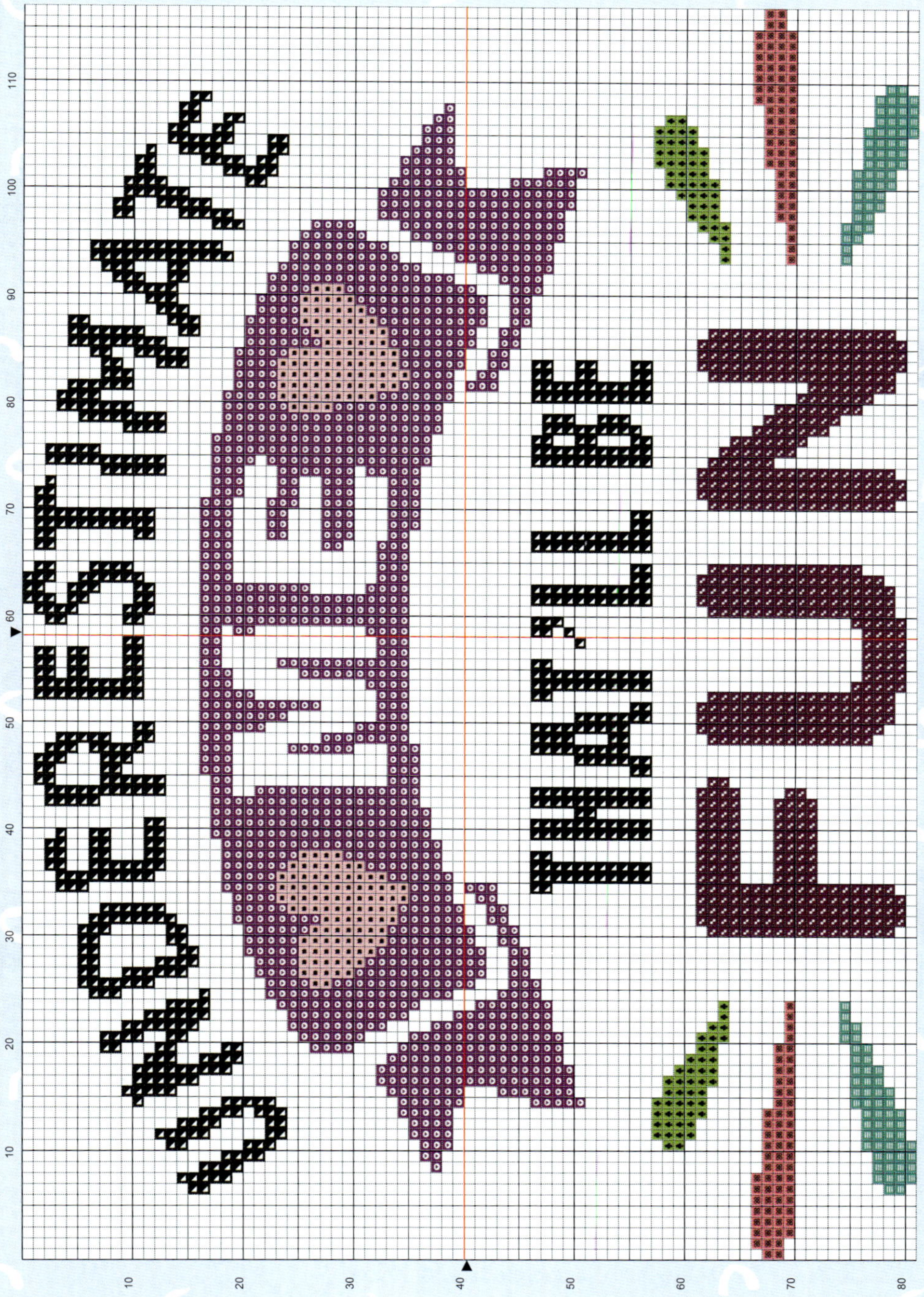

Design size:
117w x 81h stitches (8.4" x 5.8")

Instructions:
Following the general instructions on pages 13–19, stitch in 2 strands according to the chart. Allow yourself a little extra fabric around the edges if you intend to frame your design.

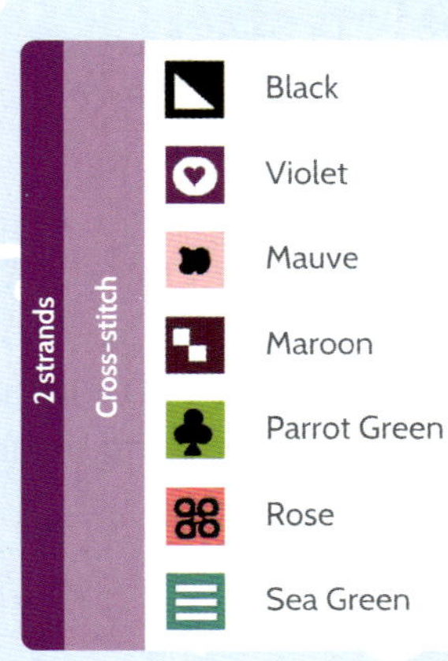

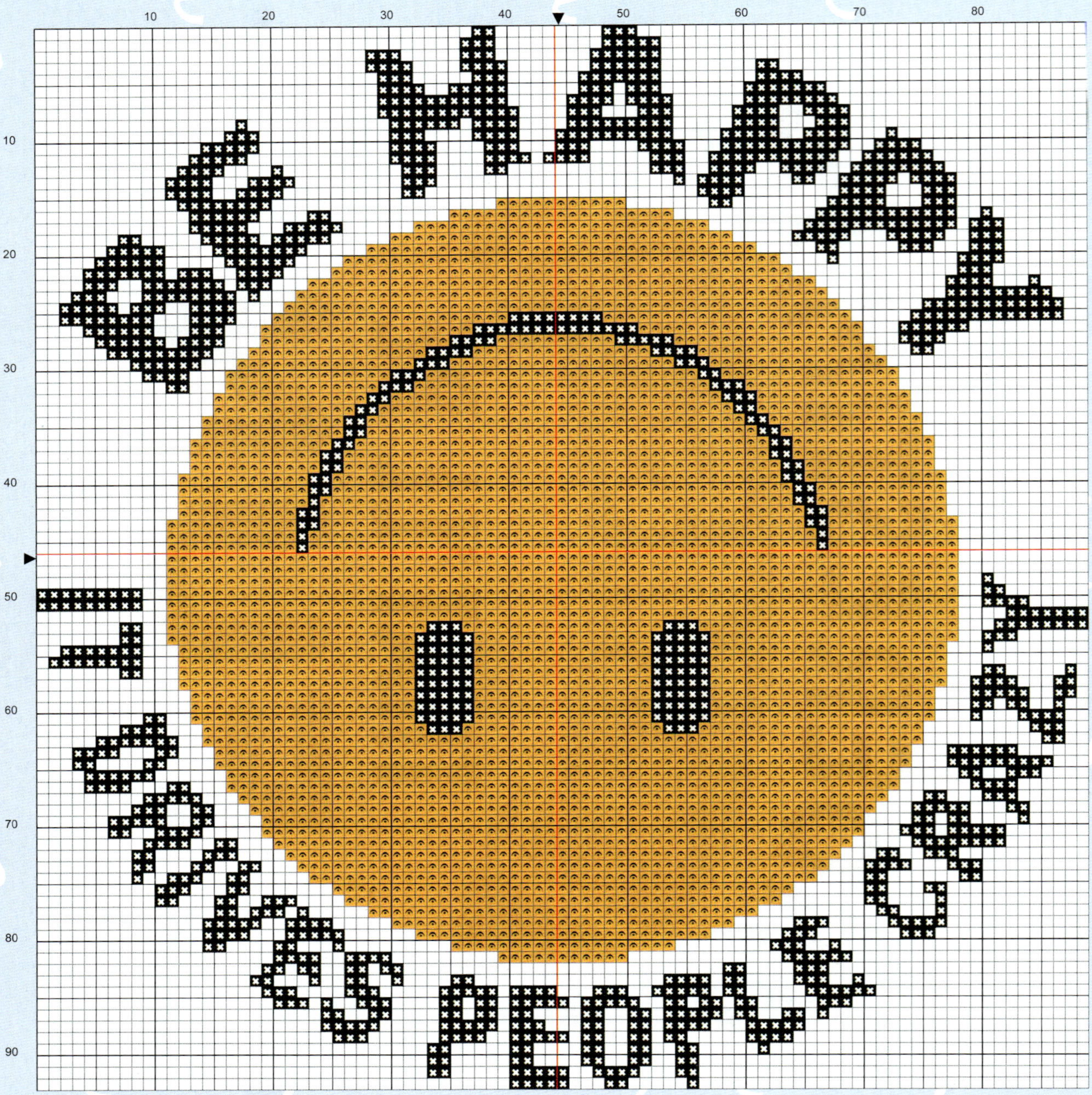

Design size:

89w x 93h stitches (8.4" x 5.8")

Instructions:

Following the general instructions on pages 13–19, stitch in 2 strands according to the chart. Allow yourself a little extra fabric around the edges if you intend to frame your design.

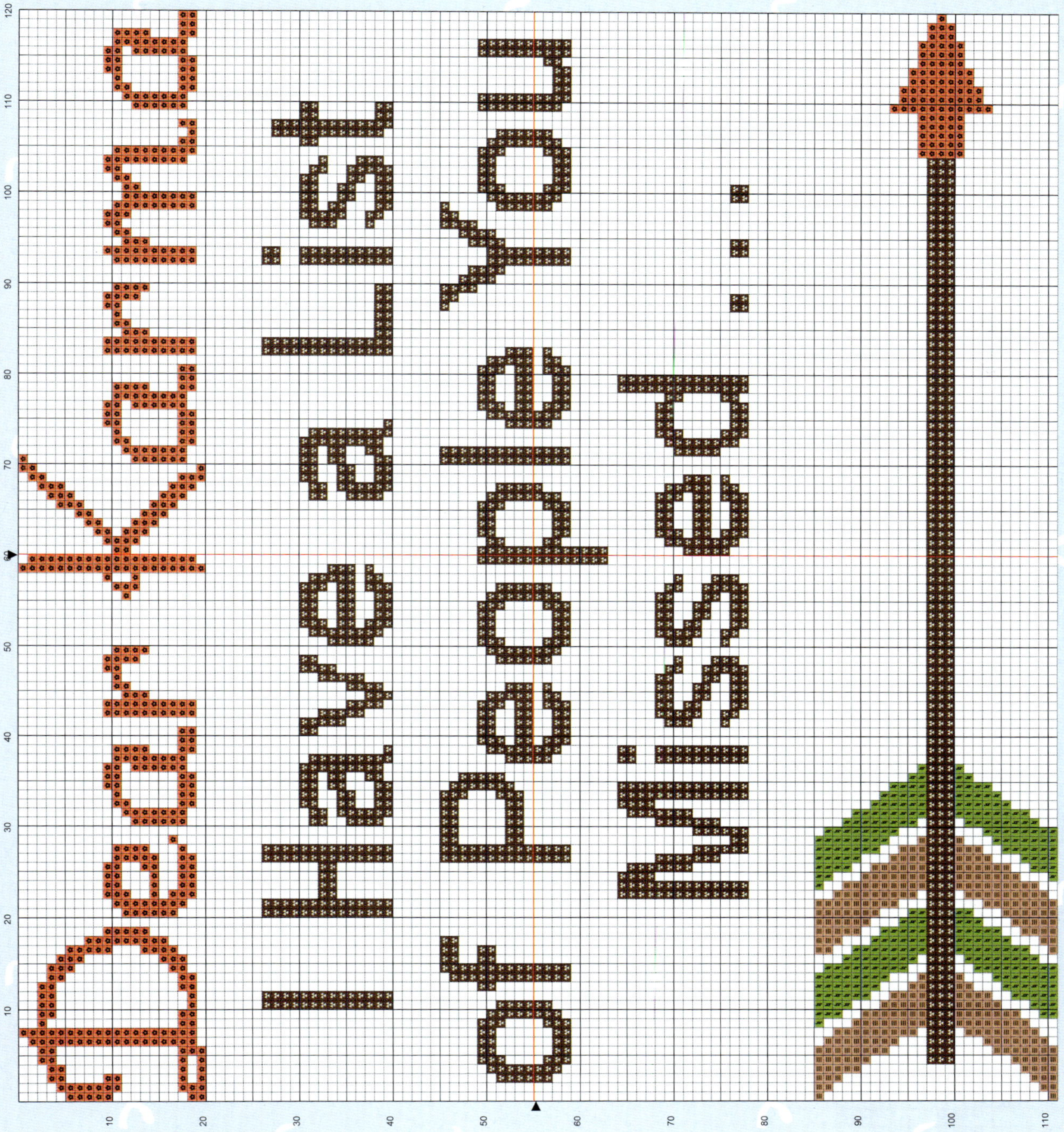

Design size:
120w x 111h stitches (8.6" x 7.9")

Instructions:
Following the general instructions on pages 13–19, stitch in 2 strands according to the chart. Allow yourself a little extra fabric around the edges if you intend to frame your design.

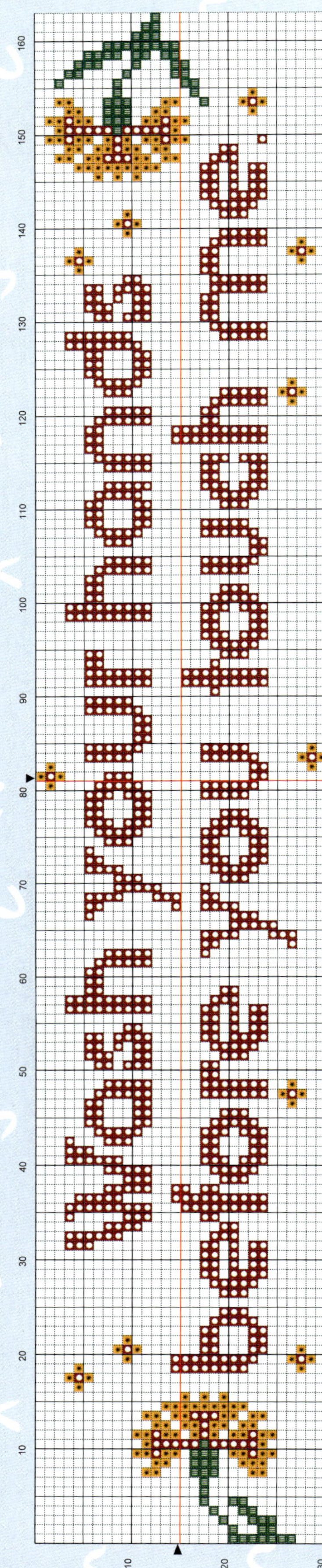

Design size:

115w x 29h stitches (8.2" x 2.1")

Instructions:

Following the general instructions on pages 13–19, stitch in 2 strands according to the chart. Depending on how you use this design, you can lengthen or shorten the border. If space allows, you can add more space between the words.

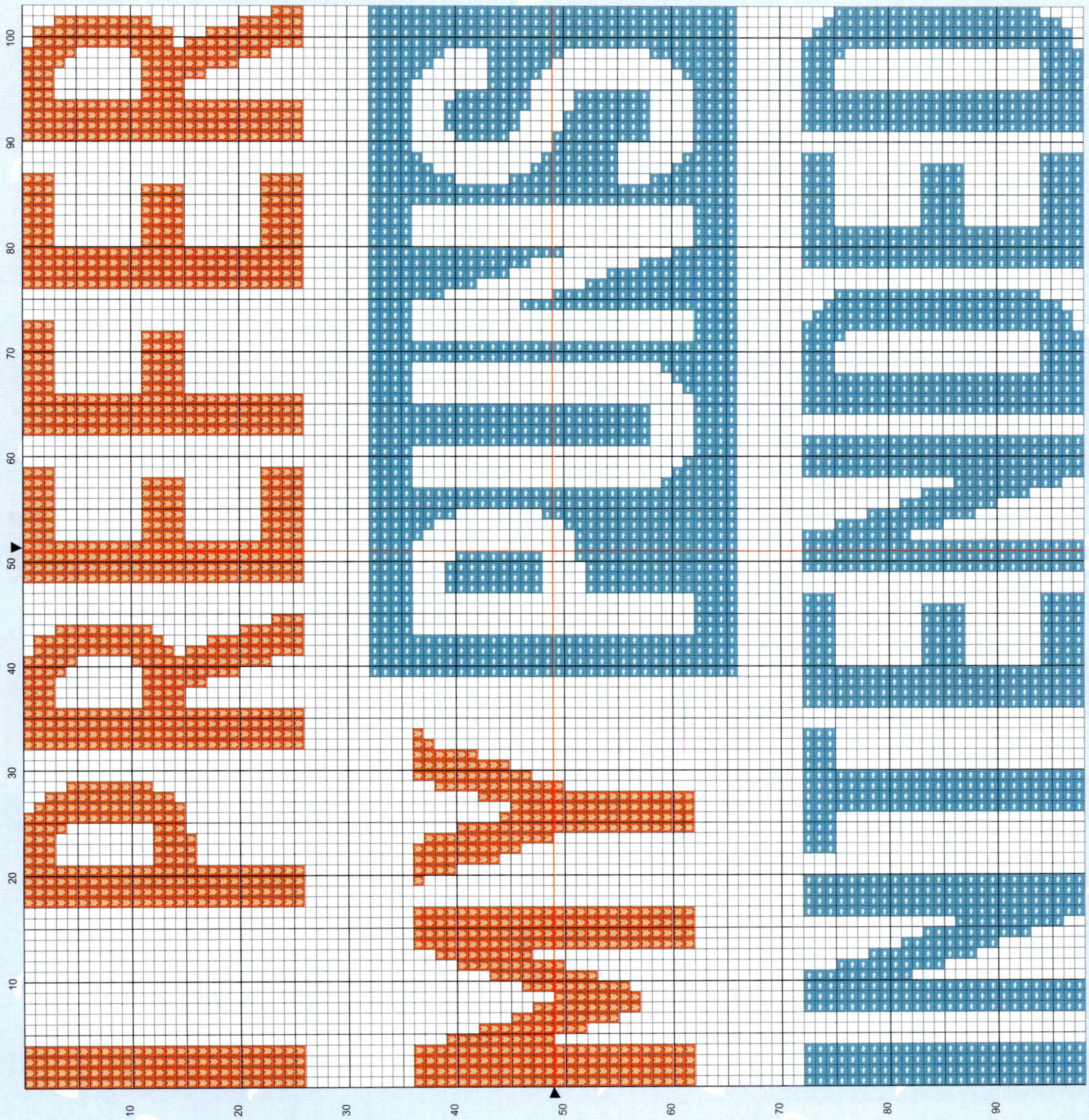

Design size:

103w x 98h stitches (7.4" x 7")

Instructions:

Following the general instructions on pages 13–19, stitch in 2 strands according to the chart. Allow yourself a little extra fabric around the edges if you intend to frame your design.

 Bright Turquoise

 Burnt Orange

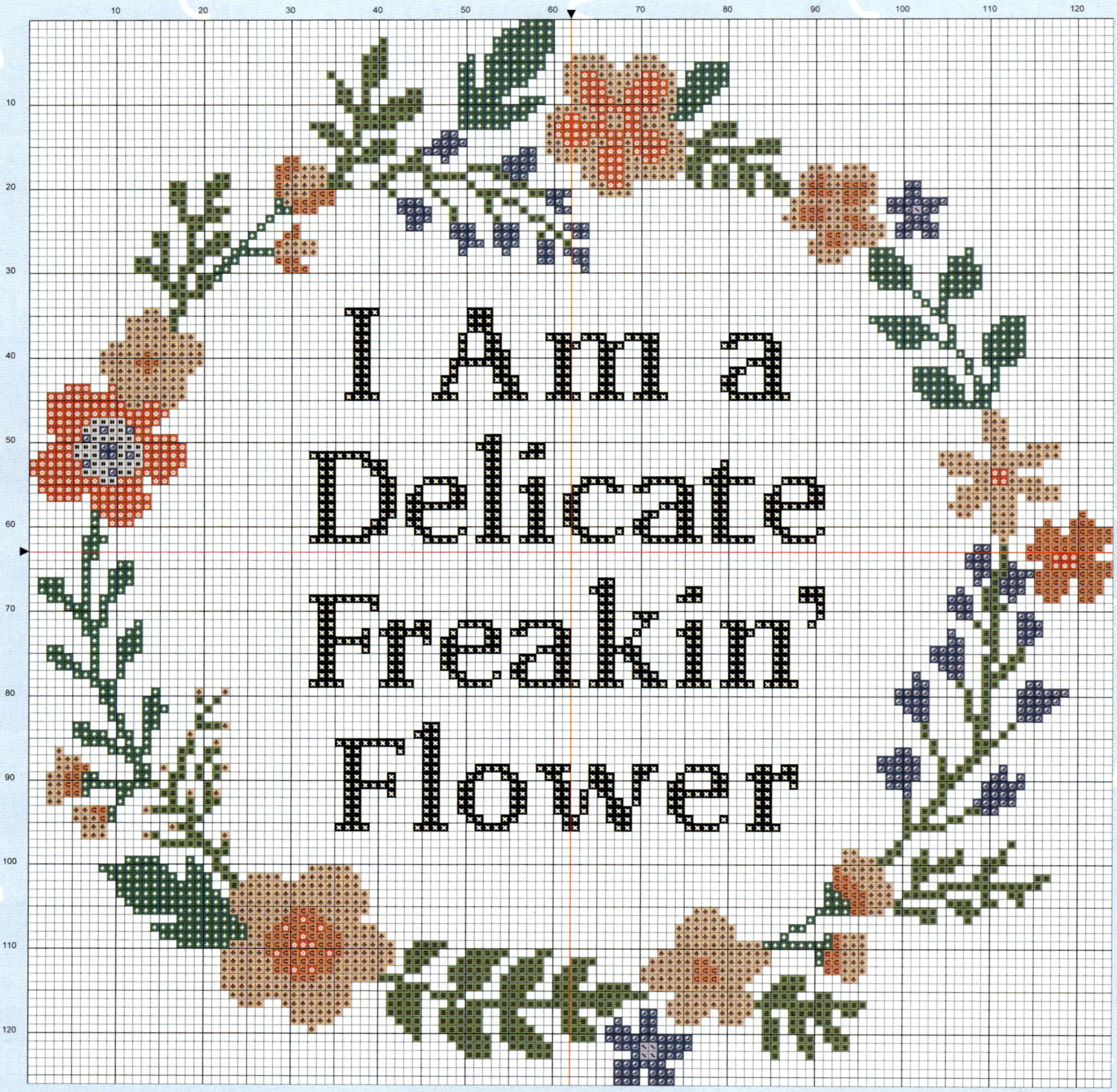

Design size:
124w x 126h stitches (8.9" x 9")

Instructions:
Following the general instructions on pages 13–19, stitch in 2 strands according to the chart. Allow yourself a little extra fabric around the edges if you intend to frame your design.

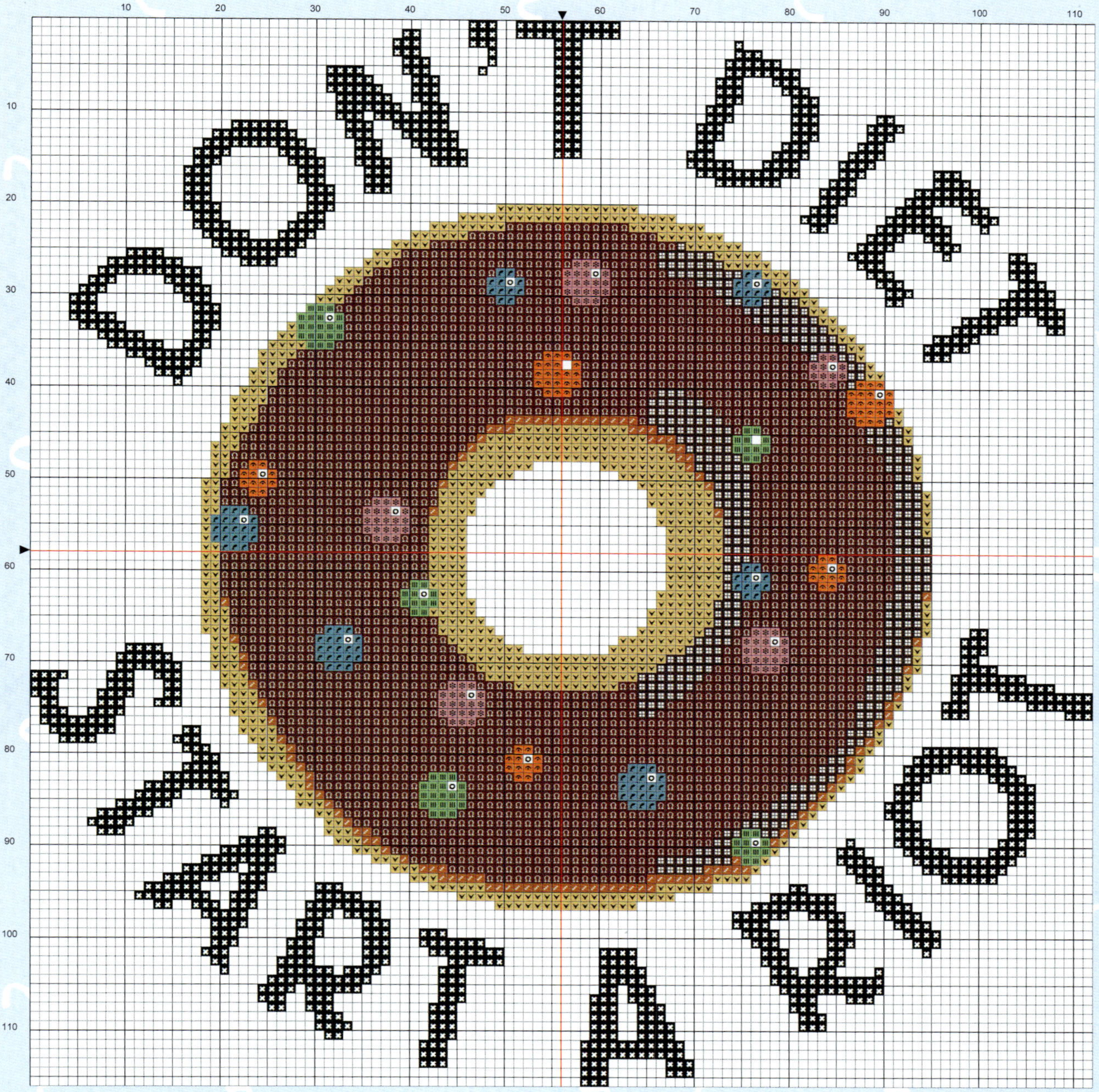

Design size:

112w x 116h stitches (8" x 8.3")

Instructions:

Following the general instructions on pages 13–19, stitch in 2 strands according to the chart. Allow yourself a little extra fabric around the edges if you intend to frame your design.

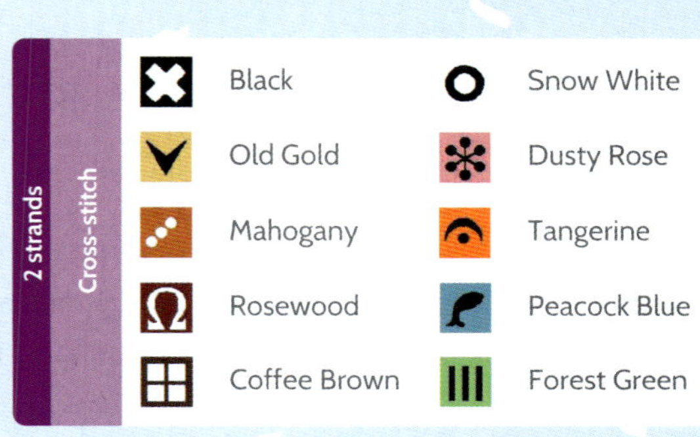

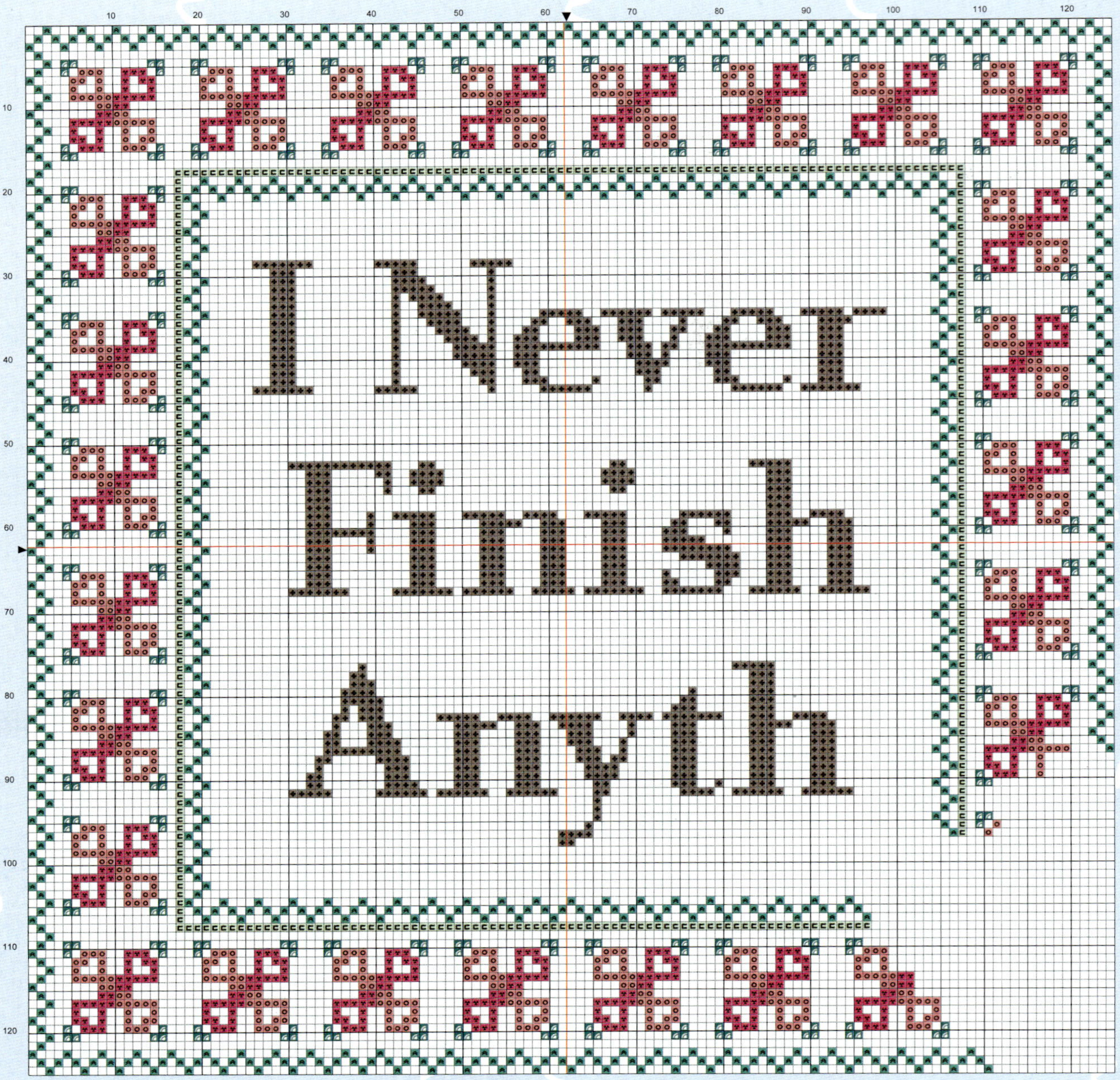

Design size:
125w x 125h stitches (8.9" x 8.9")

Instructions:
Following the general instructions on pages 13–19, stitch in 2 strands according to the chart. Allow yourself a little extra fabric around the edges if you intend to frame your design.